Winning New Business

Winning New Business

by Stewart Stuchbury

Winning New Business For Dummies®

Published by: **John Wiley & Sons, Ltd., The Atrium, Southern Gate, Chichester,** www.wiley.com

This edition first published 2017

For general information on our other products and services, please contact our Customer Care Department within the U.S. at 877-762-2974, outside the U.S. at 317-572-3993, or fax 317-572-4002. For technical support, please visit https://hub.wiley.com/community/support/dummies.

Wiley publishes in a variety of print and electronic formats and by print-on-demand. Some material included with standard print versions of this book may not be included in e-books or in print-on-demand. If this book refers to media such as a CD or DVD that is not included in the version you purchased, you may download this material at http://booksupport.wiley.com. For more information about Wiley products, visit www.wiley.com.

A catalogue record for this book is available from the British Library.

ISBN 978-1-119-27416-2 (pbk); ISBN 978-1-119-28166-5 (ebk); ISBN 978-1-119-28169-6 (ebk)

Printed and Bound in Great Britain by TJ International, Padstow, Cornwall.

10 9 8 7 6 5 4 3 2 1

Contents at a Glance

Table of Contents

Introduction

Winning *New Business For Dummies* introduces the concept of a methodology-driven approach to the science of winning sustainable new business; it ensures that you develop and maintain a constant stream of new business opportunities, along with how to close the deal.

New business is the lifeblood of every company, and in this book you're guided through the key principles of how to go about securing more than your fair share of new business success.

Having spent many years at the sharp end of winning new business, I wrote this book as a one-stop reference guide to help salespeople, both those with experience as well as those who are new to the role. It's intended to walk you through the steps and guide you around the pitfalls of what I believe is the world's greatest profession — winning new business.

About This Book

This book is intended to be a useful reference guide that you can read from cover to cover if you want to, or you can dip into the relevant chapters when you need a bit of help or inspiration. The book's easy-access organization means that you can simply and quickly get your hands on information about whatever element of winning new business you're looking for.

Winning New Business For Dummies isn't an academic, theoretical book, but one that is written from the heart by a real practitioner who gets his hands dirty in the new business trenches on an everyday basis and aims to share real-life experiences rather than highbrow theory that leaves you wondering what you actually need to do. The watch word in writing this book was *practicality.* In this book, you discover information presented in an easy-to-digest manner that will improve your customer-facing skills and set you on the right road to deliver real and sustainable new business success by making use of a structured approach to new business.

Some chapters include sidebars (shaded boxes) that expand on the core information in that chapter, should you want to explore a topic in more detail, but you can easily skip these sidebars and still get the information you need to master winning new business. (Along the same lines, feel free to skip anything with the Technical Stuff icon, too.)

Within this book, you may note that some web addresses break across two lines of text. If you're reading this book in print and want to visit one of these web pages, simply key in the web address exactly as it's noted in the text, pretending as though the line break doesn't exist. If you're reading this as an e-book, you've got it easy — just click the web address to be taken directly to the web page.

Foolish Assumptions

In writing this book, I made a number of assumptions about the typical reader. I assumed

>> You're currently working in a new business sales role and want to improve your prospect of securing a more regular flow of new business success.

>> You're brand new to the role of winning new business, perhaps even an owner or manager of SMEs (small and medium-sized enterprises), and you need a reference point to give you a head start in delivering successful winning new business campaigns.

When you pick up this book, you don't need to have previous sales experience — in fact, quite the opposite. If you're brand new to the profession, you can read and quickly act on the information presented here.

This book is intended to give you solid, practical advice on how to actually deliver new business. The working title was "Get Up and Sell Something," which sums up the approach very well.

Icons Used in This Book

Throughout this book, you see these icons used:

TIP

The Tip icon highlights specific pointers that will help you win new business more easily and effectively.

REMEMBER

The Remember icon flags important pieces of information that are critical to getting a good understanding of the topic at hand.

WARNING

The advice you find with this icon can prevent headaches when it comes to winning new business.

TECHNICAL STUFF

The text attached to this icon may not be crucial to your success in winning new business, but it may be interesting to you nonetheless.

Beyond the Book

In addition to what you're reading right now, this product comes with a free access-anywhere Cheat Sheet. To get this Cheat Sheet, simply go to www.dummies. com and search for "Winning New Business For Dummies Cheat Sheet" in the search box. Take a look at the articles in the Cheat Sheet to gain some more understanding on winning new business.

You can find additional information on the winning new business methodology on my website at www.nineteen58.com, which also contains a number of blog articles that expand on various topics related to winning new business.

Where to Go from Here

Feel free to just dive into the book at any chapter that catches your attention. You don't need to necessarily read this book from cover to cover before you implement any of the learnings. It's not linear, so feel free to jump around the content to make it work for you.

Chapter 9 on prospecting effectively and Chapter 19 on qualifying potential business contain the real keys to winning new business success, so they're as good a place as any to start reading.

1

Getting Started with Winning New Business

Chapter **1**

Introducing a Winning New Business Culture

With the possible exception of research and development, you could take away most other functions within a company and still be left with a business that existed to some degree. Try taking away new business, though, and you don't have anything left that can operate as a business entity.

Winning new business is at the very forefront of every successful company and is a cultural thing. It's not just the function of a group of new business salespeople acting independently from the rest of the business; winning new business is the fusion of different parts of the organization working together to deliver a winning solution for your clients. The specific role of the new business salesperson is to be the front end, the customer-facing part of this dynamic, building on the great things that back him up.

To introduce a winning new business culture (the topic of this chapter), you need to have a plan. I call it a methodology and refer to it a lot throughout this book. A methodology is essentially a structured approach to achieving an end result, in this case being able to successfully and constantly win new business. Think of it as a road map to guide you to your destination.

Winning new business is not an easy task, but it is a rewarding one. The buzz of securing a new deal is one of the best feelings you'll experience in your working life, and no matter how many deals you go on to win during your career, that buzz never gets lost. To maximize your chances of success, you need to bring a winning mentality to the table; be a "glass half full" type of person, a winner with a positive outlook. Pair that with a successful new business methodology, and you'll be on your way to achieving new business success for yourself and your company. New business sales is truly a profession of choice and in the 21st century has become recognized as such. Be proud to work in new business sales and wear it as a badge of honor as a career choice and not something that you stumble in to.

If there's one pointer I seek to give to a business owner looking to introduce a culture of winning new business into his company, it's to recognize and reward the new business role, not just in financial terms but as a status within your business. Don't just employ someone and then sit back and expect miracles, but support him and work with him to create the right environment, and your efforts will more than pay for themselves.

Focusing on New Business Fundamentals

The strict definition of new business is to call it the commercial, customer-facing part of your business, the part that liaises directly with potential customers and turns them into real fee-paying clients. Without this function, you don't really have a business at all. If you operate in a small business, you may not have the luxury of being able to employ a specialist for this role, so you have two choices: You either outsource the role or do it yourself. Not winning new business isn't an option.

From time to time, I come across companies that claim not to "do new business," and sometimes they really do believe that. But the reality is still that they need to win new work, and they choose to go about it via referrals and recommendations rather than have someone directly responsible for the task. It's still new business, though. These people who claim not to "do new business" are deluding themselves and are generally the ones who go on to wonder why their business isn't growing.

Winning new business is far from what many consider to be "sales," which has developed a bit of a stigma as a result generally from a lack of understanding and training. Today, winning new business is the fusion of different skill sets brought together into today's modern and highly respected profession that I, for one, am proud to be a part of. It encompasses not only selling in its traditional form but also understanding the commercial and technical considerations that make up a client-facing solution to a problem. As I identify in Chapters 3, 4, and 9, research plays a vital part in the new business role, and throughout this book, the theme of building relationships with your prospects also keeps coming to the forefront. In addition, technology is one of the key drivers of change in winning new business, and you find out how to use it to your best advantage in Chapter 4.

One more theme that's prevalent throughout this book is qualifying prospects. You discover that you shouldn't chase every potential opportunity but carefully select the ones to target based on real quantifiable data, and you find out what to look for and where to look for it. (See Chapters 9 and 19 for details.)

In the following sections, I introduce some of the fundamentals of winning new business: getting a handle on your solution, the key elements of the process, the importance of the role, and its basis in science.

Understanding your solution

Before you can go through the elements of winning new business (see the next section), you need to go through some initial stages to gain an in-depth understanding of what you're working with:

TIP

>> **Understanding what you have:** You need to take the time to understand the product or service that your company wants you to sell. Don't just assume that you know what it is; take the time to talk to colleagues in different parts of the company to get their views on what the product or service is and how they see it delivering benefits.

Don't try to reinvent the wheel in coming up with unique selling propositions. Start with what you have, and add value to it by talking to the people who work with it every day. They know better than most what key things to focus on. Discuss with existing clients how they make use of your solution, and use that information as the basis of presenting your solution to your prospects.

If you have a technical product or service, make sure you take the time to understand, at a least at a good overview level, what it does and how it does it.

>> **Understanding how it fits:** After you understand what you have, then you need to understand how it fits into your target prospect's environment. Without this information, you stand zero chance of being able to sell it successfully.

>> **Understanding what it delivers:** What are the key benefits of your solution? By now, that should be obvious to you, but you also need to dig a little deeper

to understand some of the finer points and some of the less obvious benefits that can make your solution different from competitive offerings, therefore giving you some additional advantages in selling it. Any form of differentiation is well worth investigating.

Examining the elements of winning new business

When you understand the product or service that you're working with (see the preceding section), you can then turn your attention to the six key elements of winning new business:

>> **Prospecting:** Prospecting is the early stages of winning new business, where you seek to fill the pipeline with potential clients and then set about the task of finding out as much as you can about them and their needs. A successful new business salesperson is always prospecting and always seeking out new opportunities; it becomes second nature. I talk about prospecting in Chapters 4, 9, and 23.

>> **Qualifying:** If there's one true secret ingredient to making a successful new business salesperson, qualifying is it. When you qualify, you ensure that your prospect has a real need for your solution, the authority to buy it, and the necessary budget available to pay for it. See Chapters 9, 15, and 19 for details.

>> **Handling objections:** Dealing with objections is the bread and butter of the winning new business job; you'll be doing it all day every day. Check out Chapters 7 and 10 for more on handling objections.

REMEMBER

An objection may not be presented to you in such an obvious form, but by objection I mean the need for you to cover and address any and all aspects of the proposed solution as it fits with your prospect's business and addresses his needs.

>> **Tracking:** Typically, you'll have many prospects on the go at any one time, and you can't risk having to remember every detail of every deal that you're working on. You also need to produce reports and sales forecasts, so you need a system to be able to track progress, keeping you on course for success. Generally, you'll use a CRM (customer relationship management) system here. I discuss the basics of tracking prospects in Chapter 19 and cover CRM systems in Chapters 9 and 21.

TIP

The more you use a good CRM system, the more you'll benefit from it, both in winning new business and in planning and forecasting roles. If your CRM isn't delivering benefits, then the first place to look is at your own use of it. Are you recording everything every day? There's really no excuse for not doing so.

>> **Measuring:** How do you know whether your sales efforts are on track and whether you're going to meet your targets? A wet finger in the air is one option, but these days you have somewhat more sophisticated methods, using metrics based on real activity as recorded by your CRM system. Check out Chapter 22 for more on metrics.

REMEMBER

Take the time to understand the metrics and how they relate to you and your activities. They're not based on some random set of measurements but on real data that you yourself are recording as you go about your daily tasks. It's not about big brother checking up on you; it's about using science to help you be effective in your winning new business role.

>> **Winning the deal:** This is where the real winning new business buzz comes from. Little else compares to the elation of closing a deal. It's the culmination of everything that you're working toward, and this book is focused on helping you get there more often. I don't designate a specific chapter on winning the deal; it's not as easy as that. Winning the deal is the end game in the new business sales role, and this book aims to take you through the entire process instead of trying to teach you old-school closing techniques that, frankly, have no role in the 21st century.

Knowing that new business is a company's heartbeat

Winning new business provides the momentum for business to continue, for solutions to be implemented, and for a business's economic viability. Keep in mind the importance of your role when colleagues from other functions of the company put you under pressure, and remind them that their role is to support your efforts first and foremost. Without you, they wouldn't have a job in the first place.

REMEMBER

Without winning new business, you simply don't have a business. Winning new business is fundamental to company planning. If there was a need to remove functions from a company for any reason, then new business sales would be exempt from that list.

Implementing a new business process isn't as simple as going out to hire a new business salesperson and hoping for the best. Although I'd argue that new business sales is the most important role in any company — yes, really — the responsibility of driving the company forward doesn't lie only with new business sales; support from all other functions is essential. It's important not to lose focus on the reason for the company being in business, which is delivering profit for the stakeholders.

Without a successfully thought-out and implemented new business strategy, your company won't be around long enough to make a difference. To maximize the chances of success, your company needs to adopt a new business–led approach to everything that it does. There is, however, a massive difference between having a new business–led approach and setting out to win at all costs, which I explore in Chapter 14.

Seeing new business as a science

There's been a long debate about whether sales is a science or an art form, and in my mind there's no doubt that winning new business is a science because its success can be pre-determined by following a set of well-defined processes, a methodology.

New business sales isn't about reacting to gut instinct, although you do need to recognize instinct as an important human emotion as part of the sales process. If you follow a tried and tested methodology with a solution that does its job properly, then your new business success will follow.

Don't be tempted to plow your own furrow in terms of determining how to approach a sale because you won't "know better," no matter how much you try to convince yourself. Success comes from following a replicable process or methodology, doing things for a reason rather than reacting to shifting events.

You need team effort when winning new business because you can't be expected to know every detail about your solution, do all your own research and data entry, and run a number of sales campaigns. So knowing when to delegate tasks is an attribute that you need to develop. Find out more about getting everyone involved later in this chapter.

Walking through the Steps of Winning New Business

You'll be truly successful in a new business career only if you follow a structured approach or methodology that sets out the required action steps and guides you past the noise and toward consistent success. This is one of the cornerstones of winning new business and fundamental to the teachings throughout this book.

You need to understand your product or service, understand your target audience, and know how to connect with them. There's no shortcut to success, and you have to put in the hard work to achieve the rewards.

Winning new business isn't going to happen on its own. You need to plan your approach and then take the necessary action to make it happen. A plan without action is worse than no plan at all. In Chapter 15, I discuss the importance of taking action today.

Winning new business is about developing an approach that delivers a constant stream of new business success, not just a one-off project win. You need to plan for referrals from your newly won clients at just the right moment, you need to understand and act on the importance of managing your pipeline, and you need to know and understand the importance of the metrics that I outline in Chapter 22.

REMEMBER

Follow these eight steps to winning new business, and you'll be well on your way to success:

» **Identifying:** This is the initial prospecting that you need to do, finding potential prospects, or suspects, as we call them at this stage. I discuss prospecting in detail in Chapter 9.

» **Qualifying:** Having identified potential leads, you need to qualify them, which is at the heart of any good new business methodology. Your qualification is absolutely the key to new business success, and I cover this in Chapter 19.

» **Pitching:** Presenting your solution to the correct person or decision-making unit is the traditional part of the sales cycle, and I explore this in Chapters 3, 5 and 8.

» **Responding and leading:** Responding to questions, overcoming objections (which are just another form of question really), and leading your prospect to the correct buying decision are covered in Chapters 7, 10, and 16.

» **Negotiating:** This is putting the right deal in place; you can find out about negotiating throughout the sales cycle in Chapters 7, 11, 12, 14, 18, and 20.

» **Winning:** Winning is essentially closing the deal and securing the business on the best possible terms for your company while ensuring that your new client is happy with the outcome. I explain this in detail in Chapters 7, 13, 14, and 16.

» **Delivering:** Delivering the end solution isn't the role of new business sales but rather the responsibility of your implementation colleagues; however, as a successful new business salesperson, you need to maintain accountability to your client, so make sure you stay involved. Chapter 11 covers the importance of communication at the implementation phase.

» **Getting more:** Winning additional business from the new client and securing referrals from his network are important parts of the winning new business role, and I cover these topics in depth in Chapters 11, 14, and 16.

Recognizing What You Need to Win New Business

The winning new business role is literally the lifeblood of a company (as I explain earlier in this chapter), but sometimes outside or uninformed observers see it as an expensive role to have someone good dedicated to. Let me assure you that nothing could be further from the truth; a good new business salesperson can make your company successful and is just as important as good research and development people who create your product or service in the first place. Don't be tempted to skimp on your new business efforts as this is a surefire way to failure.

TIP

Generally, having the new business function in-house is the ideal solution, although timings and circumstances may call for outsourcing part of it to a specialist. If you choose to outsource, then choose with care and ensure that the route you select is a good fit with the rest of your business.

Note also that winning new business is a company-wide activity, and although the specific responsibility may be with a named person, that doesn't excuse the rest of the company from looking out for opportunities to feed into the process. In this section, I explore that idea and other keys to success in more detail.

Involving everyone

Successful sales-led companies have a sales-led mentality where everyone in the business has a stake in its success, regardless of the actual job he performs. Everyone has exposure, in business or personal circumstances, to potential customers. Being sales led or sales aware simply means that your staff are encouraged, and rewarded, for feeding opportunities into the sales process.

The sales process doesn't involve only the new business salesperson. You also need researchers, administration people, and sales support people to be able to focus sufficient time and effort into the customer-facing part of their roles. New business salespeople need to drive the support processes and will need to be given the authority to make this happen in the most efficient and effective way.

REMEMBER

Company management needs to be responsive to requests for support in performing these other key functions. Don't hold back on this because the new business salesperson's time is his most important asset, and he needs to be able to delegate important but non-core tasks, sure in the knowledge that they'll be done effectively.

Without exception, every member of staff also needs to know and understand the basics of your product or service and be able to give a simple overview of what the company provides because you never know who they'll come into contact with. Big leads often come from humble beginnings, and when this happens you need to reward whoever was the instigator. Reward can be, but doesn't need to be, in financial terms, and often public recognition of their valuable role may be sufficient. (I discuss rewarding success in more detail later in this chapter.)

TIP

Your staff all need to know how to recognize a potential prospect and know how to feed this information into the sales process as simply as possible. This must not, however, involve new business salespeople being dumped upon; you need to have a simple process of capturing information that can be fed into the sales process with minimum direct time impact on either the information provider or receiver. Often, providing a simple lead form to fill in with all the necessary information may be sufficient, including some rudimentary qualification questions to try to minimize any waste of sales time chasing shadows.

TECHNICAL
STUFF

Getting everyone involved in understanding the importance of the sales process and having an idea of what these "people in suits" do can be the difference between successful cooperation and losing potential opportunities. I took on a sales and marketing director role in a below-the-line creative agency some years ago and discovered that the majority of the staff had no vision of what the company did outside of their narrow job view. I spent some time talking to staff and explained what my role was in helping to make sure they had sufficient work to keep them busy and any ways that could help. I encouraged them to express ideas and operated an open-door policy. This resulted in more cohesion within the business because everyone at least knew what we were trying to achieve, and it gave people a route for expressing ideas. I also made sure to give feedback on any suggestions and especially on any potential leads fed in. Of course, it met with resistance from some old-timers who "knew better," but for the majority it proved to be a valuable exercise in getting everyone to feel involved in the company's success. In truth, no real new business ever came as a direct result of staff engagement, but it at least got people pulling in the right direction.

Establishing success criteria

Success in terms of a winning new business role is easy to define in absolute terms: Either you hit your sales revenue targets or you don't. The bigger picture of success goes beyond that, however. Only by looking at the wider picture do you gain an understanding of how successful and sustainable your new business efforts really are. Typically, you need to also measure the following:

>> **Market position:** Although this may ultimately be the responsibility of marketing (see Chapter 6 for details on marketing matters), new business sales has a massive input to the success growth of your marketing reputation and position. You need to carefully consider how you measure market

position because it's too easy to fall into the trap of spending all your time on measurement and statistics rather than getting the job done. The point, however, is that over time your market position should be improving, which in turn will lead to a better sales environment to operate in.

REMEMBER

>> **Pipeline value:** This is one of the key metrics that I cover in Chapter 22 and is fundamental in understanding how successful your sales efforts are, both for the current period and into the future. A great current period and poor future quarters position, for example, doesn't equate to success and is an indicator of problems on the horizon.

>> **Successful clients:** Sales at any cost isn't a sign of success and will be short lived. You need to ensure that your new business sales efforts do in fact lead to satisfied clients, who in turn can offer pre-sales support to future prospects.

>> **Referrals:** These can provide a valuable source of future prospects who are predisposed to buy from you, and new business salespeople should be encouraged to generate a referral stream. I cover this in detail in Chapter 11.

Taking time to get up to speed

Simply appointing a new business salesperson doesn't equate to instant results or instant additional revenue; it takes time to get up to speed, however good a person you employ or however good a new business salesperson you are.

A common mistake is not taking new business sales seriously enough, or in fact doing anything about it, until it's really too late to make a difference. As a new business consultant, I've been called in too late on a number of occasions and have needed to tell prospective clients that we can do the impossible as a matter of routine but that miracles take a little longer!

Planning ahead is the key. Know your numbers, and understand the dynamics of your market. This will show you when you need to invest in new business or make some outsourcing decisions, but leave it too late at your peril.

REMEMBER

Building your pipeline takes time. Identifying and qualifying prospects takes time, especially if you're going to do it correctly, which you simply must, or it will come back and bite you later. See Chapter 9 for information on prospecting and Chapter 19 for information on qualifying. Both of these topics are fundamental to success in winning new business, so I refer to them throughout this book.

WARNING

Don't be tempted to compromise long-term success by throwing everything at short-term sales wins at any cost. That generally equates to a recipe for disaster and not a sustainable new business strategy.

Rewarding New Business Success

New business success needs to be both recognized and rewarded, as you find out in this section. New business salespeople thrive on winning and being seen by colleagues and peers as winners. Play to this in the way that you recognize and reward success.

TIP

Rewarding new business success doesn't always have to be done in a material way. A software company I once worked for had a great way of recognizing sales success. The sales director kept an air horn outside his office and would come out and set it off every time a salesperson closed a deal. This, of course, interrupted anything and everything happening in the office because the noise was unbelievably loud, but it had an amazingly positive impact on everyone. Sometimes rewarding success can be as easy as that, especially when peer recognition is important. You should have seen the way the rest of the sales team wanted the air horn blown for them.

Balancing risk versus reward

Being paid a rewarding salary, often with a well-structured commission plan, is the traditional way of rewarding salespeople. When putting together a commission plan, or accepting one as a new business salesperson, it's important to strike the right balance between risk and reward. I cover risk and reward in a deal basis in Chapter 11, but the same basic principles apply to the rewarding of sales success. You need salespeople to be hungry for success but to close the right deals for the right reasons, not chasing wrong deals just to hit a target.

TIP

You need to make sure that both the new business salesperson and the company have an equal stake in delivering new business success. This really is a vital component in structuring a compensation plan. Get the balance wrong, and problems will arise further down the line, I guarantee it. A new business salesperson needs to feel like he's more than hired help. Having some form of stake in the success of the business is important — maybe stock options or nonfinancial benefits are the key — whatever the key is, you need to find it out and use it to motivate sales behavior.

With a new salesperson, the first few months are vital for pipeline building, and, as I cover earlier in this chapter, early sales success can be hoped for but not planned for. If the salesperson is being rewarded via a commission plan, bear this in mind.

WARNING

I've seen many situations where companies try to pay a minimum wage and expect a new business salesperson to make a living wage by securing commission. I don't agree with this approach because I believe it both encourages the wrong sales behavior and also devalues the role of the new business salesperson. If you're going to pay peanuts, then expect to recruit monkeys.

Motivating new business behavior

Traditionally, sales managers were taught to motivate sales staff through money in the form of commission. Today, thankfully, this is much less the case, and although commission and salary have an important role to play, they're not paramount.

To drive the right new business sales behavior, use these three areas:

>> **Responsibility:** Agree on a sales budget — with *agree* being the operative word — instead of enforcing a set of unachievable numbers, and delegate to the new business salesperson the task of delivering them. Ask for a structured plan showing how the numbers are to be achieved. Giving ownership of the plan is the key to having it accepted. The principle is the same to structuring a deal, as I outline in Chapters 10 and 11.

>> **Accountability:** When the budget numbers are set in stone, it becomes a contract between the new business salesperson and the company, and being held accountable for delivering a budget is a big motivator for good new business salespeople. It's the closest some of them will get to running their own business; owning the numbers is key.

>> **Authority:** If you're going to delegate responsibility and accountability, you must complete the set and delegate the authority to direct resources to support the sales effort.

TIP

Two other key factors to consider: Don't keep chopping and changing the objectives — after they're agreed on, leave them alone — and have a structured plan with monthly or quarterly goals and rewards instead of leaving everything to happen in the final month. (Hint: It won't!)

Managing a house account

A house account is when the "new" part of new business sales drops off after a client has worked with you for some time. The key factor from a salesperson's viewpoint is that the sales from that client cease to count toward targets and commission plans.

TIP

You need to carefully manage house accounts because you need to ensure that sales retain a sense of client ownership, not least because they have the relationship. Often the answer is to include an element of account management as part of a new business salesperson's goals, and that is part of what the salary covers. Make sure the "rules" are clear and known in advance. Don't drop it as a bombshell and expect no adverse reaction. You've been warned!

Doing the right thing

REMEMBER

In those circumstances where an element of doubt surrounds something like a commission payment, then do the right thing by the new business salesperson. Don't let a small issue become a big one that risks taking away focus and commitment. You need your new business sales team to always be 100 percent focused and committed. Resolve problems and move on quickly, but never cut and run.

Chapter 2

Having Something Relevant to Say

So you've got an opportunity to speak to your prospect about the solution that you need to convince him is the perfect fit. You may meet face to face, or more likely, at the beginning of a sale you may just talk on the phone — the setting doesn't really matter. At every point in the sales cycle, you need to be ready to take advantage of opportunities to present your solution. When they arise, you need to be armed with something relevant to say. You don't want to waste time or risk being perceived as a time waster by talking about irrelevances.

Business cultures differ around the world, and of course you need to be sensitive to customs so you don't offend anyone, but when the time is right to discuss business, get right on with it — don't beat around the bush. Time is a rare commodity, and to get some of your prospect's time is a privilege that you need to turn to your advantage. This chapter explains the basics of saying something relevant as you try to win new business: knowing your subject and audience, properly using tone of voice, and understanding the power of silence.

Knowing Your Subject

Your first challenge in winning new business is to be able to demonstrate to the prospect that you do actually know what you're talking about and that you're someone worth listening to. I guess I'm like many typical prospects when I'm being sold to, and one thing that winds me up is when the seller just won't get on with it. Is it because he doesn't actually know much?

You need to watch out for coming across as a wise guy, though. That situation can be difficult to recover from. Luckily, this chapter guides you in the right direction.

REMEMBER

The first step is to make sure you're comfortable with your subject and have a good grasp of the basics without necessarily knowing everything there is to know. In fact, telling your prospect, truthfully, that you don't know the answer to a question is much better than bluffing your way through and exposing your weakness while also jeopardizing a sale. Your role in winning new business is to know how and where to get answers, not necessarily be a walking encyclopedia when it comes to some of the detail. On the other hand, you're expected to have a certain level of subject knowledge, and falling short here is a surefire way to a quick no — not exactly your objective!

You want to guard against allowing yourself to be sidetracked — being sucked into discussing really detailed aspects of your subject or spending a lot of time discussing aspects that aren't really relevant. By having a good, working knowledge of your subject, you'll know which questions are relevant and need focus and which ones are sidetracking so you can avoid this time-wasting trap.

The following sections go into more detail on aspects of knowing your subject as you try to win new business — namely, being perceived as an expert; using case studies, statistics, and anecdotal evidence; and concentrating on the big picture.

Being perceived as an expert

American political strategist Lee Atwater is credited with saying "perception is reality," generally taken to mean that appearance and opinion are more influential than objective fact when it comes to influencing and communicating with people. One of your early objectives is to be seen — perceived — as an expert in your field, someone who is worth paying attention to and who can provide answers to your prospect's needs. Actually being an expert is less important than having the aura of one in your prospect's eyes.

The key is to be able to back up any claims you make and generally anything that you tell your prospect. You need him to accept you as an expert in your field or, at the minimum, someone who has access to the resources necessary to solve his problem.

You'll likely be tested early in the sales process as your prospect tests the boundaries of your knowledge. Prospects often do this with subtlety, and this test is a key part in establishing the buyer-versus-seller ground behavior rules. When you notice this happening, take and retain control of the process by demonstrating your knowledge of your subject. Fail this early "expert test," and your sale is in trouble. Make sure you pass the test by having a solid grounding in your subject that will help to position you as an expert and someone who can be trusted to deliver a solution to your prospect's need.

Perhaps the greatest exponent of being perceived as an expert was Steve Jobs, cofounder of Apple. Jobs was infamous for what became known as his reality distortion field — the ability to convince himself and others to believe almost anything by using a mixture of charisma, charm, bravado, and persistence (see the nearby sidebar for more information). Few who listened to Jobs were in any doubt that he was an expert, regardless of whether he was or not. This is an extreme example, but it does illustrate my point well — being perceived as an expert will go a long way toward getting your prospect to accept what you're saying and ultimately say yes to your sales proposition.

Writing white papers, blog articles, and website posts that cover the basics of both your industry and your specific solution are excellent ways of demonstrating that you have a good, solid grasp on your subject, and you should try to make a habit of doing so.

Being able to back up any claim you make is vital to establishing yourself as an expert, and I go through some ways of doing that in the following sections. I say it's "vital" because the quickest way to lose credibility in your prospect's eyes is to overpromise and underdeliver, and if he considers that you're doing this in the early stages of relationship building, he'll begin to question the wisdom of trusting you to provide a solution to his problems.

Using the power of case studies

One of the most powerful weapons in your sales armory is testimonials or endorsements from third parties — that is, people who have experienced the type of solution that you're proposing and have found that it does what it claims to do. If you're able to talk about successful implementations of your solution in other sales situations, especially if they're in related business types, and preferably be able to back up these claims with written case studies, then you have the power of the third-party endorsement that can work for you.

THE REALITY DISTORTION FIELD

The term *reality distortion field (RDF)* seems to have made its way into popular culture. It describes a phenomenon in which an individual's intellectual abilities, persuasion skills, and persistence make other people believe in the possibility of achieving very difficult tasks. The term was coined by Apple staff to describe cofounder and CEO Steve Jobs's ability to encourage his team to complete virtually any assigned or delegated task however unfeasible it seemed to be.

There are two sides to the reality distortion field:

- The positive is that it demonstrates how Steve Jobs bent reality in such a way that a difficult or impossible task was made to appear possible. The primary objective was to inspire employees and motivate them to tackle challenging situations in pursuit of an objective. Although all good managers aim to inspire their teams in some regard, RDF implies Jobs's legendary charisma, which many believe helped Apple achieve results that otherwise would not have been possible. In this way, his distortion field was a huge leadership attribute.

- The negative is that the RDF was Steve Jobs's Achilles' heel. Many considered him so driven that he would lie, pester, cheat, or do whatever it took to succeed. In this light, a cynic would point to RDF as Jobs's ability to manipulate people to do what he wanted.

TIP

Share your sales success stories with your marketing experts so they can help develop these case studies. Check out Chapter 6 for more info.

To understand the power of the case study and third-party endorsement, put yourself in your prospect's shoes. Suddenly, you're not alone, nor are you a trailblazer. Someone else who has had the same type of problem has found that this person or company can provide a solution that works, and you're able to see the impact that it's had.

Being able to relate your prospect's situation with that of someone who has successfully bought from you or your company is one of the most powerful things you can bring to the sales table. It's always well worth reading up and learning about the case studies you have available to you.

While case studies are the responsibility of your marketing colleagues, part of your role in winning new business is to recommend to your colleagues which clients are most suitable to provide them. I cover this topic in more detail in Chapter 6.

You can give case studies to your prospect as a document to read, or you can refer to them as you discuss specific elements of a solution. They provide what's perceived as an independent view that backs up your story. By using case studies as a sales tool, you're taking your prospect on a significant journey. You're no longer selling to him; rather, you're letting the power of the third party-endorsement do your selling for you. And if the case study is related to a company, person, industry sector, or situation that your prospect is familiar with, then he'll place a great deal of weight on that. All you've done is use the material that is available to you in a professional manner, having understood your prospect's needs.

Using statistics and anecdotal evidence

Mark Twain popularized the phrase "lies, damned lies, and statistics" to illustrate the power of statistics to build up weak arguments, but using statistics and anecdotal evidence can be another key weapon in your sales armory.

Very few prospects want to be pioneers or early adopters, preferring to be numbered among the late majority (in marketing speak). In plain English, this means that if you can demonstrate that other people have successfully used your solution, then your prospect is following a well-worn path and not sticking his head above the parapet or taking an undue risk.

"Nine out of ten cats prefer Whiskers" is a claim made in a television advertisement for pet food that illustrates the power of statistics in selling — if all those other cats like it, then the chances are yours will, too. You're not taking a risk with buying the product.

Take this basic premise and make it work for your solution; find research that shows customers have successfully worked with your product or service and that it has produced outstanding results for them. I cover more on how to achieve this in Chapter 9 on prospecting effectively.

Being able to talk about your solution in terms of others statistics and anecdotal evidence does a number of key things to help drive your prospect toward that yes:

>> It keeps the focus on other people's results.

>> It demonstrates that your solution is successful.

Focusing on the big picture

While making sure you always have something relevant to say, you also want to keep your, and the prospect's, focus on the big picture — that is, how your proposed solution is going to solve his problem and make his life easier. Why is this important, and how do you achieve this?

First, it's important to avoid too many diversions into myriad detail about your product. That comes after you close the sale, because small issues that in reality are insignificant can easily derail your sale if you don't manage them effectively.

Next, a tried-and-true method is to work with the prospect at the very beginning of the sales cycle to establish terms of reference — what exactly is he seeking to do with the solution he wants? Set a series of reference points that you can check off as you cover them and agree that, as you do so, those requirements and issues are dealt with to your prospect's satisfaction. For example, suppose that you're selling office furniture to a prospect, and he says that color, height, and style are the most important features to him. You explain that your product is available in red, blue, or green and either red or blue will coordinate with the existing color scheme, so color is resolved to his satisfaction and is no longer an issue. You can then move on to the next reference point.

REMEMBER

If you get bogged down in detail at any stage, take a step back and review the big picture. Take the heat out of any sticking points by reminding your prospect of all the things you've already agreed on. Focus on the positive, and look at the big picture. Together you can work toward a solution for all the reference points you have agreed on to form the basis of the solution.

Knowing Your Audience

While knowing your subject (which I discuss earlier in this chapter) should be a no-brainer in sales, knowing your audience is a bit subtler. But if you manage to get it right, this can take you a long way toward getting to that yes that's your overriding goal in winning new business.

Taking the time to gain some valuable knowledge about your audience before diving into a sales process is time well spent. The more you're able to relate to your prospect and have something relevant to say to him, the more you'll be able to understand his way of thinking, which in turn will give you a sales advantage.

It's not just about gaining some knowledge, though; it's about how you use it to your best advantage. For example, if you discover that your prospect is very conservative, then it'd be best not to turn up at his office looking too flashy. Or if you discover that the company you're selling to sponsors a sports team or a local school or anything in the local community, then make sure you use that as a reference point when speaking to it.

You want to be perceived as the voice of experience, and you want your prospect to be able to relate to you and you to him. Having some key background information on both the company and the key people you're dealing with and then being able to apply this knowledge as you discuss your solution will increase the chances of you being someone they want to do business with.

In the following sections, I describe the power of doing background research, understanding prospects' problems, showing empathy, and solving problems professionally.

Performing and applying research

Throughout history, you see examples of knowledge equating to power, and key historical figures, such as Francis Bacon and Thomas Jefferson, understood this principle and applied it to their own situations. Your selling principle is the same: The more you know and can apply to your advantage, the better chance you have to drive the sales process toward a yes.

Can you imagine arriving for a sales meeting knowing nothing about the company you're selling to? How far do you think you'd get? Spending half an hour doing some background reading about the company will at least give you a basic understanding, and spending more time digging deeper will reap rewards. Without knowledge, you really have nothing to relate to your prospect with apart from whatever solution you're selling, and without basic knowledge of their situation, you have no idea if or how it may fit for them.

I'm sure you've been on the receiving end of cold sales phone calls when you answer the phone and someone launches straight into a prearranged script, having no idea who you are or what your circumstances are. How often do you let them get beyond the first 30 seconds before you hang up? Talking to your prospects without having some basic knowledge is almost as bad as that. You want and need to be perceived as an expert who can help them, but why would they be willing to give you any time or pay any attention to what you're talking about if you clearly can't demonstrate some circumstantial knowledge and be able to talk about their specific situation?

Often, you'll be faced with a competitive sales situation. If all the solutions being proposed to your prospect are roughly similar in terms of doing the job, then he'll generally make his buying decision based on interpersonal relationships. From the very beginning, you need to be able to rise above the noise level of the sales environment and be the standout candidate in your prospect's eyes. You can go a very long way to achieving this status by demonstrating your understanding of his situation, which you get only by having gained knowledge and using it to your advantage.

TIP

So how do you acquire this knowledge? I'm not talking about knowing everything there is to know about a person and company. I'm talking about taking the time to research commonly available facts — for example, look at the company website for background information and for latest news. If something is either relevant to the sale or clearly important in their eyes, make a note of it and introduce it into conversation. Show that you're interested.

Background research can also save you from making some big mistakes that could kill your sale. I was once the marketing director for an advertising agency where the CEO was known for being forthright and blunt. He had an unfortunate tendency to liberally intersperse every statement with a string of profanities — how he ever got to be CEO I never understood. We were due to host an important prospective client meeting, and my background research on the people involved showed that one of the key players was from a very conservative background and that he was also a lay preacher in a local church. It was obvious that our CEO was not going to do well with this audience and that having him in the meeting was a very real risk to the sale, so we excluded him. He didn't like being told that he wasn't invited, but you have to do the right thing for the right reasons.

Understanding clients' problem areas

Clients and especially prospective clients rarely want to be trailblazers. Of course, there are some exceptions, and your background research will highlight these, but in general prospects will take a safety-in-numbers approach. It's unusual to find a prospect who wants to be first to implement a specific solution that's not tried and tested.

You need to understand your prospect's problem areas, such as what he's trying to achieve with the solution he's considering buying. This may not always be obvious and may not be limited to the immediate need he tells you about, so you need to be aware of any connected activities that have an influence on the buying decision and get your prospect to tell you about all the issues involved. The last thing you need is to discover something new that delays the sale just as you're about to secure the yes.

Until you can develop a clear understanding of what your prospect is looking to achieve, you can't really propose a solution. Don't make assumptions.

Recently, I was considering a major software purchase for my business. I was looking at a project management system (or I thought that's what I wanted). I did some research and made inquiries. A software vendor picked up my inquiry, contacted me, and arranged to give me a demonstration. He did some basic qualification in terms of how many users, an idea of the budget for the project, and the technical environment it would be working in. What he didn't check was what I wanted to do with the software. He assumed that I wanted to manage projects because that's what a project management system does. Had he spent a bit more time initially checking my requirements, he would have saved himself a lot of time and effort later in the sales cycle.

The demonstration went ahead as arranged, and I'm sure the software was really good, but it didn't do what I wanted. My fault, no doubt, but it turned out that my requirement was for a document portal and information hub to share with clients so we could all see progress, and in my terminology that was "project management." That was not the right terminology, but that came to light only when the demonstration didn't show me what I was looking for. The salesman had assumed that I knew what I wanted — I did, but it wasn't what I asked for. Taking the time to understand what my real needs were would have saved a lot of time and may have led to a sales opportunity, but I wasn't going to buy something that didn't do the job.

REMEMBER

Sometimes understanding a client's needs requires a bit more digging and some risk (I cover risk in Chapter 18). You can discover other factors to investigate in understanding needs by considering your prospect's job function. If the solution he seems to be looking for isn't a generally accepted fit for his function, then you need to ask some probing questions to discover whether he's asking for the right thing or if terminology has gotten in the way.

Displaying empathy

It's important to be able to empathize with your prospect and let him know that you're working with him to solve a problem. You're seeking to be a third-party expert with a detailed view of what he's trying to achieve and the way he wants to do it. You're not trying to sympathize with him because he has a problem that needs resolving. There is a massive difference between sympathy and empathy:

>> *Sympathy* is understanding and reacting to someone's need; it's a feeling emotion.

>> *Empathy* is understanding the need from the other person's viewpoint or the capacity to place yourself in the other person's position and isn't based on emotion.

Selling based on fulfilling an emotional need isn't the same thing. When building a relationship with your prospect and demonstrating that you're the person to fulfill his needs, you need to base your help on an empathic level, showing your prospect that you understand his need and can find a solution based on that understanding.

At times in a buying cycle, the prospect will be vulnerable — for example, when he is out of his knowledge comfort zone. You need to recognize this and guide him through the decision-making process without making him feel that he's ever wrong. Prospects and clients are never wrong; they sometimes just need to be guided away from a viewpoint or course of action by someone who has their best interests in mind.

The type of relationship you're building with your prospect is based on understanding his needs, understanding how to address them, and being perceived as someone he can ask for assistance from without being subservient to because he is the prospect, and the prospect is always the king.

Prospects generally seek safety in numbers. So being able to demonstrate that your solution is tried and tested by others who have found that it met their needs in exactly the same way your prospect wants will go a long way to reinforcing you as the emphatic choice and will ease you on the way to that yes that you're looking for.

Solving problems, not making friends

In all your communication with your prospect, remember your objective: getting to a yes. You're not looking to make a new friend; you're looking to solve a business problem with a solution you're selling. Ultimately, it doesn't matter whether you like your prospect or whether he likes you. What does matter, though, and hugely, is that you have mutual respect for each other.

You need to respect your prospect's time. One of the ways you do this is by always having something relevant to say when you're communicating either face to face or on the phone. Don't phone to ask how he is or if he had a good weekend — you're not buddies. Your relationship is professional, and you want your prospect to think of you as professional and trustworthy, someone he can listen to for advice and trust to do the right thing in proposing the correct solution to his needs.

Consider the relationship you have with your bank manager. You need him to help manage your financial affairs, and you trust him because of the nature of his role in the business. You may be a bit in awe of him and may worry that he doesn't agree with requests you make. He's not your buddy, and you wouldn't consider wasting his time with small talk. This is the type of relationship you want your prospect to have with you. You're the one with the solutions to his needs.

TIP

Disagreeing with your prospect is okay, as long as you do it the right way and enable him to save face if he's wrong. How do you do that, you ask? By using the *conditional agree strategy.* In this idea, whenever your prospect says something that isn't what you need to hear in the sales process, you first agree and then bring him around to your point of view. For example, if you can say, "I understand why you think that, and of course you're right, but have you considered . . . " as a way of turning the answer around, then you show him the way you want the solution to work while allowing him to save face because you told him he was right. The prospect is never wrong, just sometimes mistaken. There are just different forms of right, his and yours, and you need to get him to agree that your form of right is the one he wants.

In all conversations, you want to be the voice of reason. You need to be the one who finds reasons things can be done rather than can't be done. It's important to do this right from the beginning because by the time the important issues come up, your prospect will be comfortable with agreeing with you — after all, you're the expert who's guiding and helping him.

WARNING

Never, ever get into a situation where you need to tell your prospect that he's wrong or has made the wrong choice because this will lead to conflict, which is the opposite of what you're trying to achieve. Even if at the end of the sales cycle you get a no instead of a yes, don't tell him he's made the wrong choice. Tell him that you understand and that should the situation change in the future, you'll be happy to present your solution again. Walk away as a professional and accept that other days you'll get the win.

More often than you may think, prospects suffer from what's known as *buyer's remorse* — when they begin to question the decision they made. If you left the door open and acted throughout with professionalism and integrity, you may be surprised to find that your lost sale eventually returns as a yes.

Perfecting Your Tone of Voice

Tone of voice is not *what* you say but *how* you say it. It's the way you express your personality through the spoken word. It's the rhythm and pace of delivery and even the order in which you say the words. Be aware of the impact of your tone of voice; although it's important to always have something relevant to talk about to your prospect, don't speak just for the sake of it.

Language is incredibly important in all sales situations, and if you're working in a different culture from what you're used to, this becomes even more important to get right. You need to be aware of your literal tone of voice — not too soft and not too sharp — and the listener's viewpoint.

In corporate communications, *tone of voice* defines how a company comes across to its audience in terms of everything that's public facing, such as literature, website, and even branding. In personal communications, tone of voice sets you apart from the next person, and how you deliver a line can convey as much meaning as the actual words you use.

Your role in winning new business is to represent the values of your business and to communicate them by using natural language — that is, the way in which you speak to your prospect. Use language that your prospect is familiar with and convey integrity and enthusiasm in your delivery. Avoid falling into the trap of becoming a walking sales brochure, though. You need to understand the benefits of your solution and be familiar with solution-specific or industry-specific terminology, but your role is to help the prospect to interpret this into natural language.

My first language is English, which in theory makes my role in sales easier because that's the primary business language in countries that I work in. I say "in theory" because the reality is that even the English language is prone to misunderstanding and nuances. Between American English and British English, there's a saying that we're separated by a common language. When dealing in Spanish, for example, the problem is compounded. The bottom line is that you need to be aware of linguistic sensitivities, and if in doubt about a phrase, don't use it.

REMEMBER

Something to watch out for and not to fall foul of is making commitments that you fail to deliver. The rule is simple but important: If you say it, mean it; and if you commit to doing it, make sure you deliver it.

Being your company's mouthpiece

When you're in discussions with your prospect, you're representing your company. But this comes with obligations. You need to be truthful, professional, and transparent. You have a responsibility to accurately portray your solution as a fit for your prospect's needs. Being your company's mouthpiece gives you an additional responsibility in that you're representing not just your own view but a corporate view. The way that you deliver messages needs to be in keeping with this fact.

Whether your prospect speaks to you or another one of your colleagues about the solution, he should hear the same messages from everyone. The message needs to be consistent to avoid misunderstandings and issues around "he said, she said" as you progress through the sales cycle.

TIP

Sometimes, especially when getting to a difficult part of the sales negotiation, it's useful to be able to fall back on a higher authority, where you tell the prospect that you can't agree on a specific term without authority from someone more senior. Use this with care, though, as you're establishing yourself as the expert in your prospect's eyes, and having to refer elsewhere can be seen as a sign of weakness.

Turn it to your advantage by letting your prospect know that whatever he wants is something special, and before you can commit on it, you need to check. This way, you retain your position as the expert and also become the prospect's advocate in seeking something special. Don't overuse this, though, or it will become self-defeating, and your prospect will want to deal with higher authority and cut you out of the loop. Then you have a huge problem.

An important part of being your company's mouthpiece is that it falls on you to set expectations on exactly what your solution is going to deliver. Rarely will you find any solution to any problem that's going to be a panacea. The rule is to underpromise and overdeliver, leaving you with a very happy customer. Get this the wrong way around and you have a problem of your own making.

Understanding the importance of words

The right word at the right time can make all the difference, just as the wrong word at the wrong time can have a devastating effect. The same word can have different meanings, especially in a multilingual setting. Words are the single most powerful weapon any of us has at our disposal and can either make or break any relationship, business or personal. So choose them and use them with care.

In winning new business, the most important word you can hear is yes, and you need to do all the right things to get to that stage — that's why you're reading this book!

REMEMBER

Consider words from your prospect's point of view. He may not be totally familiar with the solution that you're proposing, so you need to make sure that you carefully explain all the key points and show him how it'll satisfy his objectives. Use positive, action-oriented words, and try to avoid negative words. If you need to say no, then always follow it up with an alternative.

WARNING

Avoid using slang terms because they are easily misunderstood, even in a native tongue. I've heard people say that something is "bad" when they mean the exact opposite. Don't try to be clever with language; always be precise and clear.

The single most important word your prospect will ever hear is the sound of his name. In a selling situation, this can be key but can also backfire if you're not careful. You need to consider the prospect's culture as well as the perception of the interpersonal relationship between you before you begin calling him by his first name. There are two differing schools of thought here:

>> You and your prospect are equals and should address one another by given names.

>> You should address someone by his given name only with his permission.

No hard and fast rule exists here. It's up to you to decide which feels right in your situation. Absolutely nothing is wrong with asking your prospect how he'd like to be addressed. The way I see it is that I'm the prospect's equal, so I will use his name, and he is free to use mine. That's a personal choice I make, and it's difficult to define a rule that's right for every situation, so you need to go with your instinct.

WARNING

If you're going to address your prospect by his given name, then make sure you get the name right! Experience has taught me that there are fewer routes to alienating a prospect than calling him the wrong name.

Developing your own style

How to address your prospect (which I discuss in the preceding section) is the first part of developing your own style. I always use a prospect's given name because that's in my nature. My belief is that to do anything else is making myself subservient to him.

Early in your sales career, having a role model — someone you look up to and can learn from — is especially important. Take tips on how your role model approaches prospects and handles himself during a sales process, and mimic those elements that you want to put to work for yourself. I had two role models early in my career, and I'm sure that a lot of my style is an amalgamation of bits I picked up from observing both of them.

I couldn't tell what my style is today. It's just me being me, the best me I can be. If you can achieve that, then you won't go far wrong. It's when you put on an act that's not natural that you begin to experience problems.

TIP

If you're unsure of how you come across, record yourself and ask for feedback from managers and peers. Don't be afraid to ask your prospect whether you're doing a good job — the answer may both surprise you and open up new opportunities.

I'm aware of how I come across in a sales situation because I've recorded myself and asked for feedback, and the results have played a part in me revising my approach over the years. You may find, as I do, that you have a habit that you need to work on. If this is the case, put in the effort to sort it out. In my case, I would mimic accents. It wasn't something I did deliberately; it just happened. Now that I'm aware of it, I go out of my way to make sure I don't do it. Had I not checked, I would never have known.

REMEMBER

Be yourself and don't try to be someone or something that you're not, because you'll get found out and suffer the consequences.

In discussing winning new business with a prospect once, he told me that he employed an out-of-work actor to make new business phone calls for him "because they can pretend to be someone they are not and just play a role," he said. I was dumbfounded when I heard this and even more so when I discovered an outsourced new business company also did this on behalf of clients. The risk they took was astounding. How on earth can an actor represent your business without in-depth knowledge and understanding? They can't. The rationale was that they did not take rejection personally as they were playing a role. What message does this send to your prospects? That you don't care enough about them and solving their problems. "Don't worry, Mr. Prospect, I can take rejection because today I'm being King Lear." Or is it the King of Siam? Unbelievable but true. Stupidity, on behalf of whoever signed it off, of the highest degree. I hope someday to be in a competitive sales situation against one of these people!

Part of the reason for cultivating your new business style is to make yourself memorable for the right reasons. You can take tone of voice and apply it to yourself in the corporate sense of helping to define a brand where the brand is you. You can probably think of someone you know who dresses distinctly — maybe a man who wears a bow tie all the time, for example. That's his brand statement, and that's what will instantly come to mind when people think of him. Although developing a personal brand in this way as part of your style is fine to do, don't let style get in the way of substance. Ultimately, you are what you say and do, and an act will come undone at the most inopportune moment and expose you as having put on a front. Not exactly the way you want to be remembered, especially by a prospect. I look at this is in more detail in Chapter 3.

Recognizing the Power of Silence

Simon and Garfunkel sang about people talking without speaking and people hearing without listening as being the sound of silence. Silence is profound — try it and see what impact it has. In today's society, we're bombarded with noise, verbal and written, as message after message vie for our attention. When we're on the phone or in a meeting, it becomes "necessary" to fill every void with sound, or so it seems. Stop. Take a step back, and let silence have a moment. You'll be surprised at the effect it has. It forces focus and listening. It gives nonverbal communication a chance to work. The results can be enlightening.

There really is no need to talk for the sake of talking, and in a new business meeting or phone call, you can do more harm than good by following this approach. It's also often a sign of nerves, and you don't want your prospect to consider you nervous or unsure of your solution.

There is a misconception that new business salespeople must always be speaking; nothing could be further from the truth. When you have made your pitch, stop and listen to the reaction you get. This is where you will discover a lot about how your prospect is reacting and whether he has really understood what you have told him. Active listening and not repeating yourself are key, and I explore these ideas in this section.

REMEMBER

Good sale closers understand that their best weapon after they've made their pitch is to allow silence to follow. Let the prospect consider what you've said, and let him respond first. Don't be afraid of silence. One thing silence will always do in a one-to-one meeting is put the other person under pressure — pressure to speak first and potentially give away some vital information. Have the confidence to shut up and listen. You're likely to learn a lot.

Listening twice as much as you speak

You need to be alert to nonverbal communication. Facial expressions, gestures, voice tone, eye contact, and posture all tell you a story that will either back up or contradict the words you're hearing.

REMEMBER

Basically, you should aim to listen twice as much as you speak, and you will gain valuable insight that will help you in the sales process.

You can't learn what the prospect really wants if you're not listening to him — and I mean really listening. The key to the success of a sale may not be the headline features or the most obvious benefit. Maybe a small but important side issue is the real driver. Unless you get to this nugget of information, you won't get to your yes decision. If you spend the entire phone call or meeting talking and not listening, you likely either won't hear whether it's articulated or won't be able to tease it out with careful questioning if it's hinted at. I'm not suggesting that your prospect will be hiding some vital information from you but rather that he may not really know or appreciate its importance or may assume that you already know.

A typical prospect will give a lot of information and is likely to ask a lot of questions. Some have a habit of using questions as a summary, an aid to themselves. Not every question requires an immediate answer; some you will cover in other ways, such as in your presentation or proposal. Don't try to counter every objection or answer every question just so you can have the last word.

You also need to acknowledge that your prospect is right when he raises points, but again sometimes a simple "yes, you are right" is sufficient rather that a lecture. Especially at the early stages of a sales cycle, you need to get your prospect to do the majority of the talking because this is where you're going to learn a lot about the needs, about the fit of your solution, and what objections are going to have to be covered in your proposal. If you're spending too much time speaking, you're likely not listening sufficiently.

Engaging in active listening

There is a massive difference between listening and hearing. You can hear words easily enough, but are you picking up on and focusing on the real meaning?

Active listening involves not just focusing on the words but also using all your senses to take in what's being said. Is the prospect's body language telling you that this subject is of particular importance? Is your body language communicating back to him that you really are engaged with the conversation? Nonverbal signs you can give include nodding your head in agreement, smiling, and making eye contact, but beware that too much can be intimidating, such as leaning forward to listen. Don't be distracted, and don't look like you are. You need to be, and be seen to be, paying full attention.

REMEMBER

Interruptions, even reinforcement words like "yes," "I understand," and "I see," can be negative and off-putting to the prospect when he's explaining something to you. Taking brief notes as an aide memoir is far better. Asking relevant questions and seeking clarification are signs that you're engaged in active listening and paraphrasing or summarizing what you've been told will help to reinforce this view. Avoid going off topic, stick to what you've learned and probe deeper, giving your full attention to the topic at hand. Often you'll gain valuable insight by asking the prospect for more detail on a specific point or asking questions that will probe for more specific information.

If you observe a number of salespeople in action, you'll find several different styles of note taking. You need to discover what works best for you:

>> Some write verbose long hand notes, but this is often off-putting for the prospect.

>> Others rely solely on memory, making detailed notes afterward. If you can do this, it's the best way to go.

>> Others, me included, make brief notes of certain words or phrases to remind them of key points.

Go with whatever works best for you, but if it's verbose notes, be aware of its impact.

TIP

If a lot of your new business work is telephone-based, consider a call recording system to assist you with remembering detail. I do this. I spend several hours every day talking on the phone, and by not having to take detailed notes, I can pay much more attention to the conversation I'm having. There are some pitfalls you need to be aware of here, which I go over in Chapter 4.

Whatever method you use to capture information, be sure you log it for future use. This is one of the roles of using a CRM that I cover in Chapter 9.

Making sure you don't talk yourself out of a sale

There comes a time in every sales meeting and in every attempted sales close when it's time to stop talking. Recognizing when that is can be the difference between a yes and a no. Recently I was involved in a competitive pitch situation, which in my business is very rare. Three companies were invited to be present at the same time and were able to listen to each other pitch. I was a little uncomfortable in having competitors listen to me but decided to go along with it.

As it happens, I went first — luck of the draw. I did my pitch without making any reference to the competitors, exactly as I would have done had it been just me. Companies two and three followed, and at least one of them did make reference to the others, but no problem there. The meeting was then opened up to a question-and-answer session, and it quickly degenerated into a mud-throwing session with the other two companies attempting to score cheap points. I kept quiet as much out of embarrassment of the behavior as anything else. I answered questions as I was asked them and referred back to points that had been raised in initial discussions and in my pitch. The meeting leader began to summarize, and as he did the other two companies constantly interrupted by making their own points.

No decision was made that day, contrary to expectations that had been set, and we were told this was due to unforeseen issues needing to be resolved. It transpired that the other two companies had done themselves no favors by failing to keep quiet and were subsequently dropped from the buying process. My company was asked to retender based on additional requirements, and it was to be a single tender.

Two things of note came out of this: The power of silence was definitely effective, and I learned a lesson about not agreeing to be involved in such a circus again!

WARNING

There are other reasons for knowing when to stop talking:

>> You need to be wary of repetition, which is fine for reinforcing a point, but when it's done, stop.

>> Don't risk reopening closed issues for the sake of having something to say.

Don't under any circumstances lapse into any form of unprofessional behavior, such as switching out of sales meeting mode as you're saying goodbye and begin some gibberish about this evening's plans.

>> Don't tell tales out of school. Earlier in this chapter, I talk about the power of case studies, and these should always be positive. Don't go on to talk about product or service disasters or about clients that failed. That's a surefire way to a no.

If you're at a meeting, remember that the meeting starts as you walk into the building and ends only after you leave the building. Anything you say in passing on the way in or out needs to be in the new business context. Apart from a warm greeting and a professional departure, everything else is to do with the sale and getting to the yes. Who cares if it's going to rain over the weekend and spoil the camping trip? You're not making buddies; you're solving a prospect's problems and need to be seen to be the consummate professional he can absolutely rely on.

Chapter **3**

Making First Impressions Count

First impressions are made instantly and once made are impossible to undo. Whatever the situation — email, letter, phone call, or face-to-face meeting — the keys to making first impressions count are preparation, professionalism, and control. Get these right and you go a long way toward establishing yourself and setting the correct tone for your new business discussions. Get them wrong and your overall task becomes much harder. This chapter shows you how to make a good first impression with professionalism, control, and preparation — and how to maintain that good impression through follow-up and unexpected events.

Being Professional and in Control

Although it may seem obvious, you really do get only one chance to make a first impression, and that sets the tone of your dealings with that client. You have to get the first impression right to set the business relationship off on the right foot.

Your first encounter with a client is a bit like going on a first date: You're excited and a little apprehensive, and you know in general terms how you want it to work out. You arrive, and as you open your mouth to speak, gibberish comes out. All the practiced opening lines disappear from memory, and you're left floundering for something half-decent to say to avoid looking like a total idiot. A new business situation, especially early in your career, can be as daunting, but with a little fore-thought and a bit of practice, you'll be fine.

The important thing to remember is why you're there. You're not out to make a new friend; your objective is to make a strong and positive first impression and to put down a marker for the way the business deal is going to be handled. In this section, I introduce the basics of making a good first impression, with a focus on professionalism and control. Later in this chapter, I examine why preparation is so important that you need to make it second nature.

REMEMBER

In most new business situations, your interactions with a client are going to be limited and are likely to be numbered in tens rather than hundreds. You won't usually have the time or the opportunity to reestablish yourself as credible and professional if you don't get it right the first time.

Understanding the basics: Time, communication, and dress

Right from the outset, you need to come across as professional in your approach to a prospect. Often it's the little things that can make a big difference, especially when it comes to nonverbal communication. To get off on the right foot and make a good impression, especially when meeting a client for the first time, follow these basic rules:

>> **Be on time.** Irrespective of how the contact is made, being on time is important. If you arrange to be somewhere or do something at a specific time, make sure you do it. Don't be late. Fashionably late may be acceptable in social circles, but punctuality is essential in new business.

>> **Be culturally aware.** You need to act the part. By this I mean the way that your communication comes across should be in line with your prospect's culture. You need to be aware of cultural sensitivities as well as basic manners and etiquette.

REMEMBER

Age, gender, and seniority are as important as cultural issues in determining how you communicate. In North America or the United Kingdom, addressing your prospective client by his given name may be acceptable, but in Southern Europe, the Middle East, and Asia, for example, this is a big no-no unless invited to do so. Much more formality is required, unlike doing business in the United States or Western Europe. In Japan, for example, you need to dress formally for business meetings because Japanese business etiquette doesn't accept casual attire. In Spain, don't be surprised if meetings begin late and if the core of the business isn't discussed at the initial meeting. As a general rule, err on the side of caution in early meetings, and if you're in doubt, go with the formal approach.

>> **Dress well.** In face-to-face meetings, either pre-arranged or perhaps at a networking or other business event, the way you physically present yourself is vital. How you dress and your overall appearance will unlikely win you a piece of business on their own, but they can easily lose you one.

Although no absolute rule on style of dress applies across all situations, be sure you consider how you'll be perceived and dress accordingly. Old-school sales thinking will tell you to dress "better" than your target audience to gain "respect," whereas other schools of thought will tell you to dress in the same style as your audience. Being yourself and being the best representation of yourself at all times is most important. Be smart, not scruffy. Be well turned out and clean at all times. Be tidy. Should you wear a suit? That depends on individual new business situations, and being smart and appropriately dressed are the main attributes here.

REMEMBER

Some new business salespeople will tell you that they "feel the part if they look the part"; if that works for you, it's fine. My rule is to give careful consideration to how you're turned out and ensure that it's appropriate for the role you're playing in new business, for the business you're representing, and for the target audience you're dealing with.

Making the client important

In a selling situation, you need to remember that the client is king. What I mean by this is that you need to make your client important and focus on his needs, but that doesn't mean you should act subservient. Treating the client as king is a mindset that you need to adopt, and you may need to make some adjustments to your natural salesperson's instincts to gain traction here. You need to act in a professional manner at all times, and to be seen as doing so. Often, a new business salesperson likes to talk and "needs" to be talking. Remember that while you're talking, you're unlikely doing any active listening. Conversely, if you can get a client to do the majority of the talking while you apply active listening techniques, you'll gain in two ways:

>> Allowing your client to talk to you while you show genuine interest will make him feel important. The most important topic of conversation to most people is themselves and how they do their job. Showing genuine interest enables your prospect to feel comfortable when talking to you and often provides you with valuable insight into his personality that you can build on as the sales cycle progresses.

>> By listening, you'll gain valuable insight to the real needs that your solution has to address. Adopt the mindset that you're not selling to the client but that he is buying from you and you need to fully understand his requirements.

Listening is only part of the task, though. You need to show that you're interested in learning about the client's requirements or issues and how your solution will be of benefit to him in meeting those requirements. You can use this priceless insight later in the sales cycle when presenting your solution (see Chapter 5 for more information on solutions). Show your interest and accelerate your learning by asking open questions, such as "How does this . . . ?", "What would the impact be of doing . . . ?", and "What type of advantages would you gain if you could . . . ?" Ask your prospect how he sees a solution fitting into his needs. He may even tell you exactly what you need to show him or do to win the business.

REMEMBER

Active listening and open questions give your client the opportunity to open up to you about the real needs he's seeking to address. It will also demonstrate that you really have his best interests in mind when proposing a solution, especially if you don't just end with a sales pitch without first having taken the time to let him tell you what the drivers are.

Taking control

There's a difference between letting the client talk to you and allowing focus to be lost. You need to remember that you're the one with the solution to his needs and that you're the expert in your field. Taking and maintaining control of the sales process is an important step for you. Throughout this chapter, I examine some of the ways for you to put yourself into this position of control. Although you want to encourage your client to talk about his needs and potential solutions, you need to be aware of the danger of being led down blind alleys by recognizing when you're being taken off topic and returning the conversation to the key areas.

TIP

Two ways to maintain control of discussions, as you see later in the chapter, are establishing some basic objectives and having an agenda to work through. You can use these items as reference points during your discussions — either face to face, on the phone, or in writing — as a road map to closing the sale, as a means of summarizing where discussions have reached, and as a checklist of topics that you covered and agreed upon.

This style of active summary not only allows you to control the active discussion but also acts as a method of closing off objections that you've already covered. (See Chapter 10 for details on overcoming objections.) Use this to demonstrate that those areas are already agreed upon should the topic reemerge later in the sales cycle. This way, you're setting out your stall from the very beginning in a professional and concise manner while demonstrating that you're listening to and addressing requirements and issues as they arise.

If the client raises a new issue or objection, acknowledge it but know that you don't have to necessarily cover it at that moment, especially if the topic isn't on the agenda for that meeting or touch point. Let your client know that you've noted the issue and that you'll return to it and fully address it later. This way, you maintain control of where the discussion leads and can keep it on track in accordance with the agenda and objectives, and you avoid being taken into blind alleys by off-topic issues that may get in the way of your planned progress.

For example, you may learn that a side issue of the project under discussion is actually more important than you initially thought. Make a note of this, but don't allow the discussion to be sidetracked onto it until you've had an opportunity to consider the implications further. Tell your prospect that this matter is important and you'll address it at the next meeting.

I've seen lots of examples of new business salespeople not making progress in a sales cycle because they allow the client to drive the discussions and just follow the client's lead. At best, this approach will delay a sale; at worst, it will lose the sale because the salesperson never establishes and forms control.

You're seeking to make a good first impression and using that to establish your ground rules. One of the key rules is that you're driving the sales process, although you're doing so subtly. Failing to take control from the initial contact sets a precedent and once done is difficult to undo.

Setting expectations

In Chapter 19, I talk about the importance of qualifying new business opportunities. One of the key elements is not to rush headlong into meetings with everyone who comes onto your radar. This is also relevant in making first impressions count because you need to avoid the "let's meet to discuss" time-wasting trap. Your time is valuable, and you need to treat it accordingly. When you agree to meet with or have a detailed phone conversation with a prospect, you need to have a good idea of how useful this meeting is going to be in terms of getting an order. Don't agree to spend valuable time with a prospect until he's qualified.

When you do have a meeting or detailed phone call scheduled, both parties must understand why this touch point is happening and what each can reasonably expect to gain from it. This is usually defined in the form of an agenda, but the agenda doesn't necessarily have to be laid out as a formal document. Sending an email that sets out the key objectives of the touch point is a more useful tool. Use the agenda to keep the touch point on track and to ensure that you're covering the right areas. (Find out more in the later section "Setting the agenda.")

On those rare occasions where a prospect won't agree to an agenda in advance and just wants to "talk," you need to understand where in the qualification process you are and whether that justifies you spending valuable time on the opportunity. If it doesn't, don't commit to the time, and instead suggest that a meeting or conference call may not be the best way to move forward.

You need to set the prospect's expectation at each stage of communication. For example, "This is what we will be discussing, and this is what we will look to achieve by a meeting or call." Setting expectations is an important step in ensuring that your time is valued, as I discuss later in this chapter.

REMEMBER

Keep in mind that the expectation of a touch point isn't to build a friendship; the purpose is to take another step toward securing a new business deal.

Establishing trust

At the beginning of a new business sales cycle, the prospect likely won't know you and may be reluctant to provide too much information until you establish some basic credibility. You have some initial credibility by virtue of your position as a representative of your company, and you need to build on this quickly. Providing prospects with a brief outline of who you are and the role you play in new business is usually the first step to establishing credibility.

Next comes establishing trust. Active listening, as I discuss in the earlier section "Making the client important," is undoubtedly a factor, but the fastest way to establish trust is to do as you say you will. Take note of action items as they arise during your discussions, and if you commit to doing or checking something, make sure that you do it quickly and provide the results to your prospect.

Summarize the discussion for your prospect, too. You should be doing this in any case for your CRM system, as I discuss in Chapter 9, so documenting it for the prospect shouldn't be difficult or too time-consuming. Get into the habit of writing contact reports with a copy to the CRM and a copy to the prospect. You don't have to go into massive amount of detail; just summarize the main discussions and make note of action items along with the defined time frame for dealing with them. (I describe contact reports in more detail in the later section "Owning the next stages.")

Your prospect will quickly come to expect these contact reports, and they'll become part of the buying cycle as documented evidence of decisions taken and progress made. They will also serve to enhance your credibility in the eyes of the prospect and, in conjunction with ticking off your action items and keeping commitments, will quickly establish you as someone your prospect can trust to deliver. This is a good example of your professionalism and will come to be appreciated as the relationship develops.

REMEMBER

Don't ever consider contact reports and CRM updates to be a waste of your time or an inconvenience, because nothing could be further from the truth. In Chapter 9, you discover the importance of logging data into a CRM system and why you should always do so. In the same way, contact reports will prove to be a valuable selling tool as the discussions progress because they'll provide documented evidence that you've dealt with issues and closed them off.

Having your time valued

Unless you've mastered time travel, you have only a finite amount of time in each working day, and you need to use it to your best advantage in meeting your new business goals. I'm sure you have turned up for a client or prospect meeting and felt it has been a total waste of time for a variety of reasons:

>> The prospect didn't show up or wasn't expecting you.

>> The prospect was doing something else and not focusing on you.

>> You found that you were covering old ground yet again.

>> The meeting kept going off topic.

How many times have you left a meeting or finished a phone call and told yourself that it was a complete waste of time? Generally, this comes down to how the touch point was set up, and 99 times out of 100, it will be down to the new business salesperson not covering the bases.

In Chapter 19, I discuss the importance of qualifying continually and not agreeing to have a meeting until the time is right according to your qualification criteria. When it's right to have a detailed phone discussion or a face-to-face meeting, you need to ensure that it's going to be both productive and worthwhile for both parties. If you leave a meeting feeling it was a waste of time, imagine what your prospect is thinking — that you've just wasted his time, too, which won't do either your credibility or sales success any good.

In this chapter, I keep referring to the importance of an agenda, and that really can't be overstated. If you don't have a good reason to meet, then don't meet. If you ignore this basic rule, then don't be surprised to find that your time has been wasted. I discuss agendas in more detail later in this chapter.

The main premise of this chapter is to make first impressions count, so you need to start the way that you intend to go on with a prospect. Value his time and be seen to do so, and he will value yours. If you look at the earlier bullet points, I can guarantee that each of them was caused simply by one not valuing the other's time sufficiently and trying to shortcut the setting-up processes. If the worst comes to the worst and you've set up the touch point correctly only to find that one of these bullet points still applies, then what do you do? First, add it to the CRM as a warning for others in the future, and second, write a contact report in negative terms and let it be known that the touch point was a waste of time. One of two things will happen: Either you'll lose the sale, but it was unlikely to happen anyway, or you'll discover that future touch points are treated with the professionalism they deserve.

Recognizing the Importance of Preparation

Being prepared for an initial interaction with your prospect should be second nature to a new business salesperson. If you're not prepared, you risk not only giving a negative impression but also losing out on a sales opportunity. Why would anyone go into a meeting that he wasn't prepared for?

Of course, you can go to the other extreme and spend all your time preparing for every eventuality and not actually have time left to attend the meeting. I'm talking of striking a sensible balance here, of taking the time to do the basic checking on who you're seeing, what he's looking for, how your solution has worked in that type of situation previously, and the latest news concerning your prospect and his industry.

If your solution is a technical one, you won't be expected to know all the ins and outs, but you will be expected to at least understand the basics and how the solution fits with typical client situations. For more easily understood solutions, you'll be expected to know a lot about it. Although no one will expect you to know everything about your solution and its fit to a prospect's needs with no notice, you'll be expected to have a sound understanding of the basics, both of your solution and of the prospect's industry sector.

Initial meetings are the first real opportunity that you and your prospect have to check each other out, and it's important for you to create a good impression and to be seen as professional. Among the key tools for achieving these goals are agreeing on the objectives of a meeting — not just meeting for the sake of it — and having an agenda, which will help to guide you toward achieving the objectives.

Agreeing on the objectives

After you get beyond the initial contact phase and into a sales cycle, every touch point has a purpose, and the overriding objective you have as a new business salesperson is to move the discussions forward and closer to the elusive yes that you seek as your ultimate goal.

Clearly, your prospect is going to have to investigate your solution as a fit to his need and, as part of this, will need to be in contact with you. You're going to want to continually qualify the opportunity (see Chapter 19 for information) and therefore be in touch with him. In setting up these touch points, either as phone calls or face-to-face meetings, you need to set and agree on clear objectives. What are you hoping to gain from this next interaction? What is your prospect hoping to gain?

Until you understand what your prospect needs from you, doing precise preparations is difficult, and I don't suggest attending a touch point in this state. So you need to pin down the objectives and form into an agenda that you both agree on. Saying "Let's meet on Wednesday and see how things are moving along" is too loose, because there is no objective and, apart from passing some time, this statement is unlikely to achieve anything. On the other hand, saying "Let's meet on Wednesday to review the needs analysis" is much better. It's specific and measurable and will move the discussions forward. You'll both know whether you reached the objective. You may need to spell out how you go about "reviewing the needs analysis," and that is where the agenda comes in (see the next section).

Setting the agenda

When it comes to an agenda, having just the list of topics to be discussed is generally sufficient. This process allows your client to better prepare, assuming that you set the agenda, and to have no doubt as to what you're expecting him to be ready to discuss. This process also helps with making a good impression. In advance of a meeting with a prospect, you both know what you'll discuss and can arrive prepared to comment on and commit resources as necessary without having to refer to others and take up more valuable time.

Suppose that you have an objective for a meeting with a prospect on Wednesday about "reviewing the needs analysis," and that's a start, but how are you going to go about achieving this? Maybe in this example you agree that the agenda includes

>> Clearing up any points of clarification resulting from reading the needs analysis

>> Highlighting any areas of concern

>> Determining who will take responsibility for each section

>> Ensuring that resources are assigned

>> Setting a timescale for completion

REMEMBER

You don't have to formally present the agenda on a piece of paper titled "Agenda," but you should email it or at the very minimum agree to it verbally in advance of the meeting. However, as the new business salesperson, you should own both the objectives and the agenda and be the driver of the process. Without this, you lose control of the sales process, which leads to delays and potentially no order ever being received. In other words, the objectives define what you'll discuss, and the agenda defines the process you'll use to meet the objectives.

Using research (or not)

TIP

Although you should do the bulk of your preparation in advance, you'll need to account for some last-minute checks before a meeting or phone call. As a minimum, you should do an Internet search for any news about the target company that has hit that day and for any specific industry news that may be relevant. Your prospect will expect you be on the ball and to know what's happening in any relevant activity, but this also allows you to demonstrate your professionalism and understanding of the issues that affect your prospect and his business sector.

Another good reason for last-minute research is that you don't want any surprises. Imagine how you'd react if you arrived for a meeting to find that the company was in the midst of a takeover bid that threatened to overturn your project? A true story serves to illustrate my point about last-minute research. Several years ago, I was due to speak to a senior marketing person at BP about an environmental awareness campaign. As you'd expect, I did my last-minute research and found a breaking news story about the Gulf of Mexico oil spill. Easily putting two and two together, I was able to determine that today wasn't the best day to be speaking to BP about environmental issues, so I sent a message to rearrange the appointment for some other time.

When it comes to research, there's a fine line to what you should use and what you should set aside. You want to be perceived as knowledgeable, but you also need to avoid being labeled as someone who has an opinion on everything and needs to talk about it. Although research is vital and last-minute research is massively important, the real skill comes in knowing when to use this knowledge and, perhaps of more importance, when to not say anything. For example, your prospect may have just released a poor set of financial results, and you should know about this, but it may not be appropriate to bring it into discussions unless he does first.

TIP

Log each piece of research that you find into the CRM, and make it available to colleagues, current and future, who may have dealings with this company or this industry. No research is ever "pointless" or "wasted."

Answering frequently asked questions

Most companies and most solutions have a string of questions that prospects tend to ask frequently, and your situation likely won't be any different. You need to deal with company and product background questions fairly early in the sales cycle because they're pretty fundamental to a prospective customer. You, as the new business salesperson, need to know your numbers and your background as part of creating a good impression.

Moving on to more specific solution questions, you'll find that the same questions crop up time and again with different prospects, so you'll know to expect them and how to answer them. It's important to have your answers ready but to treat each question as if it's the first time you've been asked it, and not with a sign of resignation about being asked "that question" again. It's likely the first time this prospect has asked it, and the answer is clearly important to him, so treat it that way. You need to have ready answers to frequently asked questions but not stock answers.

REMEMBER

Two things to keep in mind when preparing for questions: There is no such thing as a silly question for your prospect to ask, and always bear in mind that questions equal engagement. The time to worry, especially early in the sales cycle, is if the prospect doesn't have questions to ask.

Following Up to Maintain the Good Impression You've Made

Getting in front of prospective customers and qualifying them is generally the hardest part of the sales cycle (get the scoop on qualifying in Chapters 9 and 19). After you've met with a qualified prospect and made a favorable first impression, you need to own and drive the follow-up process as it progresses into a full sales cycle.

At the end of the initial touch point, you need to establish that you, not the prospect, own the follow-up process. Failure to achieve this will cause you lots of problems as the sales cycle develops, or indeed it may not develop for precisely that reason.

Keeping to the commitments that you make in meetings or other communications is vital to both creating a good impression and to being in a position to drive the sales cycle forward. You can't expect your prospect to keep to commitments if you don't do so. Establishing a set of ground rules as to how you'll move forward is also important, as you find out in this section.

If you fail to own the follow-up process, then you're allowing your prospect to dictate the terms of how the sale will be driven. That is your job. Fail here and you lose the authority and permission to phone or contact the prospect, except on his terms. This is useless for a new business salesperson, so establishing ownership of the follow-up process is one of your most important initial tasks.

Keeping commitments

It should go without saying that when you commit to a client or prospect that you'll do something, make sure you complete it. Doing so is both good manners and part of creating a good impression for you and your company. I have come across too many instances of follow-up commitments not being kept to know that this message needs to be underlined.

Delivering on your follow-up commitments shows that you're a serious new business salesperson and one who your prospect can do business with. It also does two other key things: reinforces trust and establishes precedent.

>> Take seriously any opportunity you get to reinforce prospect and client trust in you as a salesperson. The more credit you can build up here, the easier some of the selling tasks further in the sales cycle will become.

>> Make a habit of delivering at least what you committed to and do so by at least the committed time. If you can beat either of these, then do so. You're setting an important precedent that will position you as someone who delivers and keeps commitments, someone in the sales process who the prospect can trust and rely on.

For example, if during a meeting a side issue is raised that may not be immediately important, tell your prospect that you'll address it later, and then make sure that you do so. An email follow-up telling him that you have noted the issues and will resolve it by the next meeting is a good way to handle this.

Defining the ground rules

What are you following up on? It should be in line with the objectives that you established prior to the touch point (I talk about objectives earlier in this chapter). If it isn't, then you need to revisit your objectives because something may have been miscommunicated and needs correcting. Doing so is both good practice and contributes to making a good impression.

Guard against unreasonable and unrealistic requests for more information, which can have a habit of slowing down the sales cycle and introducing additional elements that you'll need to sell around. Try to steer your prospect to focus on what is necessary and relevant for solving his problem or need. If your solution can provide additional benefits, you can summarize them simply without going into unnecessary detail. You need laser-sharp focus and may need to guide your prospect back toward the key objectives if he begins to go off on a tangent.

In defining ground rules for following up from a touch point, be realistic with timescales. You need to balance acting quickly to get to the next stage with your workload, prioritizing areas that will provide you with maximum returns. Don't promise to get something done by tomorrow in the hope that you will find time. It's better to commit a few days later and deliver early if you can than to make an unrealistic commitment and miss it.

If something is needed urgently, qualify why that is and what impact it will have on the sales cycle progress if delivered early, on requested dates, or later. If you're under pressure to provide something quicker than you know you'll be able to, then push back. Ask what the real urgency is. It may be that you need to reprioritize to meet a deadline, but equally it may transpire that the prospect has plucked a date out of the air and that the need is not as urgent.

Owning the next stages

What happens as result of a touch point is important. You've worked hard to get a meeting, your qualification is looking good, your solution is a good fit to the prospect's needs, and you have agreed to provide some additional information in three days' time. So far, so good, but now what? What is the next step in the sales cycle? Don't agree that your prospect "will look at the information and get back to you" or words to that effect. This is just about as bad as a straightforward "no thank you," because you've lost control of the sales cycle.

You need to own the next steps, at almost any cost. You need to maintain permission to instigate contact, which you lose if agreeing to let the prospect contact you.

As a tactic, you can fall back on the contact report, which I introduce in the earlier section "Establishing trust." Tell the prospect that you will, as you always do, send a contact report to document what has been discussed and decided, and leave the follow-up at that if you can't get further agreement. You can then add into the contact report that you'll speak in a week's time or whatever is appropriate. If it's in the contact report, then you have given yourself permission to maintain contact and kept the initiative.

Have a look at an example contact report in Figure 3-1 to get an idea of how this can work for you. A good contact report has the basic information of who was present and where and when the contact occurred, summarizes issues discussed and agreed upon, and specifically notes anything you feel may be contentious that you have resolved. A report protects your position should the issue be raised again as you can demonstrate that it was discussed and resolved.

CONTACT REPORT

CLIENT:		LOCATION:	
CLIENT STAFF:		COMPANY STAFF:	
CONTACT TYPE:		SCHEDULED BY:	
NUMBER:	DATE OF MEETING:	DATE OF REPORT:	

	ACTION

This contact report has been produced as a representation of the agreed actions and conversation that took place on the above date. If there are any statements that are not accurate, then these should be brought to the attention of the company immediately.

FIGURE 3-1:
A sample contact report.

....

Signed for on behalf of (company name)

Dealing with the Unexpected

Problems happen. It's a fact of life. Having a sales cycle that runs totally smoothly and according to plan is unusual. Any number of external events that you have absolutely no control over can get in the way of your progress. Accept this and move on. The mark of a successful new business salesperson is how he responds to unexpected factors, and the good ones will always be prepared.

There is every likelihood that you'll be able to make an unexpected external event work in your favor. Consider, for example, the case of your prospect canceling a meeting on short notice due to sickness. Sickness happens. Give him a few days to recover and be back at work, and reschedule the meeting. He'll likely be feeling guilty about having let you down and will accommodate a date that works for you. If you meet with any resistance, let him know that you used the canceled time wisely and did some additional background work on the project that you'd love to share with him at the rearranged meeting. He owes you a meeting, and unless your qualification was wide of the mark, you'll get another opportunity.

Consider how you should react if you're doing a product demonstration and something goes wrong. Don't fly into a panic. If you can see that something has gone wrong, it's generally better to stop and regroup. Tell the prospect the truth — something out of your control has gone wrong and this sometimes happens in demonstration situations because the data is made up and the solution can't work with an unreal set of factors. Tell the prospect that you'll work with him to define some real data based on his specific circumstances and rerun the demonstration next week. And then move on and forget the demonstration and focus on the positive.

REMEMBER

The number-one rule in dealing with an unexpected event is to act in a positive way. Make no negative comments, such as "this stupid product always falls over at this stage." Let your prospect see your true colors in these types of situations; nothing else matters as long as you're professional and not flustered by circumstances. Have confidence in your solution whatever external factor gets in the way, and let that confidence be seen.

If something external impacts your plans with a prospect, your priority becomes to ensure that you have another time and another day to regroup and move forward. This applies regardless of the circumstances. Don't make a drama out of a crisis, and don't let your prospect see that it is a crisis. Manage the situation. Take control.

Chapter **4**

Using Technology to Help

Winning new business has evolved over the years, and that evolution has become more like a revolution in the information and technology age. You need to embrace change and look to take the best possible advantage of the opportunities offered by using technology in your new business role. For business owners, you need to adopt a top-down, driven approach to gain the maximum benefit from this seismic shift.

WARNING

Technology comes with a word of warning, however: Don't expect it to do the job of winning new business for you — it won't. What it will do is massively assist you in being more productive and open up more and better-qualified opportunities. This comes at what some people may see as a cost, though, because when correctly applied, technology will also rapidly highlight problem areas and any weaknesses in your selling and qualification processes.

Creating the correct technology infrastructure is very important, and creating the right new business environment is vital. I explore these challenges in this chapter.

REMEMBER

In these days of new technical wizardry being introduced all the time, everyone has a tendency to want to use and be seen using the latest gadgets. Unless you're selling these gadgets, stop right there and put them away. Technology in a new business environment is purely a tool to assist you and should never be the focus of attention. Don't lose your selling skills, and don't water down your people skills by allowing a tool to be prominent.

Understanding the Role of Technology in Winning New Business

To gain the best possible advantage in the application of technology to the new business environment, you need to have a strategy in place. And I don't mean you should just buy new business salespeople a laptop and let them get on with it.

At the center of this strategy, you need centralized control of data, and you need to know how to turn raw data into useful information. You can find a lot of books on this subject, and I'm not trying to cover the strategy here; I'm just flagging it as something you have to put in place in order to gain any form of competitive advantage with the use of technology.

REMEMBER

Although the actual choice of technology doesn't really matter for our purposes, all the hardware and software systems should at least be compatible with each other to make information sharing possible. Without this, you're wasting both your time and money.

The role of technology in new business is twofold: automating existing processes and opening up new opportunities.

>> Automating existing processes involves being able to issue letters and quotations at the push of a button, based on predefined templates. You avoid having to reinvent the wheel for every piece of communication you need to send. Updating sales records and forecasts has always been an onerous task for new business salespeople and generally one they avoid if possible. Technology can help this be as simple as entering some numbers and clicking a button.

>> Technology opens up new opportunities in a couple of ways. First, it allows salespeople to have more time to do the real job instead of concentrating on paperwork. Second, and much more important, is that data is now readily available. In its raw form, data needs to be turned into valuable information, but you can now easily and quickly, for example, read today's industry news for sectors that you work in, which can often highlight opportunities that you'd never have previously known about. By following a snippet of data in this way, you can within a few minutes find out who the key players are, have a good idea about size and demographics, and gather relevant background information to give you enough data to begin making some qualification decisions, such as the following:

- Is this worth pursuing?

- Could there be a need for your solution?

- How could you position your solution as an important tool for this client?

- Given the size of the company involved, how would this impact your sales volume?

- Who would be the best people to contact initially?

REMEMBER

Technology not only allows you to easily identify potential opportunities, but it also enables you to do something with that raw data. You can begin to turn this into useful sales information, either for immediate use or maybe to revisit at some point in the future.

The following sections describe specific stages of winning new business that benefit from the use of technology.

Driving the sales process

If one single thing would make life easier in new business sales, what would it be?

>> More hours in the day?

>> An end to tedious form filling and procedures?

>> Easier access to sales opportunities?

>> Being able to find the history of sales efforts with a prospect?

>> Being able to quickly generate letters and quotations?

The list could go on and on. Effective use of technology can have a serious impact on just about every item you'd place on such a list and on all my preceding examples.

Salespeople previously tended to work in isolation, had their own data sources, and kept their own prospect lists. No one else knew who they were speaking to. Some organizations still work like this today, irrespective of using technology. Introducing technology isn't a panacea; to be really successful and drive forward in the way you're able to, the sales mindset needs a cultural shift.

One thing you'll quickly discover is that sales have an unquenchable thirst for data. The key is being able to turn this raw data into useful sales information, and technology can help. This is where the effective use of a CRM system comes into its own, as I discuss in Chapters 9 and 21. A CRM system can help you by keeping track of tasks that need to be performed and prompting you to do them in a timely manner, as well as acting as a central repository for all documents, logs, discussion notes, and contact reports; therefore, it builds up a complete history over time of all of your company's dealings with a prospect. You can learn a lot from previous discussions with a prospect that may predate your involvement, and having all of the data and research on hand enables you to make value-based decisions rather than decisions based on gut instinct.

WARNING

Sales research comes to the forefront, and the new businessperson's profile changes as people become much more technology savvy. Many businesses are now employing sales researchers in a new knowledge-worker role to find and process the endless amount of data that's available. This comes with a warning, though: It's all too easy to spend all your time exploring this new wealth of data and not actually doing any new business selling work. Technology isn't about replacing skills; it's about enabling you to do your job in a different and hopefully better and more rewarding way.

Researching prospects

Perhaps the most obvious role that technology can have an impact on is the ability to research prospects quickly and easily. Gone are the days of poring over trade journals and wading through business directories to identify potential prospects. In Chapter 23, I go through some technology-based information sources that may be useful to you. The following sections provide examples of how you can use technology to help research prospects.

REMEMBER

You need to be wary of data overload with vast amounts of data at your fingertips. Be sure you carefully consider ways of identifying the important nuggets and turning them into valuable information; otherwise, you experience a real risk of going from not enough data to drowning in it. You need to find a way that works for you; unfortunately, there's no one prescribed way of achieving this, but do this well and you'll be on the way to being successful in continually filling your new business pipeline with high-quality new business leads. For example: Among the daily research briefings I get every morning are snippets of information about senior staff changing jobs. If you can identify a contact who you know is moving on and find where he is going, you potentially have an immediate opportunity to contact him to wish him well in his new role and, more important, to discover if there are any potential areas where your solutions can play a role in his new company. I've used this technique to great effect a number of times, especially in companies where I've had no success previously and now know someone me in a senior role.

Compiling prospect information

Many businesses and their new business salespeople subscribe to briefing news-letters, which can be a nonstop source of initial research data as can the regular published "top 250" types of lists for your business sector.

In my business, we get around ten briefing newsletters by 9 a.m. each morning that give us a reasonable summary of activity that may be relevant to our clients. We quickly look at these information snippets and give a quick assessment on the ones we want to follow up on. We then give the snippets marked for follow-up to a researcher who uses Internet-based tools and our own CRM system to add further value to the story. When the researcher finds a good match, he adds that info to a salesperson's activity schedule to action. Any information snippet that doesn't pass the initial usefulness test isn't ignored, though. We still add it to our CRM system because it may become useful in the future. In this way, we process more than 30,000 snippets of new business information every year, and our CRM system has become a base of knowledge.

Conducting basic prospect research

Technology can help with very basic research tasks, too, of course. Just a few clicks on the Internet can help answer questions such as "Who is the CEO of United Airlines?", "Does Virgin Media have an office in Paris?", and "Did that rumored takeover of KLM ever happen?" You can discover the answers to more complex prospecting questions, such as "Who is responsible for marketing budgets at Avis?" but you may need to do a bit more involved digging, which is where the sales research knowledge role has grown up.

Tracking prospects over time

One massive benefit that can have an impact on prospect research is being able to track movements over time. For example, assume you previously dealt with a buyer at a key client, and he left to move to another job and you lost contact. Some years later, he resurfaces in a more senior role at a current prospect. Utilizing your CRM records, you can quickly get up to speed on previous dealings with him, irrespective of who in your company was involved. This info can provide essential insight into the sales approaches that may work for you now. Equally, you can find out where a key decision maker you had previously worked with now works, and that may give you an inroad to a new company.

Helping with qualification

Technology makes it easy to see the history of your company's sales activity with any given prospect. You can quickly learn from past mistakes or successes and adjust your approach or pitch based on these.

Not all qualification results in the sort of information you want, however. In Chapter 19, I cover qualification in detail. A newfound opportunity becomes much less exciting if, when looking at history, you discover a trend of the prospect changing his mind after consuming vast amounts of sales time and effort. In this case, you may want to revise your qualification status for this prospect and consider how much effort that potential sale should be given.

With technology, you can easily track changes to qualification, see at a glance the progress of a particular sale, and understand why decisions have been taken previously. You can identify qualification patterns, which can provide valuable insight into sales management with regard to forecasting, as I discuss in Chapter 21. No longer do forecasts need to be made by sticking a wet finger in the air; you can now make them based on qualification and historical precedent.

REMEMBER

One of the main advantages technology helps with qualification is that of exception reporting, which can quickly identify any sales activity that is displaying early signs of trouble and needing intervention or more help. Chapter 9 covers using a CRM system to help with tracking qualification and reporting on exceptions, which are a solid part of a new business methodology.

Keeping on top of everything

Technology in new business helps not only the individual salesperson but also sales management. The individual is helped by having access to information, automation of routine tasks, easier reporting, and forecasting. Sales management gets a complete top-down view of the overall sale position; by using exception reporting then early intervention in problem cases, technology can often make the difference between being aware of information, and therefore being able to act on it, and losing a key opportunity.

Sales management also needs to pay careful attention to fully exploit the advantages of technology in automation and sales processes. The benefits are available to be exploited both by new business salespeople and sales managers alike:

>> Automation can be a great time saver but, unless set up with care, can also lead to some silly errors. Basic things like always getting the prospect's name spelled and formatted correctly in correspondence is an example. Too often, I receive emails and letters addressed to me with my name either misspelled or, even worse, addressed to "Mr. QZXCVB" or similar. These basic errors can always be tracked back to the care taken in setting up the automated process and, unless done correctly, can negate any benefit gained by sending them. In my case, they're always consigned to the trash, unread.

Automated action prompts can have a time-saving effect as well as assist in driving a sales cycle, especially in the early stages. For example, if in your research you identify a new prospect and add him to your CRM, then you can send an introduction letter and schedule a follow-up call without any sales intervention. This is a simple example; many more complex situations can benefit from carefully considered automation.

>> New processes are required as the benefits of the application of technology begin to be realized. You need to keep an eye on this because it's a moving target. Adopting new processes and workflow allows you to take maximum advantage of your investment in technology, and while no two situations are identical, it's one of the single most important actions for you to keep abreast of.

Adjusting to Technology in Your Business

The first thing to accept when applying a technology solution to the new business role is that you're not going to get perfection — such a thing doesn't exist. Also, you're chasing a moving target as your needs and the capability of your technology platform evolve. Don't expect, or wait for, perfection, but that's not to say that you shouldn't expect to make some very significant improvements and indeed giant leaps forward. The following sections note some ways in which you and your company need to adjust to the use of technology in winning new business.

REMEMBER

You need to recognize that you'll need to make some changes to the way you work, and although change is sometimes a frightening thought, nothing succeeds without it.

Everyone needs to buy in

Clearly, you're going to have to make investments in equipment, hardware, and software. But don't forget that investment in training will be potentially even more important. Getting all the staff onside and buying into the new platform and changes is an essential part of rolling out a technology solution.

In my experience, any new platform succeeds or fails based on the buy-in from the users. You need to sell the benefits to each person involved because everyone's role will have to adapt to get the maximum benefit out of technology. Doing a selling job on salespeople may seem a strange concept, but they're going to gain massively, even if they may have some in-built resistance to change. High on their "don't want" list is likely to be sharing "their" information and adding knowledge to the CRM system. I know; I've been there! Adopting a dictator approach won't get you far because salespeople are ideally placed to subtly sabotage the process. You need to get them onside and committed from the outset by focusing on the benefits to them.

Securing everyone's buy-in to the effective use of technology is important in order to make a solution truly valuable. One way I have found of achieving this is by using data only from the new systems in internal meetings and essentially ignoring anything not included in a CRM system, including requests for additional sales resources. "If it's not in the system, then it doesn't exist" is a mindset to adopt in order to lead from the front. This works in reverse also; if sales managers want information, point them to the CRM and tell them that it's all there and that you don't have time to do things twice.

Note: Other considerations include addressing integrity and security of your information. This topic is beyond the scope of this book because it's a complex subject in its own right, but you do need to be aware of information security and integrity and at least have a set of policies in place to cover it.

Technology is not a cure-all

Technology — whether it's new laptops or tablets, presentation software, CRM systems, automated quotation systems, or any combination of them all — won't deliver benefits on its own. You need to allow time for new systems to settle in order to begin to deliver benefits, and don't underestimate the amount of management time this will take up.

Putting a laptop or a tablet into the hands of a new business salesperson isn't going to make him more productive overnight, and it won't turn an underperforming salesperson into a world beater, either. The successful rollout of technology platforms into new business quickly identifies weaknesses in both personnel and processes. Applied correctly, technology guides you to problem areas, and as a manager, your role becomes one of mentoring and eliminating weaknesses through training, procedures, or personnel management.

You, perhaps for the first time, will be given a helicopter view of your new business situation, with real data backing up accurate forecasting of sales. Yes, you'll need to make adjustments and, more likely than not, will have to make some tough decisions, but you'll base them on factual performance data, not instinct. A few weeks ago, I saw a tongue-in-cheek advertisement for T-shirt printing with a slogan that said something along the lines of "Managing director: We do precision guesswork based on unreliable data from sales staff." That sums up the typical instinct-led sales management approach before technology is applied.

REMEMBER

Don't shoot from the hip; understand what the sales reports tell you. Examine the numbers, but don't become a spreadsheet warrior who can't see the forest for the trees. Technology is an augmenting science and not a replacement for common sense and solid sales management.

Don't hide behind technology

As a typical end-user of new technology solutions in your company, the new business salesperson is both exposed and empowered: exposed because the numbers don't lie, and empowered by having information vital to his role at his fingertips. Embrace the change, and rise to the challenge of redefining the way you approach the new business role.

REMEMBER

There is little to be gained from fighting the implementation of a new technology platform; it's going to happen regardless of what you want or think. Use it as a springboard to more success, but don't try to hide behind it when things go wrong. Take responsibility; be a leader. Accept that it's not "the computer's fault" when things go wrong, and be professional. Understand and accept that systems will show weaknesses in your processes and techniques, but learn from this and become better for the knowledge. Technology can enhance your sales skills (not water them down), give you much better information, and really empower you to drive new business forward, making you even more invaluable in your role.

How many times have you complained about not having enough prospects to go after? How many times have you complained that you didn't know the history of an account? How many times have you complained about not hearing about an opportunity soon enough? Well, with technology you have the answers to all of these and lots more areas available to you on demand, so how are you going to use the newfound position of knowledge to the best advantage in your new business role? You're going to have to make changes to adapt to the new reality you find and to be able to take advantage of the new opportunities opening up to you. How much more new business will you be able to close?

Distinguishing between Different Selling Aids

Technology has many uses in new business, but to the mainstream new business salesperson, these can be distilled into three specific areas: prospecting tools, presenting tools, and recording tools. I explore these areas in depth in this section.

REMEMBER

In adopting new ways of working, you need to consider what works for you and how you're going to adapt your workflow to take maximum advantage of it. One way of working likely won't suit every new business salesperson, even within the same company, so take the time to plan your use and figure out what's going to work for and deliver the best results for you.

WARNING

Be aware of paralysis by analysis. Paralysis by analysis comes about when the reams of information now available to you get in the way of doing the job rather than help you. "There must be 50 ways to leave your lover," Paul Simon wrote. One way is enough. You can apply the same principle to information. There are dozens of ways to look up revenue figures for your prospect. Find one way, use it, and stick to it. The figures won't change if you use a second or third tool; you're just wasting time. Your CRM may have three or four ways of reporting forecasting based on the data it holds. The figures won't change whichever way you look at them, although you can analyze them in different ways. Unless you need to do so as part of your job, don't. Stick to one way.

Prospecting tools

Technology perhaps delivers its greatest benefit in the new business role as a prospecting resource. As a new business salesperson, you now have in your control access to the greatest prospecting resource known to man: the Internet. This needs to come with a warning, however, because it's also the biggest business time waster known to man.

You need to understand how to find prospecting data quickly and efficiently and to develop a workflow that suits your needs. Following data trails can be both interesting and rewarding, at times. But you need to know when to stop.

TIP

You also need to get into the habit of searching your own CRM, which will likely contain a goldmine of relevant prospecting information. There's no catchall workflow, so I walk through some examples here. Figure 4-1 shows a prospecting workflow for a new business salesperson who has recently been given a new brief. This workflow instructs you to search the CRM first to pick up all the previous research and historical information, and if these searches don't give sufficient numbers, turn your attention to the Internet to widen the search, ensuring that you add all information you find to the CRM.

You have a pre-defined set of information sources that you work through first (you can find examples of these in Chapter 23). Your colleagues in marketing probably have given you a list of data sources, too. (I discuss marketing in Chapter 6.)

Don't fall into the trap of becoming just a prospecting expert, though. Your role is much wider than this. Some of you may have dedicated research and prospecting staff available to you who take care of this task, but you still need to spend time doing your own research because you may find valuable information that others may not realize the significance of. The key rule with prospecting is to always seek to add value to data snippets, either from personal experience or from linking together data snippets and articles.

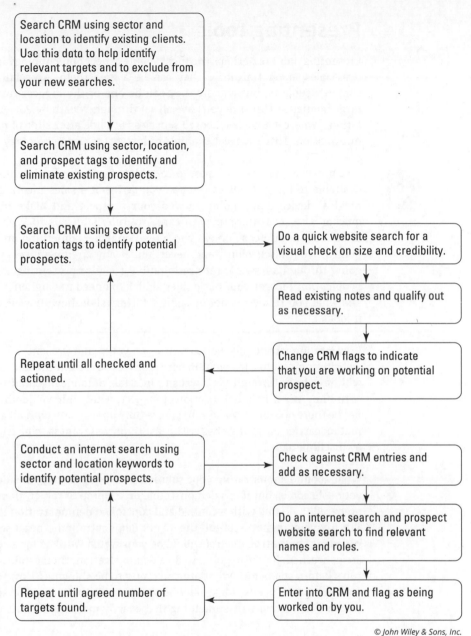

FIGURE 4-1:
The workflow for using a CRM system and the Internet for prospecting.

Search CRM using sector and location to identify existing clients. Use this data to help identify relevant targets and to exclude from your new searches.

Search CRM using sector, location, and prospect tags to identify and eliminate existing prospects.

Search CRM using sector and location tags to identify potential prospects.

Do a quick website search for a visual check on size and credibility.

Read existing notes and qualify out as necessary.

Change CRM flags to indicate that you are working on potential prospect.

Repeat until all checked and actioned.

Conduct an internet search using sector and location keywords to identify potential prospects.

Check against CRM entries and add as necessary.

Do an internet search and prospect website search to find relevant names and roles.

Repeat until agreed number of targets found.

Enter into CRM and flag as being worked on by you.

© John Wiley & Sons, Inc.

REMEMBER

Having the Internet and your internal CRM as resources means that you never have an excuse for not having enough prospects.

Presenting tools

Presenting aids are perhaps the most visible aspect of technology in the new business salesperson's armory. They can be a great help, especially in explaining complex subjects, but equally they can be one of the biggest turn-offs for your target audience. I'm sure you have all sat through "death by PowerPoint" presentations, where you've been bored senseless by slide after slide of poorly presented information. That's a great example of how *not* to use technology in presenting.

REMEMBER

Just because you have a laptop or a tablet, don't think it's either necessary or desirable to bring it out as soon as you arrive at a sales meeting. It's not some magical device that's going to woo your prospect and make him sign up any quicker. Use presentations with care. My rule is always to keep your laptop or tablet in your briefcase unless you intend on using something on it to augment a point in your discussions, and never, under any circumstances, would I suggest going through a PowerPoint presentation if you're presenting to fewer than six people. Don't forget your basic sales skills! You need the audience to focus on you and what you're saying, not on some arbitrary slideshow, however cool you think it looks.

Presentation technology works even when you're not present, of course, and your website comes into the equation here. You can be certain that any serious prospect will have been through your website in a fair amount of detail before you meet with him. And if he's not a serious prospect, you will have qualified him out and not be there of course. Make sure you're fully up-to-date with all aspects of information carried on your website. The last thing you want is to be tripped up by your own selling tools.

What about demonstrating your solution in use? Obviously, this depends on what your solution is, but if it's demonstrable on a laptop or tablet, then you need to be prepared to do this with a canned and controlled demonstration if at all possible. Try to avoid ad-hoc seat-of-the-pants demonstrations, because in these cases you're not in control. *Control* should be your watch word as far as demonstrations are concerned. If you're going to do a demonstration, then establish some ground rules before you begin. What are you going to be showing? How will this fit with your prospect's needs? Make sure he understands that he will be seeing a simulation and not necessarily something that exactly matches his situation.

TIP

Try to limit the amount of focus on the demonstration to no more than five minutes, and return to a discussion with you as the focus as soon as possible. Understand the limitations of technology as a sales aid and use accordingly, not allowing it to take your place as the focus of the discussions. Technology has yet to ask for the order!

Recording tools

As you may guess, I place enormous importance on the recording of information, and I can't stress enough the importance of adding all your information to the CRM. The CRM becomes so much more than the sum of its parts; it becomes a true knowledge base for the company to use, both now and in the future. It's perhaps the single biggest new business asset that you have, and I cover it in more detail in Chapter 9.

REMEMBER

You need to understand and accept that information is a company asset and not the private domain of individual new business salespeople. This is a step-change from old-style selling and comes as a culture shock if you're not use to it. Get used to it. You'll quickly find that you reap the benefits of shared data.

Some companies may need to make some policy and procedure changes to fully underline the importance of sharing information. For example, old-school sales-people would jealously guard "their" information and be reluctant to share it with anyone. The Information Age demands that information be shared and available to all in a controlled manner, and if your colleagues are reluctant to adopt this policy, then some changes to employment contracts may be necessary to insist that they comply.

WARNING

Should you use your laptop or tablet to take notes during client and prospect meetings? Surely, if I'm advocating the importance of technology and capturing data, then this is a good idea? I'm less sure of that fact, unless you're selling real-time note capture. In fact, you shouldn't use technology as a matter of fact in any meeting unless it is to demonstrate a specific agreed point, and then put it away again. You need to have the prospect's attention on you and your attention on him, without unnecessary distractions. Using technology in no way replaces some of the basic principles of selling that have stood the test of time, and this is a prime example. People buy from people, not from a laptop or screen they're being shown. Technology is always subservient to the new business salesperson driving the sales cycle.

2
Planning for New Business

Chapter **5**

Presenting Solutions

The most important person in the sales cycle is your prospect. Your prospect may be an individual or a decision-making unit (a group of people who make up a team that drives the buying process and arrives at a purchase decision), and a decision-making unit is likely to have at least one key driver who is your target. To deliver a successful sales cycle to its conclusion, you need to place yourself in your prospect's position and consider how you present your solution in his terms.

Your approach requires flexibility and a focus on can-do solutions, looking beyond the obvious areas for key buying clues. You need to present yourself as the prospect's champion and demonstrate that you're on his side and have only his success in mind when proposing a solution. Achieve all of that and you'll be well on the way to presenting a winning solution to your prospect. Get the full scoop in this chapter.

Being Solution Oriented

If one key selling skill or attribute rises above all the others in terms of being solution oriented, it is one of attitude. Your attitude to building a winning solution is often the key that unlocks the sale. You need to be seen as a can-do person who the prospect can rely on to build a solid working solution that delivers on his needs.

Your focus is on finding solutions that deliver the prospect's objectives, not on locating obstacles along the way.

TIP

The good news is that you don't have to do this all alone. Generally, you have a number of in-house resources who you can call on. And even if you're a one-man operation, you build a team-based approach with your prospect, involving him from the very early stages in shaping the solution, so that it becomes "our solution" and not just a solution that a new business salesperson is proposing. Giving the prospect an early sense of ownership can be vital when the going gets tough in a sales cycle, which it often will do. If you achieve buy-in, then he'll work with you to find paths around obstacles. This collaborative sales approach often marks the top new business salespeople.

In addition to attitude, you need to develop and demonstrate another key skill to be solution oriented, and that is critical thinking: the ability to analyze a situation and devise a strategy for dealing with it.

The following sections delve into the details of these two skills.

Understanding the prospect's problem

You should never go into a sales situation with a ready answer before taking the time to listen to and understand the prospect's problem area. Understanding what he's trying to achieve, why he's trying to achieve it, what impact not having a solution has, and the impact a successful implementation will deliver provides you with the information you need to structure the presentation of your solution both in his terms and in a way that focuses on alleviating the key pain points.

If you go into a new sales situation with your solution already in mind, you're likely to miss any key buying signals that would point you in a different direction. Don't assume that you know better than your prospect does about what his business needs are. Maintain an open mind and be solution oriented rather than product oriented as you begin a new sales cycle.

In the early discussions with your prospect, active listening provides you with reams of useful information, not only about the specific problem area but also about how it affects his business and the benefits he expects to achieve from a successful purchase. You also find out what success means in his terms. These are all vital pieces of information that you'll return to time and again during the sales cycle. Active listening, which I cover in Chapter 2, is a real key to coming to grips with what your prospect is really trying to achieve.

Always accept that the prospect's problems are real, even if in absolute terms your solution considers them to be side issues to a greater big picture. I cover this in detail in Chapter 7.

You need to be objective in your approach to understanding your prospect's problem areas and ask open questions to delve deeper into any key areas or areas that aren't obvious to you. For example, ask "Why does that . . . ?" and "How does that . . . ?" type of questions, and above all, get the prospect to open up to you, and demonstrate that you're interested. I was once discussing outsourced new business with a prospect, and although he seemed to have a real need, he was reluctant to accept that outsourcing was for him. I attempted to discover the real issue by asking questions around previous experience and discovered that he had in fact tried it before but with mixed results. After I got the objection into the open, it was much easier to deal with.

You need a degree of flexibility in the early stages because you don't know where the discussions will lead. Right from the beginning, you need to demonstrate that you're on the prospect's side and can provide a level of support necessary not only to solve the problems but also to ensure that he's going to be successful with your solution. Time invested here pays for itself many times over as the sales cycle develops.

In the preceding example, I was able to show the prospect that we could be flexible in our approach and build in sufficient checks and balances to ensure that he always felt in control of where our new business effort was going to be invested. I offered to give him access to our voice recordings so that he could understand for himself how we positioned him, and although this would be an inconvenience to set up, it gave him the assurance that he needed. In fact, he never asked for any recordings and was satisfied that I was confident enough in our solution to make the offer.

Of course, you're also qualifying while listening, and as you understand the prospect's problem areas, you'll also have a very good understanding of how well suited your solution is and be able to qualify the sales opportunity accordingly. (Find out more about qualifying in Chapters 9 and 19.)

Thinking outside the box

Sometimes, the answer to a problem area is not immediately obvious and may not be what you consider to be your solution's key selling point. It may be that success in the prospect's terms means implementing only part of what your solution is capable of and maybe utilizing some elements of his existing systems or processes. This is not necessarily a bad thing for you; it just requires you to be able to think outside the box and not try to pigeonhole everything into your terms.

REMEMBER

Nothing the prospect wants to do is "wrong," even if it seems strange to you. Challenging assumptions is fine, and you should do so but in a positive and constructive way. For example, a client once wanted all of our call notes to be provided in electronic format so that he could incorporate them into his own CRM system. We did this for many years, and I know from firsthand experience that he never referred to them.

Don't be afraid to think the unthinkable — for example, that maybe your off-the-shelf solution isn't the right one. Be prepared to walk away from a sale if you see that you're unable to deliver the necessary solution but not before exploring all the potential avenues, including working in partnership with others to provide a sum-of-the-parts solution. In Chapter 10, I provide more information on walking away from a deal.

Thinking Like Your Prospect

To be able to present a winning solution that captures your prospect's imagination and propels you toward the elusive yes decision, you need to be able to think in the prospect's terms, understand his driving forces, and align your presentation to match them. The following sections help you accomplish these tasks.

TIP

Don't assume that you know what your prospect's driving forces and buying criteria are — find out for yourself. Here are a few pointers:

>> Get to know how your prospect reacts to key situations by using your powers of observation during your dealings with him. For example, if you discover that he is a sports fan, position your objectives using sports analogies.

>> Read and understand any notes or research snippets contained in your CRM to understand why any previous sales campaigns have failed to convert into new business wins. (I introduce CRM systems in Chapter 9.)

>> By using open and searching questions, probe for nuggets of information. Your prospect is your entry point into his organization and the focal point for everything you need to learn about how your solution is going to be used. He is the expert in his organization, so tap into that resource. You can, for example, ask for his opinion on the best way to introduce your solution to different areas of his business.

Understanding the prospect's view of risk

Anything that your prospect does involves inherent risks — a risk of not solving existing problems if he takes no action, a risk of making the wrong buying decision regardless of which solution he goes for, a risk of being seen as indecisive by colleagues, and a risk of being perceived as a failure if the chosen solution doesn't deliver the promised benefits, just to name a few. Rarely is a risk-free option available. Even the do-nothing approach involves risk. Your prospect likely has a degree of exposure by virtue of the fact that he's leading the search for a solution, which makes him either a hero or a villain in his business, depending on the outcome of his buying decision.

The prospect's attitude toward risk and the risk-to-reward ratio are important considerations. One of your jobs is to discover what his attitude to risk is, which will give you some pointers toward what level of solution you should be proposing. If you understand the element of risk that he's exposed to, you can use this information by focusing some of your presentation attributes to directly addressing the risk.

Risk is always a potential barrier to closing a sale, and understanding both the prospect's exposure to and attitude toward risk becomes important for you in driving a sale. Is risk a perception, or is it real? Ultimately, the answer to this doesn't matter. What matters is how you approach it with your prospect and how you help him to minimize his exposure by being onside with your solution.

REMEMBER

You need to tailor your solution to match the level of risk your prospect is prepared to take, so don't go for an all-guns-blazing solution if you're dealing with a risk-averse prospect, because a mismatch will lead to the sale being lost in the vast majority of cases. For example, if he is risk-averse, then be wary of proposing a brand-new solution where he would be a pioneer.

WARNING

A prospect who has a rather gung-ho attitude to risk is almost as bad as one who is extremely risk-averse, and you have to steer a careful path toward presenting a solution that delivers against the requirements at what your company perceives as the lowest level of acceptable risk. Just because your key contact may throw caution to the wind doesn't mean that you can, or that his colleagues share his view. You need to be professional in your approach and be seen to be doing the right thing. For example, don't be tempted to introduce a brand-new, untested solution because you think it may suit the needs. Never lose sight of your professional approach to winning new business and your fundamental need to ensure that you do the right thing for your prospect, even when he cannot see it for himself. (I provide more information on risk and managing its perception in Chapter 18.)

REMEMBER

Some prospects will require more support than others as they come to terms with a decision that carries an element of risk. Show them that risk is inherent in everything, including the do-nothing option, and assure them by words and actions that your role is to support them and to see that the solution is implemented successfully. I talk about building trust in Chapter 3, and this is a clear example of that requirement. If you've established trust in your prospect's eyes, then overcoming the inertia of risk will be much easier.

Mitigating the perception of risk

As I note in the preceding section, risk is inherent in everything, so acknowledge it and move on. If you discover that your prospect is overly risk-averse, you may want to revisit your qualification of the opportunity because sometimes the time investment required is disproportionate to the reward and it's better to move on.

Assuming that isn't the case, how do you mitigate the perception of risk? In this section, I explore a number of ways to do so.

REMEMBER

The bottom line in mitigating the perception of risk is to accept that it's real and use a combination of the following techniques to find the optimal way of making your prospect comfortable in dealing with you.

Establishing trust in a professional manner

Being the prospect's champion, building him up in his colleagues' eyes, and supporting him are part of relationship selling. As you establish a business relationship and associated trust, the fear of risk occurring diminishes. Keep in mind, though, that one of the basic premises is that you're building a business relationship and not a friendship. Keep it professional. (Chapter 3 has details on maintaining your professionalism.)

Supporting your case with external resources

Your support resources should include case studies of similar buying situations, and you should use these to demonstrate that your prospect is not being a pioneer. Few things are as powerful as third-party peer endorsements, and if you can show that others in his situation have benefited from a similar solution, that will go a long way to mitigating risk. If you're able to support this with qualitative data from external resources, then it becomes an even more powerful sales tool. Research reports, opinion pieces, articles, and studies all have an important part to play. (Flip to Chapter 2 for more about case studies and the like.)

Maybe even more powerful than case studies are personal recommendations from existing clients. These need to be handled with care because you're not realistically going to allow your prospect to talk to a dissatisfied client, and he'll be aware that you're going to introduce him to your most powerful advocates. But sometimes it becomes a useful sales tool and, as long as you manage it carefully, can offer powerful mitigation.

Maintaining transparency

Being transparent is a key element of mitigating the perception of risk. If you're being economical with the truth, then expect to be found out and suffer the consequences. Keep in mind that just as you have technology resources for research, so does your prospect, and it would be naive of you to think that he won't be using the Internet and social media to research your company and solution.

If your solution has had a bad review for any reason, then assume that your prospect will be aware of it. To mitigate any damage, you should be prepared to be up front in discussing the review, any lessons you learned, and changes you made to avoid it happening again.

Managing your prospect's expectations

From the outset of a sales cycle, you need to be engaged in managing expectations, both in what your solution will deliver and how you'll support the prospect through the sales cycle. Be clear about the scope of your discussions concerning budget, capabilities, scope, timescales, and so on, and document them in contact reports as I outline in Chapter 3. If you do this from the outset, you establish yourself as someone who is reliable and in turn goes a long way toward mitigating risk.

Where you're dealing with a decision-making unit, make sure you've covered all the bases as I outline in Chapter 19. This should ensure that you know all the stakeholders and can be prepared to overcome any risk elements that they may introduce.

Considering contractual obligations and accountability

Some contractual considerations, such as trials and guarantees, can play a part in mitigating risk, and although you shouldn't enter into these lightly, they can provide a high degree of risk mitigation. Be wary of allowing all the risk to sit with your company, however, because any successful implementation requires a significant element of commitment and resources from both parties.

Many years ago, in fact my very first consulting project, a client requested a legal personal guarantee of my performance. I signed it — partly because I had nothing to hide, partly because he asked for it, and partly because I didn't know any better. With the benefit of experience, I caution against doing something like this because it tends to imply an unreasonable measure of control is required by the buyer. In this specific case, I discovered that all their sales contracts also demanded personal guarantees from clients. It didn't take me too long to work out why they weren't being very successful!

TIP

Senior management accountability is another element that may help you. Introducing your CEO as part of your presentation, whether physically or in writing or even video, can demonstrate that he's accountable to your prospect.

Structuring your solution in the prospect's terms

Any sales cycle is also a buying cycle for your prospect. Understand that it's your prospect's needs that are being met and it's the solution to his problem, so you should seek to structure the solution in terms that he's familiar with. Don't assume that your prospect is an expert in your field. You have to guide him through the attributes of your solution and how it's going to fit within his business, meeting his buying objectives. Simple things like using his industry's terminology and avoiding product-speak go a long way here. Be sure to speak in his terms, and avoid the temptation to use your industry terms and acronyms, assuming that he understands. One of the roles of a new business salesperson is that of a communicator, so use your communication skills to speak in business terms and try to fit this into his language wherever possible.

If you have to quote metrics, use ones that apply to him and not to your solution. During your discussions, you'll have picked up many clues about the style of person you're dealing with, so use this information to structure your proposal in a way that will be both meaningful and understandable to him.

In Chapter 7, I discuss using your prospect's terminology as well as some of the potential pitfalls of not doing it correctly. If your prospect is driven by metrics, for example, then careful use of metrics can be an aid to him understanding the impact of your solution.

TIP

Don't assume that you understand language that he's using if it's specific to his business or industry. If you're in any doubt, then check and clarify because this is a sure way to store up future problems if not addressed at the time.

Considering All the Angles

In driving a sales cycle, it's important to be able to take a top-down view of where you are. Use this view to ensure that you've covered all the possible angles relating to the sale of your solution. Have you discovered the prospect's needs? Have you covered these needs in sufficient detail? Have you delved a little deeper than the needs you were given to discover what lies behind them? For example, does the prospect want a 2-centimeter drill bit, or does he want to be able to drill holes to achieve a bigger objective? Have you discovered what this bigger objective is? And are you able to address it?

The following sections provide pointers on how to consider all the angles when you present a solution to a prospect.

Changing the rules

Have you considered your competitive standing with respect to the potential sale? Assuming that most solutions on a prospect's shortlist will be able to deliver the fundamentals, what have you discovered about the real need that enables you to present something a little different, which also covers the bases?

Don't be afraid to change the rules in a sales cycle, especially in cases where you're not in pole position to win. If your solution fits all the buyer's criteria but you're still not winning the deal, look for some other key hooks. Re-examine the needs analysis for clues (I discuss covering the prospect's needs in Chapter 7).

PROMOTING A PROSPECT AS AN INDUSTRY LEADER

Have you considered promoting your prospect as an industry leader? Getting him on board as a client could open up a wide range of benefits to him if you suggest that he writes a positioning paper, for example, or speaks at a conference that you're promoting. Let your prospect see that working with you can further his career, but do it in a professional way. Years ago, IBM salespeople were renowned for going over the heads of their prospects and "reporting them" to their own senior management for considering buying from anyone else. Hopefully no one does anything like that these days — they wouldn't last for two minutes if they did. There's a massive difference between promoting your prospect's interests and undermining him.

What can your solution offer that, while not fundamental to the main objectives, can provide an attractive additional or alternative benefit?

Find this key hook and bring it to the forefront of your solutions pitch, taking the major areas as already covered. Play the gorilla against the mainstream challenger by going for the additional benefits as a game changer. You may discover that the final solution isn't necessarily the same as the initial problem.

If your prospect has a choice of two solutions that both address the fundamental needs, but your solution also helps in some peripheral areas, then switch his attention, and that of any relevant member of the decision-making unit, to focus on delivering added value as a by-product of your solution. Change the rules of the sale in order to play to your strengths.

Focusing on the real problem

A prospect's real motivations in exploring potential solutions aren't always immediately obvious. Sometimes the real needs — and therefore the real benefits — in a buying scenario aren't the obvious ones, and sometimes they're well hidden. Take the time to explore under the surface of the obvious and see what you can discover. To provide the best advice and deliver the optimal solution, you need to discover the key drivers, and if they're not clear, don't be afraid to ask for the prospect's help in uncovering them.

Your prospect may ask for a 2-inch drill bit when what he actually wants is to be able to drill a series of 2-inch holes in order to install a new window. By asking what he is setting out to achieve, you may be able to steer him in a better direction and focus on the actual need and not the perceived means of getting to it.

Keeping your prospect on board and engaged with you is important, so don't dismiss what he tells you about problem areas, even if they seem weak to you. Keep digging and exploring how the current operations work and where shortcomings occur, and eventually you'll uncover what you need to know to present a winning solution.

Unfortunately, and for reasons best known to themselves, you'll occasionally come across prospects who have no intention of buying from you. Your qualification should weed them out before you spend too much time or resources on them (see Chapters 9 and 19 for more information), but you do need to be aware that this happens. Bear this in mind if you're having trouble focusing on the real problem. You should be seen as an expert in your field and one who can help, so if you're being kept at arm's length from discovering the real motivation, then revisit the qualification before spending too much time on it.

Don't be prepared to accept confidentiality as a reason for not giving you the information. If you're going to propose a winning solution, then you need the real facts, and you should be prepared to sign (and even suggest) a nondisclosure agreement. I've done that many times, and it should, at a stroke, remove any barriers to being given the real story.

Using existing resources

Sometimes part of the solution lies with the prospect himself and his existing resources. It's not always necessary to drop something that he has working to some degree and maybe just needs augmenting or enhancing. Good business can still be won in these cases.

For example, your prospect may want to focus on specific demographic targets and may have already invested in data sets of prospects. Offer to use this data as part of your solution so that the investment isn't a wasted effort on his behalf.

Equally, you may have implemented a similar solution with another client and may be able to reuse some of the work from that project. You don't necessarily have to start from scratch each time, so consider what existing resources can play a part. Can you learn lessons from previous implementations?

Be aware of blatant copying, however, as no two solutions should really be identical. Position yourself as an expert who can guide your prospect through a solution based on past experience and lessons.

Chapter **6**

Marketing Matters

Full disclosure here: I've worked on both sides of the marketing and selling fence and have seen both the collaboration that's possible as well as the animosity that occurs when things aren't the way one party expects them to be. The sales joke of "I'm from marketing, and I've come to help" does ring all too true at times, but it's when these two functions align successfully and cooperate fully that great things can happen that support new business sales efforts. Real success comes only when the functions work well together and share insight, understanding, and experiences to produce a winning solution.

In this chapter, I focus mainly on sales and marketing being separate functions in a company, but of course in many small and medium-sized enterprises (SMEs), the same person is responsible for sales and marketing, and here I highlight the different parts he needs to understand and play.

REMEMBER

A longstanding debate is whether sales or marketing is the senior function and the senior career path. This misses the point because they're interrelated, and each has its own values. Marketing matters because it sets the scene for the sales environment and warms the prospect up to enable new business sales to bring in the business and associated revenue. One can't thrive without the other.

Understanding the Role of Marketing in Winning New Business

A classic definition of marketing is that it focuses on what has become known as the four Ps: product, price, promotion, and place. Another, perhaps easier, way to think of the marketing function is that it

>> Creates the public face of the business

>> Sets the direction in terms of who the customers should be and what they should be offered through what sales channels

>> Sets the pricing to ensure maximum revenue and profitability

>> Feeds all of this info into the selling function to actually deliver the new business success

The following sections go into more detail on the role that marketing plays (and doesn't play) in winning new business.

REMEMBER

A well-run marketing function creates the right environment for new business sales success by attracting the prospects with the right solution offering at the right price. You can think of marketing as preparing the ground in preparation for sales to work on it.

Harnessing the power of the brand

The 21st-century world has become very brand savvy, especially with consumer products. Brand champions have appeared all over the place, but what is a brand and how do new business sales harness its pulling power? Hundreds of books explore the power of the brand, and *Branding For Dummies*, 2nd Edition, by Bill Chiaravalle and Barbara Findlay Schenck (Wiley), is one of the best if you want to read up on this subject.

REMEMBER

In terms that you need to understand for winning new business, branding differentiates products and seeks to create an aura of desirability for a product or service. It warms up your audience and gives them a powerful set of expectations before you even begin to talk to them in your new business role.

Branding is often the very first thing that comes to the public's mind when they think about a particular product, and they're predisposed to have a view about it, rightly or wrongly. So the brand is powerful. If you're selling a solution with known brand attributes, then you should, in theory at least, have a head start in terms of your prospects knowing what to expect. For example, when prospects look to buy personal computers, they are likely to recall the "Intel Inside" branding over some generic brand, so if your solution uses Intel chips, then marketing has given you a head start.

Working with sales, not against it

If the marketing function is about discovering the needs of prospects and working to stimulate the potential customers by making them feel the need for your solution, then the role of new business sales is to take this and show the prospects how your solution fits into their unique situation and deliver the results and benefits they seek.

If marketing and sales don't work together for the common good, it'd be like one part of your organization telling prospects that they need a blue solution and another saying that all they can have is a red one. As a new business salesperson, it's your responsibility to understand how your solution is positioned in your prospects' minds before you even set foot in the door. Everything that you say and do in a new business sales situation needs to align with your company's public information flow or marketing communications.

REMEMBER

The marketing function, especially in larger companies, is likely the custodian of the CRM system, which is so important in new business sales. Irrespective of who "owns" the data, it's your responsibility to ensure that all customer feedback and sales experiences are logged so marketing staff can view them as needed. (Flip to Chapter 9 for more about CRM systems.)

You need to keep abreast of new initiatives and new products or services being planned so that you're not taken by surprise, of course, but also so that you can begin to consider how to introduce new solutions into your prospect and customer base and to be aware of the effect of solution changes in your existing sales pipeline deals.

However frustrating you may find working with a marketing function that doesn't seem to understand your day-to-day new business sales needs, it's your responsibility to work with them to close the gaps. Don't be tempted to do your own thing contrary to the marketing plans.

Having worked on both sides of the sales and marketing divide, and having seen firsthand the in-built suspicion that each has for the other, I can only conclude that time spent battling your colleagues is time wasted, and that the time would be much better spent in being in front of your prospects. In your new business sales role, try to spend some time with your marketing colleagues and share firsthand experiences of working with the positioning messages that they produce.

Give open and honest feedback, but don't provide it in a confrontational manner; your objective is to help get a better understanding of your solution in the minds of your prospects, and by working together with marketing, you can influence this process.

Equally, be generous with your time and experiences when marketing colleagues ask for help. The old adage of "I'm from marketing, and I've come to help" as salespeople fall on the floor laughing has no place in the modern-day process of winning new business. Take the responsibility on yourself of providing feedback and building relationships with marketing colleagues. It will be worth your effort in getting the end result to work better with your prospects.

Developing strategic and tactical approaches

Strategic and tactical approaches are both necessary and complement each other:

>> Consider a strategic approach as being the grand plan — the "What are we going to do?" For example, it may include ways of ensuring that all the decision-making unit roles are covered (see Chapter 19 for more about the decision-making unit).

>> A tactical approach is more about the "How are we going to do this?" It's the actual on-the-ground plan of who does what and when.

Another way of looking at this is to consider the strategy as defining the outcome and the results of implementing your solution, so, for example, a senior-level salesperson perhaps focuses on those people in the prospect's organization who don't have day-to-day involvement in using your solution. Tactics involve operating at a features and benefits level with those directly concerned with the detailed implementation of the solution. As a new business salesperson, you need to be able to handle both types of situations, switching from strategic selling to tactical selling depending on your audience. Your marketing colleagues provide the necessary information to enable you to talk knowledgeably at both strategic and tactical levels.

Marketing functions define the overall strategy and positioning messages that reflect your solution and generally are the first things that your prospects come into contact with. Your roles in winning new business are to understand this positioning and to be able to articulate it in terms of how the solution addresses a prospect's business needs.

You need to understand your audience on each occasion that you meet with them and ensure that you're approaching the sale in the correct way, covering all the bases of the decision-making unit. Different sales approaches cover different buyer influences and must work hand in hand to succeed, so it really is important that you understand how to position your solution in both a strategic and a tactical way.

As a new business salesperson, you need to be able to address strategic issues, such as the direction that your prospect wants to move his business toward, and to have an understanding of why your solution will enable him to achieve this objective. Your role is not just to get a product or service sold to a prospect regardless of it being a good fit for him; your role is to ensure that whatever you're selling is a good fit for him and will assist him in moving in the right direction as he pursues his strategic goals.

TIP

A tactic that often works well is to involve a marketing manager directly in your sales cycle, arranging for him to present to a group of your decision-making unit to perhaps cover long-term plans for your solution and ways that the prospect's industry is having to adapt to change, along with the steps being taken to ensure that your solution is at the leading edge of this change. A presentation along these lines is a good example of the fusion between sales and marketing and also delivers a number of significant benefits:

>> It demonstrates to your prospect that he's important enough to be given a view of future direction.

>> It enables a perceived expert to deliver some selling messages on your behalf. Because they come from an "expert," they may carry more weight in the eyes of the decision-making unit.

>> It helps your marketing colleagues gain firsthand feedback from real customers.

I've personally used this tactic many times to great effect in my new business role. And when I was working in a marketing role, I was often brought into such a sales situation, so I can confirm that it works well from both a sales and marketing perspective.

Knowing what marketing can't do

Marketing will be a great help to you in your new business sales role, but you need to understand that it's not a panacea. Marketing is no more the magical solution to every possible problem than sales is. Keep in mind the following:

>> On its own, marketing isn't going to deliver sales on a plate. You need to work with its output and turn it into your selling advantage. Don't just take marketing material as it arrives; take the time to read and understand it, ensuring that your sales message is consistent, and make any changes as necessary.

>> Marketing isn't always in front of the prospect in the way that you are, so your input to the marketing process should be valuable as you build those internal relationships.

>> Generally, marketing isn't driven by today's activities; it's not at the very cutting edge of new business sales, which is your domain. A prospect is unlikely to get very excited if you show him a copy of your latest ad. It's your job to help the prospect see the benefits to his situation as a result of you interpreting the ad's message in his terms and demonstrating how he can benefit from the solution. (Chapter 10 builds on this tactic as a way of overcoming objections.)

>> Marketing is unlikely to dig you out of a hole that you've gotten yourself into by failing to understand or communicate the right messages. You need to take responsibility for yourself.

REMEMBER

Being on Brand and on Message

Every new business salesperson has a responsibility to be on brand and on message all the time. New business sales have no room for mavericks who think they know better, because that simply stores up future problems for the business to have to sort out. Individuals with a unique style are most definitely the correct types to have in new business sales, but they need to understand and buy in to the values and attributes of their organization.

The following sections provide pointers on how you can remain on brand and on message when you win new business.

Don't reinvent the wheel

Marketing likely has well-researched and thought-out reasons for defining a set of solutions and associated brand attributes, so don't reinvent the wheel by putting your own spin on them. Take advantage of the marketing work that has been done for your benefit, and put it to maximum use by making sure you understand it thoroughly.

I was once a product marketing manager for an international technology firm and had a fantastic new product to work with; I thought it was going to walk off the shelves when prospects saw it. The problem that developed was that some members of the sales team were more excited by the brand name, which was catchy, than by what the product actually delivered. The product was an integrated spreadsheet and data management system, well ahead of its time. Some of my sales colleagues took the brand a bit too literally and were telling prospects that it would give them perfect insight into any data they used it on. While it was good, it wasn't that good! When they took the time to read the marketing literature that was produced for them, it was obvious what the benefits really were, and having understood the product, they were able to sell it successfully.

Some years later, I switched sides from marketing to sales, and I always kept the lessons I learned from my marketing role as I helped my prospects see the real business benefits of solutions I was selling them.

REMEMBER

Marketing materials — brochures, ads, websites — set up prospect expectations long before you get in front of them. Use these resources in your sales cycle and give feedback to marketing on the relative success and usefulness of each of them. You're a key resource to your marketing colleagues because you're the one who sees the real day-to-day impact of the work they do. Build these relationships and forge close links to help both functions deliver stronger marketing communications and make your role easier in the process.

TIP

Find your own way of communicating the marketing messages in terms that your prospect can accept and desire, but don't make it up as you go along; that is simply a recipe for disaster that any professional new business salesperson won't want to be associated with. My earlier story of introducing an integrated spreadsheet and data management product provides a good example of how a simple message can be misinterpreted by new business salespeople who make it up as they go along instead of taking the time to learn and understand.

Understand your branding

Earlier in this chapter, I cover the importance of the brand. I can't overstate the importance of taking the time to understand your branding. I don't just mean remembering a strap line but also being able to articulate the brand values in your prospect's eyes and being able to explain how that benefits his unique situation and why it's a better fit than any competitive offering. If you don't understand this positioning, then make sure that you fill in the missing knowledge before you go anywhere near a prospect because this will kill your sale better than any competitor can.

REMEMBER

The following are some guidelines for better understanding your brand:

>> Make sure that you read, understand, and digest all the internal communications regarding your brand and its positioning. Don't dismiss it as "marketing hype"; it's part of your toolkit, and you need to know how to use it.

>> Understand how your solution fits into the bigger picture of your prospect's business and what role it plays for him. You need to be able to understand the bigger picture rather than just the narrow niche you may be selling into at any given time. Understand how different parts of the solution tie together with your prospect's unique way of working and demonstrate to him that the real benefits are there for the taking.

>> Take the time to keep up-to-date with the contents of your website and blog or news items. Your prospects will, and you need to be better informed than they are about your own business. Make it a matter of routine to spend time each week refreshing your understanding of current messages, campaigns, and client-facing communications.

Avoiding a Reliance on Marketing

As I explain earlier in this chapter, marketing has a massive role to play in supporting your new business sales efforts, but don't just rely on marketing to spoon-feed you information and sales support. You're responsible for generating today's revenue — you and no one else. Your new business sales role is the most important one in the company. Nothing else will succeed or even exist for very long without you. You truly are the linchpin. The following sections explain how you can take the work that marketing does and go to the next level of winning new business.

Taking responsibility

As far as your prospect is concerned, you are your business. You are the point of contact, and you are the one who is championing his cause. You are the one who is going to provide the solution to his needs, and you are the one who will hold accountability and take responsibility. Lead from the front, show your prospect that you always have his best interests at heart, and build that trusting relationship that I discuss in Chapter 3.

Internally, you're the one who delivers today's revenue that enables your company to thrive. Don't wait to be spoon-fed leads and marketing messages; get out there and do your own prospecting and build those relationships using your knowledge and experience. (Don't know where to start? Get the full scoop on prospecting in Chapters 9 and 23.)

Revisiting prospects after a marketing change

Over time, your company's product line and marketing strategy will change — that's a fact of life. The need for new business success will never change, though, because new business is the lifeblood of a company.

Today's product or solution may not be right — indeed, it won't be right — for all your prospects, but solutions yet to be delivered could change that in the future, so never give up on a prospective opportunity if it's not right today. Add the details into the CRM, and revisit it in the future. (Flip to Chapter 9 for an introduction to CRM systems.)

Supporting and feeding back

Give your marketing function the benefit of your experience with prospects and customers. You have an obligation to keep them abreast of how their work, branding, positioning, and communications are being received where they really matter — by your prospects.

Find your own case studies and, when relevant, feed them into marketing. Have them make these studies into formal case study material, but don't wait for this to happen. Talk about your customers' successes with implementing your solution, and make sure your prospects get to hear about successes in using the solution. Nurture your own references so that if you're asked to provide a user reference, and you decide it is the right thing to do, you have people ready and willing to assist you. Chapter 5 covers some of the issues around user references.

Keep your relationships between new business sales and marketing both open and strong, and you'll reap the benefit in having the right tools provided for your sales tool bag.

In smaller organizations, you'll often find that sales and marketing fall under the remit of the same person, and that person could even be you. If that's the case, then wear your different hats accordingly. Being able to differentiate strategic work from tactical work will be your greatest asset. And, of course, you have no option but to work closely with yourself!

Chapter **7**

Making It Easy to Say Yes

Winning new business is all about getting your prospects to accept your offer in the quickest and easiest way possible. In other words, your task is to get your prospects to say yes, and you need to make this as easy as possible for them. The easier you can make this, the quicker you can close the deal. Although that may sound simple, it's not quite as easy as it sounds. But don't worry. In this chapter, I cover tried and tested strategies that help make your task of getting to a yes both quicker and easier.

Making Your Customer Comfortable

Some people say that you should ask only "yes" questions — questions that make it more difficult to say no to you later. Others focus on positive body language, such as nodding your head a lot to get your customer into a positive frame of mind. These two examples may well be true and may assist in setting a positive tone, but in any serious winning-new-business situation, you need a lot more to help you.

Before getting into how to make your customers say yes, consider the customer's point of view. First of all, you're asking your customers to make a commitment to buy something they may not know much about from someone they may not know very well. You're asking them to take a leap of faith, which may not be a comfortable or natural response for them.

One of your first objectives in winning new business has to be to make your customers comfortable with you and your product or service. If you win this battle for heart and mind with your customers, get them on your side, and show them that your objective is to help them reach their objectives, winning new business will be a lot easier. On the other hand, if you alienate your customer, you'll have a near-impossible job of getting to that yes decision.

TIP

One way to help your customers feel comfortable with you and to encourage them to open up is to ask them questions. Find out what problem they're seeking a solution for. The more you can get customers to talk, provided that you actively listen, the more you'll learn and the more comfortable you'll make customers feel with you.

Note the difference between selling and order taking. If customers often come to you knowing exactly what they want and waving an order or payment at you, then you're an order taker, and much of this advice won't necessarily apply to you. For the majority of people involved in winning new business, that's a pipe dream!

REMEMBER

When the sales cycle reaches a natural conclusion — that is, you've put together a straightforward proposition, covered the issues, and handled the objections — a key moment comes in getting the yes (as I explain in the rest of this chapter): asking for the order. Some buyers want to be asked and won't give you a yes until you do. Amazing as it may seem, I know of cases where a sale has been lost simply because the salesperson didn't have the confidence to ask for the order at the right time.

Creating a Straightforward Proposition

Often the initial sale to new customers opens all sorts of potential added features or services you can offer them. You want to avoid the temptation to load the first deal with extras and options, preferring instead to make it a nice and straightforward proposition to sign them up as your customers. You do so by keeping the sale uncomplicated and using the prospect's terminology, as I explain in the following sections. You need to be mindful of the lifetime value of new customers, but don't try to get them to commit to everything at the same time because then you risk both delaying the decision and complicating the initial sale. Remember that your task is to make it easy for your prospects to say yes to your offer.

TIP

With new customers, your goal is to establish trust quickly and to let them see that you're interested in solving their unique problem rather than leaving them thinking that you're concerned only with the size of your own commission check. Take the time to really understand what they want to achieve. Do some background reading on trends in their industry that may be driving the buying process. Doing so can help you understand some of their pain points.

REMEMBER

Your *unique selling proposition (USP)* is whatever sets your solution apart in the way that you want it to be perceived by your prospect. USPs generally are defined by your marketing colleagues (see Chapter 6 for more on marketing). Make sure you fully understand your USP and use it as the focus of your sales efforts. Don't reinvent the wheel with every (or any) sales situation you find yourself in. If your offering does a, b, and c, don't push on d, e, and f. This is where the importance of qualification comes in (see Chapter 19), but the basic message is to keep your selling efforts focused on the big picture by majoring on the areas that give you the best chance of winning — and that is your USPs.

Don't overcomplicate

You likely know better than your customers exactly how your range of products or services can solve their immediate needs, fit in with other systems they have, and overcome potential problems. The first sale you make to new customers may be only the tip of the iceberg in terms of everything you can do for them, so don't overcomplicate it. Focus on solving the initial need. Letting your customers know that your solutions can provide much more and that they're buying into a long-term solution is fine, but don't focus too much on the future. If you do, you run a serious risk of delaying your sale. Instead, keep customers focused on the here and now and on the initial problem that you're solving.

REMEMBER

Any presentation or discussion about the capability of the solution needs to be straightforward and easy to comprehend. Don't get sucked into product-speak or sidetracked by other things you can do. You need laser-sharp focus on pitching an easy-to-understand solution to a stated need.

I have seen many examples of salespeople losing a piece of business that really should have been won by overcomplicating matters, even when the customer was saying yes. One particular example involved a salesman having gone through the basics just fine and essentially having won the order, but then he went on to discuss some completely irrelevant technical considerations that the customer hadn't even thought about and that wouldn't ever be something that was important in delivering the solution. The net effect was that he worried the customer — who delayed the decision, spent the next few weeks deciding how to cope with some imaginative future need, and canceled the entire order process.

REMEMBER

There's a big difference between not overcomplicating and leaving out important information. You need to ensure that your customers have all the pertinent information as you guide them to making an informed choice.

Use the prospect's terminology

When creating a proposition, discuss the merits of your solution, using language that your customers are familiar with. Take the time to understand the vocabulary used in their line of work. Your customers don't need to know that your "widget type 7 interfaces to a type 9B and is driven by software version 8.6"; they need to know that your solution will work with whatever they're currently using and that existing staff can use it without massive amounts of re-training.

For example, if a customer refers to clients, then you should use the term *clients* yourself and not *customers.* If a customer uses the term *training,* make sure you don't say *skill sets* or *education* — stick to *training.* Your objective is to make your customers comfortable in dealing with you, and using a common vocabulary is a big part of this.

REMEMBER

The last thing you want to do is alienate customers by talking in terms they either don't easily relate to or may consider complicated. On the other hand, if a customer is using terminology that you're not sure of or don't understand, don't just go along with it and echo it. Check. Ask questions. Not knowing doesn't display a weakness; rather, it demonstrates that you're actually listening and are acknowledging the customer as an expert. It also shows that you're keen to ensure a good problem-to-solution fit while also ensuring that clarity and understanding occur in your communications. Customers love to be seen as experts and will usually be only too happy to explain in terms that you, as deferential to their knowledge, will understand.

You also need to be aware of natural language. Even English has different dialects, so you want to make sure you and your customer are talking about the same thing. If one of you isn't speaking in your native tongue, this becomes even more important. Nothing is wrong with seeking clarification if in doubt rather than continuing based on your assumptions only to find you were wrong and have delayed getting to the yes decision.

Covering All the Issues

Your customers will likely tell you about all the problems they're seeking to address, but don't assume that you know better than they do. Early in the sales cycle, you need to discuss with your customers exactly what issues they expect to resolve with the solution they're going to purchase. Addressing the needs early in your discussions is vital in getting a sale to close. You also want to make sure that whatever you're proposing does indeed cover all those stated needs or that you show why the customer doesn't need to address any specific needs at this stage.

The last thing you want to happen is having a customer ask about something that you either don't expect or haven't satisfactorily addressed right before closing the deal. Your objective is to get to a yes as quickly as possible while making sure you address all the customer's considerations. In the following sections, I go into detail on avoiding the introduction of additional elements and focusing on the customer's needs.

Here's an example: Years ago, I was about to close an order for PR services with a new client (a software company selling database solutions to a niche sector). I thought I had covered all the bases, but literally, as the customer's pen was poised over the order form, he asked, "You can guarantee press coverage, can't you?" Thankfully, I was quick on my feet with a truthful answer that also demonstrated that I knew what I was taking about, without putting him down in any way. What I told him was, "Yes, I can guarantee you press coverage as long as you do exactly as I ask, but you won't necessarily thank me for it." Puzzled, he asked what I meant. I told him, "If I ask you to streak across the Centre Court at the Wimbledon Tennis Tournament, I can guarantee that you will be front-page tabloid news, but that won't help your business!" He got the point I was making about guaranteed coverage versus relevant coverage, but with hindsight I should have covered this during the sales cycle. He signed the order, though!

Avoid introducing additional elements

If your solution addresses all the customer's needs and also does a lot of other things, don't get sucked into focusing too much on what else your customer can do with your solution. If it isn't broken in the customer's eyes, then don't try to fix it. Making your customer aware — at least on a superficial level — that your solution will enable him to do x, y, and z better that he currently does is completely fine and even encouraged. But if z is the only thing that is driving the customer's purchase needs, that is where your entire focus needs to be. Maybe y can help him better if he changed some aspects of his business, but introducing this when it isn't a key requirement is asking for trouble and at an absolute minimum will cause a delay in getting your sale.

In some cases, introducing additional elements can lead to losing a sale altogether. The customer either becomes too focused on a non-core element or becomes concerned that something on the periphery isn't quite right for the future and so decides to do nothing.

WARNING

Being mindful of the lifetime value of a customer (see the nearby sidebar for more information), you can explore this area after the initial sale is made and implementation is underway. You want to avoid doing it too early, especially during the initial sales process, because your initial focus needs to be on closing the "now" sale.

THE LIFETIME VALUE OF A CUSTOMER

You will often hear marketing people talk about *lifetime value (LTV)* of a customer, but what is it and why is it important?

The lifetime value of a customer is the profit that you expect to generate from sales to a particular customer in the future. It assumes that the majority of your cost in acquiring the customer is spent upfront. Although you'll have customer service and service delivery costs in the future, your rate of profit per customer increases over subsequent sales as you lose the majority of the customer acquisition cost after the initial sale is concluded.

The initial process of winning a new customer is nowhere near as profitable as keeping and servicing that customer in the future and is why money spent on retaining customers has a higher value return than money spent on winning them in the first place.

As far as winning new business is concerned, you need to be aware of a customer's LTV, but your focus needs to be on the acquisition phase — winning that first order for something that is required *now,* without getting caught up in trying to sell the customer everything he may need in the future.

After covering the customer's requirements, don't then get sucked into peripheral areas. If the customer takes the conversation into these areas, bring the discussion back to what you've both agreed the objectives are and ask the customer to affirm. If the customer opens up more areas of importance that suggests that he hasn't thought through what he's trying to achieve, revisit the objectives that you've agreed on to understand where the new requirements have arisen. (Chapter 3 provides more detail about agreeing on objectives.)

Focus on the prospect's needs

In all likelihood, your customers are speaking to you about your solution because they have a specific problem that needs solving. Your first task in getting a yes is to discover exactly what that perceived need is and then focus your selling messages on how your solution is going to address that need or needs. However, you want to avoid getting sidetracked by elements of the solution that, although exciting to you, aren't part of the core issue that your customers are trying to solve because you run a risk of losing focus on addressing the key issue. The narrower you can make the key issue, the easier it will be to address it and get to the yes decision faster.

I recently was given a demonstration of a software system that was going to make it much easier for me to quickly identify target prospects according to the salesman. He had correctly identified my core need as fast access to quality data that was 100 percent accurate. The salesman kept straying away from this core need in his demonstration, though, by showing me lots of different things that I could do with searches and lots of interesting but irrelevant information I could discover. When I managed to focus his attention back on the core need of accuracy, I quickly discovered that the proposed solution had some glaring problems. Rather than try to address my issue, the salesman ignored it and continued to push other features. By failing to focus on my core requirements, he quickly lost any chance of making a sale.

Sometimes your customers will know exactly what they want and how they want to achieve it, in which case your primary objective is still to focus on how you're going to meet their needs better than any competitor. In these cases, how you focus on ensuring their needs can be met is often the key differentiator in making sure you, and not a competitor, get the yes vote.

REMEMBER

By having laser-sharp focus, understanding your customers' needs, and then meeting their needs, you'll quickly gain the respect you need to be perceived by customers as someone they can do business with. Forget the size of your commission check — that will take care of itself. Focus instead on the needs of your customers and then how your solution is going to meet those needs. Keep this at the forefront of your mind when looking to win new business, and you'll be on the right track; lose sight of this, and you'll soon discover that you're in trouble.

Taking Away the Risk

In Chapter 18, I go into detail about risk and ways of mitigating against it. Here, I cover the perceived risk to customers. When trying to make it easy for customers to say yes, you need to remember that one of your main duties is to make customers feel comfortable with buying your solution. They may feel like they're taking a risk in doing something, or anything for that matter, and they need to feel confident in both your proposed solution and your integrity in selling the right thing.

Presenting your solution in as straightforward a way as possible, using the customer's terminology and focusing just on his core needs (as I describe earlier in this chapter), will go a long way to making your customer comfortable with his purchase decision and steer him away from worries about taking a risk.

Put the customer at the center of your solution, and you won't go far wrong. Consider how the solution looks from his perspective. Have you covered the perception of risk and removed it as far as possible? If your solution calls for a leap of faith from the customer, then you're likely to be in trouble, so remain customer-centric in considering the risk factor. In the following sections, I discuss getting your customer's objections out in the open, building on your customer's trust, and thinking about performance-related payment.

Generally, the higher the perceived risk, the longer it will take to get to the yes that you're seeking.

Getting objections in the open

An objection in a sales process is simply a reason for your customers not to accept your solution or an issue that needs to be overcome to get to the yes.

In any remotely complex sale, you'll likely have customer objections to overcome. The important thing to remember is that you need to discover what these objections are as early in the sales process as possible. Doing so enables you to present your solution in a way that deals with each of the objections. The last thing you want is to be ready to sign the order when an objection rears its head for the first time. That will lead to at best a delay and at worse a lost sale.

To bring out the objections, you can ask upfront whether the customer has any reason not to buy your solution. However, this approach may still not get the objection into the open and may make you seem pushy. So you need to find ways around this.

Another approach is the trial-close approach. Here, when discussing the key issues from the customer's perspective, you can ask a question like, "If we cover x, y, and z, is there any other reason you may not go ahead?" This approach gives the customer an opportunity to disclose any hidden agenda that you have yet to uncover, and it enables you to put down a marker that is difficult for the customer to turn back from later. You're not asking for an order at this stage; you're merely covering the bases and ensuring that you both understand what needs to be achieved to progress the deal to a yes. It also shows the customer that you're professional and serious about meeting his objectives. If you get any form of pushback from the customer at this type of question, then you need to consider your qualification criteria (which I look at in Chapter 19).

Objections in a typical sales situation include the following:

>> Affordability

>> Complexity

>> Compatibility

>> Trust

I talk about trust in the next section. The other standard objections should be covered early in the sales process. In Chapter 10, I look at the importance of overcoming objections in more detail.

REMEMBER

You never want to dismiss or ignore anything that your customer says to you that implies a problem or concern. If you commit to come back to him with an answer to any question, then make sure you do. Unless you take note of these issues and adequately address them, they're likely to come back and bite you.

Building on trust

In winning new business, you're not setting out to become best buddies with your customers, nor are you looking to become a "yes man" to their every whim. You're building a business relationship based on supply and demand of a product or service that you're providing. You need your customers to be able to trust you to sell them something that will meet their needs and to ensure that you're perceived as an expert in your field who can be relied upon to be responsive, open, and trustworthy. You want to be someone who they can happily go to for advice on the solution and who they're happy to refer to friends and colleagues with similar needs.

This trust is something that you earn; it's not yours by right. Your customers are many times more likely to say yes to someone who has established this trust bond and has proven to deliver on commitments. This is why it is important not to overstate your benefits and to always do things that you say you will.

WARNING

When you're involved in a competitive sales situation, it can often be tempting to trash your competitors and to expend negative energy in running them down or showing why they're not the right solution for your customers. This approach is unlikely to help you build trust, and you should avoid it at all costs. Doing this is risking telling your customers that they're wrong in considering any alternative — and who are you to tell them they're wrong? Your energies will be much better and positively spent by focusing on how your solution can meet their needs. Although you may need to reference competitive offerings, you should always do so in a professional manner. If your competitors do the opposite, then that just adds to your credibility and helps in the trust-building stakes.

Trust works the other way also; you need to be able to trust what your customers are telling you in regard to both their objectives and their proposed solution. See Chapter 20 for more details.

Considering performance-related payment

In a complex or financially large sale, especially where the product or service is delivered over time, offering a structured payment plan based on performance criteria that you determine with your customer can both benefit the customer and show him that you're confident in your offering. Remember that your objective is to get to a yes decision as quickly as possible and that you want to make it easy for the customer to give this to you.

I cover how to structure a deal in Chapter 11. Don't be afraid of the concept of performance-related payment, but you need to ensure that you build in safeguards for your business as well as for your customer. Performance-related payment can be a bit of a minefield, and you shouldn't agree or enter into it lightly. But in the right circumstances and handled in the right way, it can be a powerful tool in your mission to get to a yes as quickly as possible.

WARNING

If your specific sale doesn't lend itself to performance-related payments for whatever reason, don't be afraid to rule this out because it will apply only in some circumstances. If structuring a deal this way is obviously going to lead to delay, then stay clear of suggesting it.

Generally, I am wary of proposing performance-related payment and don't consider offering it upfront. I am inclined to hold it back until one of two things happen: either the customer raises it as an issue or it becomes obvious that you're not going to get to a yes quickly — and then only if the qualification criteria are met. If the customer raises it, then you can turn this to your advantage by, for example, making it conditional on an order date being agreed.

TIP

Your company sales guidelines or terms and conditions of business are likely to have a bearing on the parameters you have at your disposal in this area, so make sure you're completely familiar with them. You don't want to be in a position where you have to tell customers that you don't know or will have to get back to them if the issue is raised. Remember that you're positioning yourself as the expert and as such you should be well versed in both the product or service specifics as well as the commercial terms.

Chapter **8**

Elevator Pitching

I t may seem a little ironic that a chapter about an elevator pitch, which by its very definition is short and succinct, should take up so many pages!

Elevator pitching is about being prepared to take advantage of an unexpected opportunity to promote yourself or your solution in a slightly unusual way and is not confined to use in elevators! The term dates back to the early 1980s and is generally used to describe encountering an unexpected opportunity in passing, such as during an elevator ride, to address someone you wouldn't normally get an audience with. (*Note:* Don't get hung up on the word *pitch;* what I discuss in this chapter is a prepared introduction that offers something compelling and worthy of later follow-up. It's not intended to be a full-on sales pitch — in fact, far from it.)

When developing a winning impromptu introduction, you need to follow some basic rules. Your pitch should be

» Interesting

» Memorable

» Succinct

I explore how to put together and deliver an elevator pitch in this chapter. You just may win new business because of one.

Take the time to develop an elevator pitch, because you never know when it may come in handy. How many times have you attended chamber of commerce–type events and been asked to give a one-minute summary of your product or service? Your elevator pitch, or a version of it, is ideal for this type of event.

Breaking Down the 60-Second Pitch

So what exactly is an elevator, or 60-second, pitch? Think of it as an opportunity to deliver a high-end but basic introduction, enough to spark interest in your listener. It's a primer to your overall message and not the message itself. You need to set it out as a means of providing your audience with just enough information to give them a clear sense of what you're talking about without overwhelming them and leaving them wanting to know more.

Specifically, your 60-second pitch isn't an unexpected information dump. That simply leads to your audience tuning out the noise and seeking to get away from you as quickly as they can. You don't want to come across as the party bore.

A good elevator pitch should take about as long as the typical elevator ride, so around 60 seconds. You should use natural language and not something that sounds like you're reading from a prompt card or autocue. A quick and concise introduction, well delivered and in the right circumstances, can be a deal changer and a life changer. It can just be the most important 60 seconds you ever spend, so it's worthy of a great deal of thought and preparation. Your delivery needs to come across as natural and not canned in any way, and anyone who has ever delivered a set of prepared remarks understands that getting the tone right is one of the most difficult and most important aspects.

The only one way to achieve this is through relentless practice in front of a mirror. Spend time rehearsing your pitch and your delivery; you'll be thankful for the effort when you face a live opportunity to deliver it.

The following sections explain what to include in your pitch, when to use it, and when not to dive right into it.

What to cover

Both what you say and how you say it — in other words, the content and structure of your pitch — are very important. In planning your 60-second pitch, you need to focus on a number of key areas:

>> **Introduction:** The introduction is where it all starts. You can't just launch into a spiel without letting your audience know who you are and why you're qualified to address them on your subject. You need to introduce yourself by name because this is one of the key things that you want them to remember.

TIP

Make sure that you include your name at both the beginning and the end of your 60-second pitch. You need to do it twice both to reinforce it and to give your audience a second chance to remember it. Remembering who you are is vital for others to be able to engage with you in a follow-up, and to assist in this, make sure you provide a business card as you part.

>> **Language:** Using plain language is important because you need to be able to communicate in a clear and concise manner. Avoid MBA-speak, corporate-speak, and acronyms at all cost. Your native language contains more than enough vocabulary to enable you to craft clear, unambiguous sentences and articulate a message without having to rely on made-up words. Your audience won't have the time or, likely, inclination to try to decode anything else.

WARNING

Don't hide your message behind a cloak of Ivy League hyperbole. If you mean something like "we use it successfully," don't say "we eat our own dog food" as an example. This is especially true when working in multinational or multicultural environments. Imagine what something like "eat our own dog food" sounds like to non-native English speakers and what they're likely to think of some stranger accosting them with such rubbish. Moving your sale forward is the most unlikely outcome of such an encounter.

TIP

Practice your 60-second pitch in front of your significant other and get some honest feedback on your language. If your significant other understands you, try the same with your parents or neighbors. Keep refining your language until you're able to convey your message in a form that's immediately understood by all.

>> **Making each word count:** Put 60 seconds on a timer (do it now), and see just how long a time it is to fill. Don't feel the need to fill exactly 60 seconds, either. If you can get your clear message into 50 seconds, then stop there and don't fill the remaining time with waffle. The only really acceptable repetition is your name and maybe the name of your company. You should aim to develop your 60-second pitch in as few meaningful words as possible.

>> **Being relevant, specific, and tangible:** Your message needs to be relevant, specific, and tangible, and you need to continually refine it until you achieve these goals because anything less won't get you the result you want. Give your audience just enough information to stimulate a desire to know more. You're not going to move your sale forward if you don't communicate what you're talking about and why they should be interested in listening to you. Get to

the point, make the point, and finish with a call to action, which can be a request to speak again, for example, depending on your objectives (which I cover later in this chapter).

>> **Conversational delivery:** Your 60-second elevator pitch isn't a sales pitch and you're not trying to close a deal. Your aim is to start a dialogue and sow a seed for future follow up, so keep the tone conversational in nature as if you're talking very briefly, one on one, to someone who could assist your sales cycle.

>> **High level rather than detail:** You won't have time to go into any detail, nor should you in this situation. Keep your 60-second pitch aimed at a high level and focus on a key benefit as part of your unique selling proposition (USP; see Chapter 7). Detail is for another time and, more than likely, with a different audience. Your role here is to get to that other time and place, and your 60-second pitch audience could be the key that you need to unlock the path. Give them a reason to do this.

TIP

Express your USP in an end user's terms rather that some internal or marketing-driven soundbite. Leaving out your USP is like forgetting to go to work — it's that important.

>> **Relevance to your audience:** To keep your pitch relevant, prepare a few different versions, in varying lengths of perhaps 30, 40, and 60 seconds, to cater for slightly different audiences, circumstances, and time opportunities. You won't know in advance who you'll have a short opportunity to speak to, so have versions that are relevant to a CEO, a finance director, and a marketing director, for example, who each have a slightly different view on and interest in your subject area. Each variant of your elevator pitch must, however, be consistent and convey the same message but be expressed in slightly different terms.

TIP

By definition, you're going to use your elevator pitch to introduce yourself to someone who doesn't know you, isn't expecting to meet you, and is therefore extremely unlikely to hang around when the elevator has parked to wait for you to finish. My rule is to ensure that I deliver just enough of the right type of information in the right way to catch the attention of my target audience and make them receptive to a follow-up.

Here's an example of an elevator pitch that takes all the preceding guidelines into consideration:

My name is Stewart Stuchbury, and I'm the CEO of N58 Consulting Group. We help clients win more new business than they can achieve on their own. Let me briefly share a recent success: A graphic design company approached us from a referral and asked if we could help them. They were excellent at what they did but poor at winning new business. We developed a replicable plan for them so that they understood their ideal prospects, how to contact them, and how to win real business. Their sales were up by 60 percent after the first quarter. It would be good to have an opportunity to discuss how we might be able to help you. Here's my card with my direct contact details. Do you have a personal assistant I could talk to about scheduling an appointment, please?

When to use it

A key to successful elevator pitching is knowing when to use it. Generally, any chance encounter with a key stakeholder is an open invitation to engage with him and not one that you should pass up lightly.

However, as you know, people are busy and have their own agendas to deal with. If you approach your audience at an inopportune time, then you're likely to have the opposite effect than the one you hoped for. Use your eyes to observe the environment and determine whether now is the right moment. Hold fire if you can see that now is obviously not a good one; otherwise, go ahead and engage. (See the next section for more information on when *not* to use your elevator pitch.)

REMEMBER

Engage your audience first, and give them a moment to react before you launch headlong into your pitch. If they have a level of interest high enough to want to turn it into a conversation or to ask questions, then allow that to happen without trying to force-feed them your rehearsed ending. An impromptu pitch that leads to a compelling conversation is about as high as you could hope for, so if it moves in that direction, then go with the flow.

TIP

You need to have a good, solid opening to get you started, which is why I suggest you begin by simply introducing yourself (as I note in the preceding section). Nothing like the sound of your own name and position gets the sales juices flowing. Avoid being tongue-tied or star-struck by solid preparation, and remember the way you deliver your pitch is as important as what you actually say.

A 60-second pitch can also be a useful social tool, and you can use a version of it to introduce yourself at a networking event or party, quickly getting beyond who you are and allowing more time for interaction and conversation. Just remember that your audience has changed and that you're not seeking an ultimate close to a deal.

Another key use for a 60-second pitch, and one that I use a lot in my business, is for a phone conversation introduction. Especially in a first call with a potential prospect, having a succinct introduction helps you avoid the cringeworthy opening of "How are you today?" as if you really care what the answer is. This is such a powerful tool that forces you to really think about your opening impression that

I make all the new clients I work with develop a 60-second pitch for use in exactly this situation. (I discuss first impressions in detail in Chapter 3.)

When not to dive straight in

In the preceding section, I mention being aware of the environment and considering whether it's appropriate to launch into your pitch. This consideration sets you apart from snake-oil salespeople who'll launch into a pitch at their granny's funeral if they thought it'd give them an advantage. Throughout this book, one of my recurring themes is the need to be professional, and that comes above everything else in my mind. Don't try to score cheap points.

TIP

Read the body language of your audience before and during engagement, and you'll see whether they're receptive to you. Don't waste your time and reputation if they're not because it really won't get you anywhere. For me, knowing when not to pitch is as important as the way you deliver your pitch. You can acknowledge someone without pitching to him if the circumstances are right, and you can even use that in a follow-up, saying that you saw him and realized that he was busy but you wanted to bring something to his attention, and then you can give the gist of the pitch, asking for an opportunity to discuss with him in person.

I'm sure that many people (myself included) have encountered a situation where on their way out of a prospect's building, they happen to notice the managing director arrive with an entourage who he's in deep conversation with. Unless the world is about to end, this isn't a good time to dive into a pitch. Again, it comes back to being aware of and sensitive to your environment.

WARNING

Do not, under any circumstances, use a chance encounter to deliver bad news or a complaint of any kind. It's not the time or place to leave negative feedback about a member of the decision-making unit, for example. (See Chapter 19 for more about decision-making units.)

You need to leave room for your audience to respond to you, so don't deliver your 60-second pitch and then just wander off. Allow your audience a moment to consider what you've said and let them offer to engage further if they want to. This is the Holy Grail of the 60-second pitch, so make sure that you do have more substance behind it.

Of equal importance is knowing when to shut up. After delivering your pitch, leave your audience to do the talking until you're fully engaged with them. Consider what your objectives for this encounter are and secure them first. (I discuss objectives later in this chapter.)

You're seeking to use your elevator pitch as a springboard to enable you to move forward in your sales cycle, so don't create a poor impression or make a nuisance of yourself. I cover the importance of making a good first impression in Chapter 3.

Setting Your Objectives

Even with an elevator pitch, you need to establish some objectives and understand what you're looking to achieve from an unexpected encounter. Without an objective, you risk your pitch being a wasted opportunity to win new business. Three key outcomes are

>> Securing another opportunity

>> Making yourself memorable

>> Getting gatekeeper information

I examine each of these in turn in this section. These objectives are fairly obvious, so you should also set some sales cycle–specific ones for yourself, bearing in mind that you don't know who you're likely to encounter.

When establishing objectives, ask yourself this question: Are your objectives reasonable and attainable in this type of encounter? You need to be honest with yourself here. You're more likely to successfully float an idea than to be able to secure a signature on an order. Set your reasonable objectives accordingly — for example, to gain the name of a personal assistant for a follow-up or to get a direct line contact number or email address as well as permission to contact the person again.

Securing another opportunity

An unexpected 60-second pitch is, by its very nature, limited in what it's able to achieve at the time, although the long-term implications of this event can be much more compelling. Recognize, for example, that you're not going to finalize a deal in 60 seconds, so don't expect to. Your mindset shouldn't be on closing a sale or really even on selling at all. One of your primary objectives needs to be to secure a follow-up, where you can fully state your case and progress your sales cycle. Your 60-second pitch is a primer toward reaching this objective.

Go in to your 60-second pitch knowing the ideal outcome you want to achieve and ask for it. Engage with an open question, perhaps along the lines of "How would an additional 3 percent on your top line change the approach to your investment in automation? I have the figures on my desk and would be happy to go through them with you." Then arrange to set up the follow-up meeting. A word of caution here: Don't oversell and underdeliver. If you're promising something of substance to secure a meeting, make sure you deliver it.

Always have a business card with you, and offer it as part of establishing the next step or contact. Attempt to maintain control by asking for contact details to confirm an appointment, but accept gracefully if the person declines and says he'll contact you. This is one of the very few times I suggest that you readily accept not being in control of a follow-up because you've just dropped in, out of the blue, and he needs to have an opportunity to show that he has an element of control and hasn't been hijacked by a stranger who's now trying to dictate terms.

Where you've given up control of the follow-up, always write or email preferably to confirm your discussion point and state that you look forward to hearing from him as agreed. Writing may be necessary if you can't secure an email address. Or you can try phoning his assistant to either secure his email address or ask her to prompt him to arrange the follow-up meeting. But don't be pushy here.

As in all things, ensure that you update the CRM with the full details and a contact report. Send your new acquaintance or his assistant a copy of your contact report, and also send a copy to your key prospect so that he doesn't find out later that you've gone over his head. (Flip to Chapter 9 for more about CRM systems.)

Making yourself memorable

The person you get an opportunity to deliver a 60-second pitch to, who could potentially open up doors for you or get you past an obstacle that you've been struggling with, is going to be busy and in demand, with his own set of issues to resolve. It almost goes without saying that the more potentially useful a contact is, the busier and more preoccupied he seems to be. You therefore have to grab his attention with a memorable, well-prepared pitch.

In Chapter 3, I cover the importance of making a positive first impression. An elevator pitch is your first impression, so you need to be memorable and for the right reasons. It's easy to be memorable for the wrong reason, and at a stroke this can finish off any credibility that you had with that company as well as finish off any opportunity of winning new business with it.

Here are a few pointers for making yourself memorable in the right way:

» As in most new business sales activities, be prepared for a variety of scenarios. I'd even suggest that you limit an elevator encounter with a senior member of a prospect company to something simple, such as "Hello, Mr. Jones, I'm John Smith from ZYX Corp. Pleased to meet you," unless you have planned your approach in detail and have a well-rehearsed elevator pitch ready.

» In delivering your 60-second pitch, remember to keep it human and let your passion shine through. Even if your target audience hasn't fully grasped the significance of your message, let them see the passion in your delivery, and all isn't necessarily lost should the message not hit home.

» Don't spout information, and avoid jargon. Speak clearly and concisely, using native natural language, as I discuss in the earlier section "What to cover." The style and tone of your delivery should have a smooth conversational flow and most certainly not feel like an aggressive sales pitch.

REMEMBER

» Stick to the big picture, and don't attempt to get involved in detail because this is simply not relevant at this stage. Use the time wisely. Rehearse again and again until your timing, tone, delivery, and body language are as you want then to be. And then rehearse some more. In fact, always be rehearsing as you never know when an opportunity will present itself.

» Don't stumble around looking for something to say, but do be prepared to respond warmly to any attempt to engage that the prospect makes. You may even find yourself on the end of his elevator pitch and learn a thing or two from it.

Getting gatekeeper information

At the very least, one of your objectives should be to secure access to a gatekeeper and clues as to how to work through one. By *gatekeeper*, I mean a secretary, an assistant, or someone in a similar role who guards access to the decision maker by fielding email, calls, and letters. A gatekeeper will also often be the custodian of the decision maker's diary and, in controlling all external access, is a very important target of a new business salesperson.

Don't think of gatekeepers as the enemy or as obstacles to be overcome, however much they may give that impression. You should always seek to make them a valuable resource. Gatekeepers can be a fount of knowledge and generally love being asked to help.

Try asking for help and see the response it brings you. I do this a lot, often whether I need help or not, because it makes gatekeepers immediately feel important and engaged in whatever you're discussing. Never, ever patronize a gatekeeper, or you risk never getting in contact with the decision maker again. Asking for help brings the gatekeeper into your camp and can be illuminating. If, for example, you're finding it difficult to speak to the decision maker, then ask the gatekeeper how you should go about getting an opportunity.

If you ever make a commitment to a gatekeeper, then make sure you keep to it, to the letter, because it will be remembered. You need to show that you're reliable, and when he enables you to speak to the decision maker, it is safe in the knowledge that you do as you commit to do. He will have done his job in vetting you and letting you pass as someone that can be trusted.

As an objective of your 60-second pitch, therefore, access to or information about a gatekeeper is important. You can then use this direct referral from the decision maker to the gatekeeper to your advantage as he will be much more inclined to help you if the decision maker has told him to, which is essentially what a referral is.

When you get a referral from a 60-second pitch to a gatekeeper or elsewhere, you need to act on it quickly before it gets forgotten. It's no good going back to a referral after six weeks — even six days is far too long. It needs to be within one working day while the lead is warm.

Embracing a Listening Opportunity

The environment of a 60-second pitch can also be a great place to listen as well as speak. For example, listen for feedback from your audience and what clues you're given about how to proceed.

As I cover earlier in this chapter, finding a senior-level contact unexpectedly isn't always an invitation to engage with him. But even when you can't interact directly, what can you find out by using your powers of observation? It's not eavesdropping if you happen to overhear a conversation that is relevant to your sales opportunity. If he didn't want it to be overheard, he should have taken more care where it was being discussed.

When you've delivered your 60-second pitch, give him a chance to speak and take careful note of how he responds to you. Look and listen for any clues. You may be given pointers to people in the organization who you've never heard of so make sure you note names and titles. Don't be afraid to ask for his help after making your 60-second pitch. Ask for his recommendations on who you should speak to.

When following up, be sure to use the referral you've been given. Being able to say, for example, "Mr. Jones suggested I contact you," is a powerful door opener, especially if Mr. Jones is a senior manager. Your reaching out will carry more weight than if you begin from a cold contact. Always assume that someone will check with Mr. Jones, though, so don't overplay your hand here, and use the referral route only if you were actually given it.

TIP

Another route that you can use, having spoken to the senior decision maker and given your 60-second pitch, is to contact his assistant, explaining that you've spoken to Mr. Jones, and ask for the contact details for the senior contacts in the functions you need to get into. You then have a legitimate reason to contact them directly and use the opening of "Mr. Jones's assistant suggested speaking to you." I've used this technique with a fair degree of success.

Chapter **9**

Prospecting Effectively

Identifying the right sales opportunities to pursue — known as *prospecting* — is one of the most important aspects of winning new business. You have a limited amount of time to spend on each stage of the sales process, so making the most of it is key. If your initial prospect identification isn't spot on, then you risk wasting your most valuable resource: time.

You may have the greatest product or service to offer, your presentation skills finely tuned, your objection handling rehearsed to perfection, and your 60-second intro word perfect, but if you're talking to the wrong profile of prospect at the wrong time, then you're not going to win.

You can spend time on literally hundreds, or even thousands, of potential opportunities, but only a few of them will be the right profile of prospect. The right profile of prospect is one that is in the right market at the right time, with a set of needs that your solution can address. You can't and shouldn't chase everything that moves. Your prospecting efforts need to be more akin to a finely tuned sniper's rifle rather than a farmer's shotgun. Targeting effectively is the name of the game. When I was branding my company's new business service, I called it Targeted Lead Generation for exactly that reason.

Prospecting effectively takes a little time to master, but it's time well spent and will reap rewards as your sales efforts move forward. In this chapter, I cover four of the fundamental areas that you need to master: knowing your targets, conducting research, performing first-level qualification, and keeping records.

If you learn only one lesson about the secret to winning new business success, learn to prospect effectively, and you'll be halfway toward your objective of getting to as many yesses as possible.

Understanding Your Targets

Taking the time to understand the profile of your ideal target prospect is time well spent. You'll need to pass over some opportunities because they're not the right fit for your solution. Of course, in some situations, you can make your solution fit with a bit of tailoring and with your prospect compromising on his requirements; however, these situations are generally not worth pursuing because somewhere along the sales process, the prospect will decide that he needs a better fit. Knowing this at the outset will save you precious time, so make sure you really understand your product or service and what your ideal prospect looks like. And then look for and sell to just that type of prospect, with a laser-sharp focus.

How good a fit does a prospect have to be? You should address this question as part of your sales planning. Don't get too carried away with identifying prospects who are an exact fit because you'll be leaving a lot of good opportunities alone, but equally don't spend time focusing on those prospects who only halfway fit because you'll be wasting your time. You need a process of determining the key characteristics or profile of an ideal prospect, which I cover in Chapter 19.

After you identify the profile of your ideal prospects, you need to focus on some basic areas to understand your targets. For example, you need to deal with a key member of the decision-making unit (DMU), as I outline in Chapter 19, but in your initial prospecting work, you'll likely find a contact who doesn't fit within the DMU or who isn't a key player to getting to a yes. So you need to find out who you need to speak to and where your initial contact fits in and then have a plan for getting to the key contacts via your initial contact. Don't allow your initial contact to feel unimportant, however, just because he's not part of the decision-making process. You need as many internal champions as you can find to help build your case, so treat every prospect member of staff as important, but make sure you understand who the power players are.

To understand your targets, you need to apply some common-sense qualification criteria. For example, ask yourself, "What can my/our solution do for them?" or "How can I/we help them?" If you don't have clear answers, then move on to the next prospect. Be selective with your time and use it wisely. Don't chase leads that aren't going to turn into new business.

The following sections cover several types of information you need to understand about your prospects: basic demographics, the details to focus on, and timing.

Needing some basic demographics

REMEMBER

Later in this chapter, I talk about the importance of demographics in winning new business, but demographics aren't everything. In terms of understanding your targets, the basic demographic information you need is, at a minimum:

>> **Geography:** Geography is important because you need to be able to service the prospect if he becomes a client, and if he's hundreds of miles away or in a different time zone, can you effectively do this? Also, you'll likely need to spend some time during the sales process with a prospect, and if he's too far away, is it an effective use of your time?

>> **Business sector:** Business sector is important because you'll know where your solution is best suited, and if the prospect you're looking at isn't an obvious fit, then nine times out of ten, you're better off passing him by.

>> **Company size:** Company size is important for a number of reasons:

- Is the company the right profile for your solution?

- Do you have the right supplier profile for it to buy from you?

- Is it likely to take too much resource to sell to or service?

REMEMBER

After you establish some demographic qualification criteria, know that these aren't set in stone. You'll likely have some exceptions that may lead to solid new business wins. Although demographics are important, they're not the be-all and end-all of prospect qualification. Apply a measure of common sense to your criteria because you'll know better than anyone what a "good fit" really looks like.

Also, nothing is wrong with a prospect appearing to come out of left field, as long as you've followed your prospecting rules and accept that you're following something out of the ordinary. To spend time on this prospect, however, you need to be confident that it's worthwhile and generally that means having a manager or peer check your prospecting logic. Rarely is "because I know best" going to lead to new business wins.

TIP

You may want to set yourself some ground rules about investing a maximum amount of time in investigating left-field opportunities. Depending on your product or service, you may want to allow 5 or 10 percent at a maximum of your prospecting time for following your instinct, but don't forget the basic prospecting and qualification rules, ever.

Sharpening your focus

When prospecting, your objective is to identify opportunities that have the potential to result in a new business win somewhere down the line. You need to be time efficient and highly targeted in your approach, accepting that you can't go after every potential opportunity, simply because you won't have time.

Earlier in this chapter, I talk about the finely tuned sniper's rifle versus the farmer's shotgun. Keep that image in mind as you prospect for opportunities. You'll do better if you pursue opportunities that are highly qualified and are a very close fit to the profile of your ideal prospect instead of scattering resources around and hoping that you hit something that is of interest, largely more by luck that judgment. This attribute sets highly successful new businesspeople apart from run-of-the-mill salespeople.

REMEMBER

Taking a highly targeted approach to prospecting allows you to quickly home in on those opportunities that should result in a discussion about how you're able to help. You have a reason for speaking to the prospects, in that their profiles are a good match for your product, service, or experience, and therefore you have something of relevance to offer them. From the prospects' point of view, they're far more likely to invest some of their time in listening to someone who is relevant to them and can offer added value.

TIP

Understanding the profile of prospects you need to go after is the first step. Your next task is to begin looking for those prospects who meet your stated requirements. I outline a number of information sources that you can use to identify key targets in Chapter 23, so use them as a guide to help you find your own ideal data sources.

You can't afford to be too blinkered in your prospecting approach, however, because you risk missing some potentially good opportunities. Good new business salespeople allow some "what if" time to explore non-obvious opportunities. For example, early in my new business days, I came across a company that needed new business help. As far as demographics were concerned, it was a reasonable fit; it was based close by and was an ideal size of company for us to work with, but it operated in a sector in which we had no previous experience. However, because the company provided a business-to-business service (an area in which we were highly experienced) and because the opportunity seemed interesting, it was worth having a discussion. This company became our biggest client, and we worked with it successfully for seven years. Had I been too limited in my prospecting approach, I would have missed it.

TIP

Establish a set of rules for going outside of being highly targeted in your prospecting opportunities. As I note in the preceding section, my rule of thumb is that when I'm not busy, I'll spend up to 10 percent of my prospecting time investigating left-field opportunities as long as I can see and be able to articulate how our products or services can provide the prospect with a key advantage. If an opportunity fails this test, then I ignore it and move on.

About 99 percent of my success in winning new business comes from being highly targeted and knowing exactly what I'm looking for when prospecting. This is also what I tell clients to do and is one of the foundations of any successful new business campaign. Exceptions always exist, and as I highlight in this section, some of them will be very lucrative, but approach them as exceptions and with a very clear set of rules.

Knowing that timing can make a difference

In the majority of sales situations, you have a window of opportunity — that is, a set of circumstances that results in a prospect being in the market for a product or service. If this isn't the case and no compelling time-driven reason exists for a prospect to make a buying decision, then carefully consider whether you should be investing your valuable time with him because he may decide to postpone any decision. You need to qualify the buying criteria and get the prospect to a point where the time to act is now.

Where timing is an issue, you need to understand what the time window is and what the driving factors are. Find out what factors you can influence and focus on these without wasting your time trying to change immovable objects.

If, for example, you provide a service based around annual reports for corporations, then your window of opportunity is going to be in the three months immediately preceding a company's year-end. Outside of this time frame, you may have some interesting discussions but nothing is going to happen in terms of sales activity because it would just not be relevant. Avoid this time-wasting situation by understanding your prospects' timescales.

When your prospecting uncovers an opportunity but you're not yet in the time window, your role is to keep the prospect warm until he's ready to act. In time-driven sales situations, you likely won't be able to influence the timescale in your favor — that is, to get the prospect to buy according to your timescale and not his. Understand the factors that are driving the timescale and whether the window of opportunity is real or just a buyer-driven benchmark that has no basis in reality. If it's the latter, then you have an opportunity to influence and change it, but if it's really time driven, you need to accept that and act accordingly.

When the buying window is some months away, there's no need to go all in with guns blazing. Instead, plan your campaign according to the reality of the prospect's buying and action window. Until that window gets close, your role is to keep the prospect warm, keep in contact, keep qualifying, and keep feeding relevant information until the time is right for a full-fledged sales push.

TIP

Depending on your product or service and the business sectors you're selling in, you can likely predict some buying windows or seasons. If so, use this to your advantage by getting your prospects into a position where you're ready to sell to them at the right time — where they know you and your solution, are comfortable with the solution fit, and are ready to press the yes button as soon as the window of opportunity opens.

Time windows may be seasonable or driven by budget cycles or other external influences. It's important to understand how timing influences your prospects, which is likely to differ among business sectors. Getting the timing of your sales campaign wrong will lead to frustration for both you (because you won't be winning new business) and for your prospects (because you'll be wasting their time as well as demonstrating your lack of understanding of their situation). Getting your timing right eases the sales process and helps you to be much more time efficient. I expand on the importance of timescales as a qualification element in Chapter 19.

Recognizing the Importance of Research

Today more than ever before, with information on almost anything available at your fingertips, you have no excuse for not researching your prospects and opportunities thoroughly. I can't overemphasize the importance of research as a sales tool. As a prospecting tool, research can both save you a lot of time and give you valuable insight into your prospects.

REMEMBER

Research is part of both qualifying and prospecting, and it's one of the cornerstones on which new business sales success is built. It's not something you can skip over or opt out of if you're to be successful in new business sales. Good research will set you apart in a competitive sales situation and can often be the key factor in turning a sales situation into a yes. Successful new salespeople will always be prospecting, researching, and qualifying new opportunities, and you need to make this one of your defining characteristics. It really is that important.

Research can also save you from embarrassment. To illustrate this, a few years ago, I was due to speak to a prospect early in the sales cycle. Prior to picking up the phone, I did a Google search on the company just to check for anything new. It's just as well that I did because unknown to me (I hadn't seen any news reports that day), the company had been involved in a major environmental disaster. Can you imagine the response I would have gotten had I called and tried selling some service or other?

The following sections walk you through the steps to performing research to prospect effectively and win new business.

Doing your own research

Timing can be everything. You can use timing to your advantage if your research shows an opportunity that needs action immediately, but you need to be aware of competitors having access to the same information and be prepared to react accordingly. You can subscribe to a number of press information services (I cover some of them in Chapter 23), but you need to recognize that your competitors are also likely to have access to the same information at the same time. Potential prospects face being bombarded with calls from suppliers, so you need to develop a way of being different from the crowd. How you do this depends heavily on your business and your solution, but a good rule of thumb is to consider whether whatever you're going to say is something that can add value to the recipient. I advise that unless you can add value, then you shouldn't call a prospect.

Some business sectors have research companies that make a living out of doing research for salespeople, generally selling the same research data to dozens or even hundreds of competing organizations. Although the quality of this data may be fine and even highly accurate, the fact that it's made available to so many people waters down its effectiveness. Imagine being on the receiving end of countless phone calls all spurred by the same bit of research.

WARNING

Beware of the potential of research leading you down dead ends, though. However tempting it is or however interesting a story may seem, you need to recognize where research for sales ends and chasing a story begins — unless you're a journalist, of course, in which case why are you reading this book? Internet access and the advent of 24-hour news can easily lead you into far greater depth than you need for the purposes of sales research and can become a massive time waster.

So while accepting that research is vital in a sales environment, I suggest that you treat bought-in research with a measure of caution and, if possible, rely on your own, or in-house, research to provide you with an element of competitive advantage.

Researching prospects can be seen as a boring and repetitive part of winning new business, but don't let it become mundane. Keep your mind fresh for spotting opportunities as they arise. Develop a lateral thinking mentality when researching; ask yourself, "What does this mean for us?" or "How would our solution help with that?" and see where the answers take you.

REMEMBER

Research in prospecting is more than just looking for new opportunities, though. It's important to also research people — decision makers and key influencers — who have a role in your prospects' decision-making units. You also need background research on the company you're going to be dealing with. This is important for two reasons:

>> To make sure it meets your company's qualification criteria

>> To enable you to demonstrate enough knowledge about your prospects when speaking to them

You need to talk from a position of knowledge, being seen to be interested and knowledgeable about your prospects and, therefore, in their eyes, be the right person to propose a solution to their needs based on understanding them.

It's often said that information is the fount of knowledge, and you gain knowledge from researching information. Your research objective in new business is to be able to build up a knowledge base that you can dip into whenever necessary, maybe to demonstrate understanding of a situation or maybe to be able to apply your knowledge to a new situation that you uncover. Later in this chapter, I talk about how you can use research knowledge to add value to your company's sales database or CRM systems.

Finding resources that work for you

The secret of good sales or prospecting research is often the source of your base information. One of your first tasks is to be able to identify good, reliable, and consistent sources of information that you can use as the basis of your research knowledge. In Chapter 23, I go over some good data sources; in this section, I look at some areas you can investigate.

First, it's important to do some research on your sources. What type of hit rate do they have in terms of accuracy? How reliable are they? Where does their information come from in the first place?

You need to develop a systematic approach to prospect research and find a way of doing it that works for you and delivers the results you need. In the 21st century, you'll never be short of sources to look at, both online and offline, and part of your challenge will be to decide which sources work best for your specific needs.

Personally, I use both online and offline resources and subscribe to daily digests of information from newsletters and research clippings of services that focus specifically on my areas of interest. I get between 8 and 16 of these each day (the volume is dictated by the publishing schedule). I then back this up by looking at industry-specific publications relevant to anything I'm working on at that moment. I could probably spend my entire day reading research, which clearly wouldn't get me very far with the rest of my role. So I scan the headlines only and then save all the data in a form that I can later retrieve by a keyword search. I delve in to details only as the need arises, but I feel safe in the knowledge that I have the data instantly available to me.

TIP

It's a good idea to subscribe to the best business newspaper that covers your region. You'll often find that they, too, offer an electronic business news update. In the United Kingdom, I use *The Times* for this. It produces at least two digests daily, one first thing in the morning and one during the afternoon, which I make sure to read and file. Depending on your geographic location, you may want to look at *The New York Times, San Francisco Business Times, The Wall Street Journal, Reuters,* or whatever is best suited to your location. Industry-specific publications are also great sources of research information and usually published in paper format with an online option.

Surrounding yourself with data is not the objective, though. The objective is to be able to distill information into research knowledge that you can make use of in your new business sales drive. To avoid information overload while being able to process information, you need to develop a series of triggers — things to look for, action points. If you do as I do and save research into a tool such as Evernote, you can then use the automatic indexing to find these triggers. I cover this a bit more in the later section "Adopting an effective workflow," and Chapter 23 lists some good data sources that you can use as a starting point.

REMEMBER

The bottom line with prospecting research is that you need to allocate an amount of time to do this every day. It needs to become a habit, and when done correctly it will yield important information to help you win new business. No one said it was easy, but it will pay dividends.

Reading between the lines

Research is so much more than just gathering and storing information. It's about interpreting and disseminating information into knowledge. You shouldn't just rely on something that you read; you need to test it, which I cover in the next section, and put it into context so you understand what the data is telling you.

For example, say you read an article that tells you one of your prospects is about to appoint a new finance director or chief financial officer (CFO). What does that tell you and what should you do about it? If you're close to reaching a buying decision with that prospect, then the news may set off alarms that spending plans or purchase authority may change. If you've been struggling with getting budget sign-off, then this may signify a change of position and could be good news. No obvious fallout from such an appointment may exist, but you need to note it and maybe mention it when next speaking to your contacts to show that you're on the ball and checking that it makes no difference to your sales proposition.

TIP

Sometimes research information you come across will lead you off on a tangent and lead you to uncover more information or even a new opportunity. Research tangents are fine to follow, but be aware of going down dead ends. Experience will soon lead you to the right decision, but in the meantime it can be a steep learning curve. Talk to your peers and ask for the benefit of their experience because rarely does one answer fit all.

Does anyone else in your company need to know about research snippets you've gained? Do they have information that you could benefit from knowing about? Figure 9-1 shows a CRM system my company used to evaluate a potential prospect. The first thing you may notice is that we had some discussions with this company in 2011, 2012, and 2013 so it came onto our radar several times without converting to a client. A quick scan of the historic notes shows that the company already uses an outsourced new business team and has used them for many years. Because of this long-term relationship, this client will be difficult to win, so we'd be better off spending our time on other opportunities rather than wasting resources on pursuing this one. (Later in this chapter, I talk more about CRM systems.)

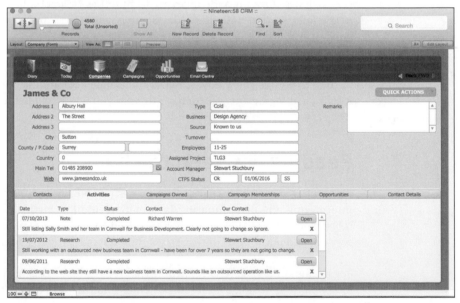

FIGURE 9-1:
Information in a
CRM system.

Source: Stewart Stuchbury

Another thing to be aware of with research is not to use it as an excuse to delay action or to not do something. Sometimes delaying an activity is the right path to follow based on a research snippet, but don't assume that will always be the case. A general rule is to continue along your sales process unless you see a clear benefit to waiting.

Testing your assumptions

All sorts of information can be passed off as research, and not all of it is either correct or helpful. Don't necessarily assume that something you read is actually true. Test it, ask about it, and challenge it if in doubt. Does this new information fit with what you already know, or is it something completely new? Is it in keeping with what you'd expect?

WARNING

Be aware of red herrings getting in the way of your sales process. Would you believe a reporter who tells you the earth is flat after all? Of course not, because everything else you know tells you otherwise. Treat suspect research data the same way.

Performing First-Level Qualification

Qualification is never finished. As a new business salesperson, you need to be qualifying from the first moment a new prospect appears on the horizon right through until the order is signed. It's a way of life. If you're always qualifying, then you likely won't get any surprises as a sales campaign develops and you'll be able to stay one step ahead of the curve.

In first-level qualification at the prospecting stage, you'll focus most of the qualifying effort on qualifying out those companies or opportunities that aren't going anywhere. This is a necessary step.

WARNING

Don't get bogged down with opportunities that are unlikely to become sales opportunities. When you come across opportunities that are interesting, maybe from a personal point of view, there's nothing wrong with looking at them and spending a bit of time wondering "what if?" as long as you recognize the difference between interest and qualification. For example, I'd love to sell new business consulting to Apple and will spend time researching them, but I also recognize that it's unlikely to be a real sales opportunity.

First-level qualification is about asking yourself whether an opportunity is realistic for a sale. In this section, I go over some of the things that you need to cover at this stage. (Chapter 19 goes into more detail on qualifying potential new business.)

Considering demographics

An obvious starting point in first-level qualification is that the prospect's demographics need to be right. As a first level of qualification, some basics include

>> **Location:** The prospect is located in an area that allows you to service it in both a sales cycle and later as a client.

>> **Sector:** The business sector that it operates in is one that your solution is at least a decent fit for.

>> **Size:** Company size is important — too big and you may not be able to cope, too small and it may not be able to afford your solution.

Based on your experience, you should be able to gauge how much prospects are likely to spend on a solution such as yours based on how big they are and how important the need you're offering a solution to is. At the first-level stage, you have to estimate a lot of this information, but if your experience tells you there's a mismatch here, then it likely won't go much further and you should generally qualify this prospect out.

REMEMBER

As part of a first-level demographics qualification exercise, you need to consider how good a fit your offering is likely to be for the prospect. Again, this is based on estimates of need, but knowing your product or service as you do, you'll have a good feel for how it's likely to work for any given situation. If you're not comfortable with the fit, then qualify out and move on.

Checking annual reports and public information

Where does first-level qualification information come from? Your own CRM system is an obvious starting point to see what you already know about prospects. Because colleagues may have looked at them in the past, you may have a lot of information already available at your fingertips.

Figures 9-2, 9-3, and 9-4 show a typical use of a CRM system. In these scenarios, colleagues supplied information about a prospect as part of their prospecting efforts. This tells a story of a prospect that seems to be a good fit at first glance:

>> Figure 9-2 shows that the prospect was actively looking to work with the company after getting additional staff in place.

>> Figure 9-3 shows that there was a long series of communication with the prospect over several months.

>> Figure 9-4 shows that maybe it's not such a good prospect after all, because the timescale is constantly slipping and the requirements appear to be changing.

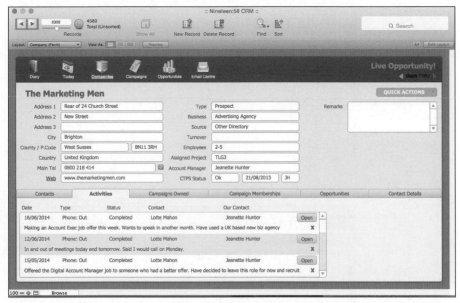

FIGURE 9-2:
The CRM system shows conversations over an extended time period.

Source: Stewart Stuchbury

You can use this historical information to get a feel for an opportunity and make a judgment on committing time and effort to it.

The next obvious places to look are at online resources, and among the best for this type of activity are LinkedIn and Facebook business pages. These resources are useful for both finding company profiles that are good fits and identifying decision makers. Use this data as a guide only, though, and be sure to cross-reference it with other data sources to improve accuracy.

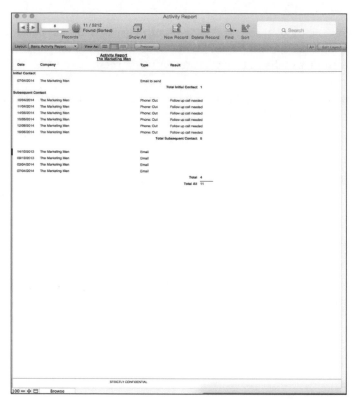

FIGURE 9-3:
A CRM activity report showing lots of contact points.

Source: Stewart Stuchbury

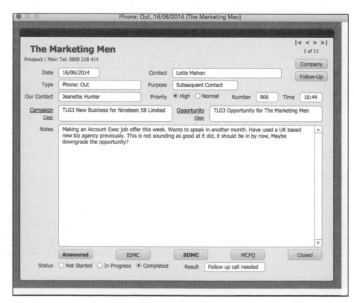

FIGURE 9-4:
The notes of a telephone call in the CRM system.

Source: Stewart Stuchbury

For public companies, annual reports are a great source of information. While the financial data is interesting and informative to the qualification process, the rest of the document is often used as a company insider sales brochure and as such can often contain real nuggets of qualification data about both the company and the key individuals you may need to deal with or be assessed by.

Online reviews and write-ups on the prospect's business are another good source of data you can use for first-level qualification, and the same is true of articles in trade publications. You can identify decision makers and influencers from these articles and have a good idea of whether the type of business they operate in are likely to have a need for your type of solution.

REMEMBER

In all of this, one of your key tasks as a new business salesperson is to make sure the information you're gathering turns into useful knowledge for the business to act on, either now or in the future. For this reason, you need to get into the habit of logging it into the CRM system. See the later section "Adding value to CRM systems" for more information.

Covering the decision-making unit

In Chapter 19, I talk about the decision-making unit (DMU) and its role in the new business process. At the first level of qualification, the types of questions you need to consider are how you're going to approach the DMU and where your entry point will be based on the prospecting information you've discovered. For example, if you know that a prospect is experiencing rapid growth and opening new sites, you may consider how your solution can help and what role your solution would most assist. That should give you a clue about how to approach the prospect when the time is right.

In addition to considering who to approach, you also need to prepare your reason for contacting the prospect and figure out how you're going to quickly engage his attention with your product or service. If it's not obvious based on the prospecting information you've uncovered, then the prospect has most likely failed your first-level qualification test and you should move on to another target.

Do you have suitable case studies prepared that you can use to attract the attention of key members of the DMU as an introduction? Great, if you do from a prospecting point of view. Again, if you lack a suitable "in" to the DMU, then you need to consider how strong your first-level qualification is.

REMEMBER

You're going to qualify out more prospects than you qualify in at the first level, and that's fine. It's the entry point to your sales funnel, and your objective is to whittle down the numbers until you're left with well-qualified prospects to spend your valuable sales time on.

Noting that some prospects aren't right

Right at the outset of your career in winning new business, you need to under-stand that you're not going to sell to everyone. Part of your role is to qualify out those potential opportunities that aren't going to convert into new business wins, and the sooner in the prospecting process you do this, the better.

A prospect may not be right for lots of reasons; here are some of the main ones:

>> **Legal or ethical reasons:** Legislation or company policy may bar you from dealing with some types of prospects; if so, they are automatically qualified out.

>> **Cultural reasons:** Cultural or even language reasons may get in the way of being able to deal with some business or personnel types. Even in the 21st century, this is not an uncommon occurrence. If you face this roadblock, these prospects are automatically qualified out regardless of how good a fit your solution may have been.

>> **Competitive reasons:** Competitive reasons for qualifying out a prospect can be a bit of a minefield. Trading laws in some regions prohibit you from denying a service to a company on competitive grounds, so you need to tread carefully here. You may have non-compete clauses in existing contracts that prohibit, for example, sales to named competitors of existing clients. One of your competitors may be interested in looking at your solutions and you'd be unwise to entertain him as a prospect, unless of course it is to feed him incorrect data, but that is a whole other topic.

TIP

Some companies that your prospect research highlights may just be entirely the wrong profile for your solution. In this case, not only are they qualified out, but you may also want to examine how they even got onto a prospecting list in the first place. This examination may result in you making changes to the research parameters that you specify, but don't worry about doing this as it is a constant learning process.

Keeping Records

In any professional sales environment, keeping accurate records is important. Doing so assists not only yourself in running a current sales cycle but also col-leagues and future colleagues with campaigns to be run in the future.

In the past, salespeople have been poor at both keeping and, more specifically, sharing records and information. In writing this section, I feel like the poacher turned game keeper in that I have been just as guilty as anyone else in keeping "my" information to myself in times gone by. In Chapter 1, I write about introducing a winning new business sales culture, and in respect to record and information sharing, sometimes a cultural shift is required. The benefits to the company and also to individual salespeople make it well worth the effort, though.

The following sections explain the value of CRM systems and a structured workflow to keeping and sharing information.

REMEMBER

Data elements and basic information combine together to help make knowledge, and sales knowledge is what you're trying to capture. You need information that will help you or a colleague turn a prospect into a customer. And remember this works both ways: Information that you gain from someone else will be vital to your sales efforts, too. You need to keep all the research and prospecting data that you collect on prospects, and the sum of all the data in turn becomes the company's knowledge base. It's no wonder that in my business the companywide CRM system is called Knowledge Base, because that's exactly what it is.

Adding value to CRM systems

First, what do I mean by the term *CRM system*? It has come to have different meanings, and dozens of software CRM products are available on the market. Ultimately, it doesn't matter what type of system you use or what label you attach to it. Some call it a database, others just a sales system. What I'm describing is a system to keep track of all the data you collect on a company along with all the interaction you have with that company.

TIP

Any system is only as good as the data that it holds and the use it's put to. There really should be no reason for every piece of data that you have about a prospect not to be included in this system. How do you know whether a piece of information you've found is relevant? Often you don't know, so include everything. Only by aggregating this data can patterns begin to emerge that can give you clues as to how to approach a sales situation with a prospect.

Adding all the prospecting data to a CRM saves someone else from reinventing the wheel the next time that prospect comes onto the sales radar. Because you're laying a lot of the groundwork and the information is instantly available to be looked at and worked on, you further add to its value.

Historical sales data can often hold the key to unlocking a future sale. Figure 9-5 shows a CRM system displaying a research snippet that highlights that a prospect is actively involved in building its business and therefore is likely to be a good fit for some services.

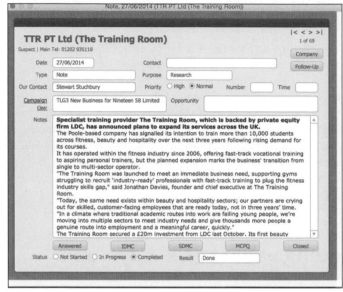

Source: Stewart Stuchbury

FIGURE 9-5:
A research note logged into a CRM system.

Adopting an effective workflow

Implementing the steps outlined in this chapter requires a lot of effort, so how do you go about achieving it in practice? The only effective way to be able to do this is to adopt a structured workflow, a set of routine steps that you repeat for each prospecting step and each opportunity.

A workflow needs to be specific to each salesperson's situation. For example, Figure 9-6 shows the workflow that one of our clients uses for this purpose. This will give you an idea of the type of steps you need to include as you tailor your own workflow.

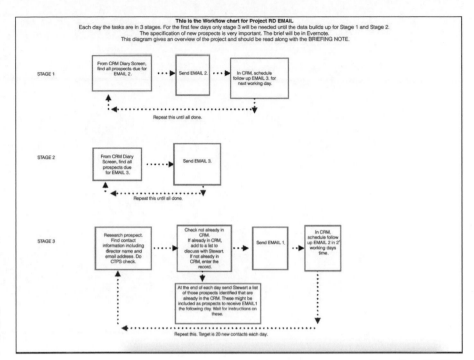

This is the Workflow chart for Project RD EMAIL
Each day the tasks are in 3 stages. For the first few days only stage 3 will be needed until the data builds up for Stage 1 and Stage 2.
The specification of new prospects is very important. The brief will be in Evernote.
This diagram gives an overview of the project and should be read along with the BRIEFING NOTE.

STAGE 1

From CRM Diary Screen, find all prospects due for EMAIL 2.

Send EMAIL 2.

In CRM, schedule follow up EMAIL 3, for next working day.

Repeat this until all done.

STAGE 2

From CRM Diary Screen, find all prospects due for EMAIL 3.

Send EMAIL 3.

Repeat this until all done.

STAGE 3

Research prospect. Find contact information including director name and email address. Do CTPS check.

Check not already in CRM. If already in CRM, add to a list to discuss with Stewart. If not already in CRM, enter the record.

Send EMAIL 1.

In CRM, schedule follow up EMAIL 2 in 2ⁿᵈ working days time.

At the end of each day send Stewart a list of those prospects identified that are already in the CRM. These might be included as prospects to receive EMAIL1 the following day. Wait for instructions on these.

Repeat this. Target is 20 new contacts each day.

FIGURE 9-6:
A sample workflow diagram.

Source: Stewart Stuchbury

3

Making New Business Happen

Understand that objections are just questions that need answers.

Structure a winning deal.

Be confident to say no to prospects when necessary.

Know that your winning solution puts you in a strong position to ask for the order.

Recognize why you need to avoid hard selling and be action oriented.

Chapter **10**

Overcoming Objections

I n this chapter, I examine ways to deal with objections, both serious and time-wasting ones. By *objection*, I mean anything that your prospect tells you is a reason for not buying your solution or for delaying a decision. It can be as simple as he doesn't like the color of the filing cabinet or as complex as he doesn't believe that it will fulfill his needs.

Your role as a new business salesperson is not necessarily to solve all the objections you receive but to demonstrate how your solution meets the needs, to address complex objections, and to work around simple objections, such as convincing your prospect that the color doesn't matter.

REMEMBER

In overcoming objections, a lot of your success comes from your professional approach. Don't be fazed by objections; they are just part of the sales cycle, and they'll always exist. Be firm in addressing objections, don't allow yourself to be messed about, and remember that you control the ultimate sanction: to walk away.

Taking Care of Real Objections

One of your first challenges in overcoming objections is to recognize when you're faced with a real one rather than a noise-level one. What's the difference?

>> A real objection is valid in the context of your sale. It's something that you need to consider and that if left alone may kill the sale on its own. For example, your prospect is concerned that the solution you're proposing may be contrary to his health and safety policy.

>> A noise-level objection isn't a showstopper but has to be addressed before it becomes a bigger, and then a real, objection. For example, a software system has only one level of sign-on authority, but your prospect really would like to have two levels for convenience.

You need to treat the different levels of objections in different ways, as you find out in the following sections.

Handling noise

As far as your prospect is concerned, unless he is playing games (which I address later in this chapter), any objection that he raises is valid and needs answering, however trivial you may think it is. An objection that you consider noise may be a big deal to your prospect, so never dismiss an objection as being irrelevant. Let your prospect know that you consider the only silly questions to be the ones left unasked that continue to cause worry.

You know much more about your solution than your prospect does, so something that you take for granted may be a big deal for him, or he may not fully understand it. You need to take the time to understand the concern and satisfy it before moving on; otherwise, it will fester, and a noise-level objection can become a deal breaker.

Your role is to guide the prospect through his discovery process as part of his buying cycle, and in doing so you need to address all the issues, real or imaginary. You can deal with the noise-level ones easily and quickly. I'm not talking about dealing with a prospect who objects just for the sake of it but rather handling reasonable objections that you consider to fall into the category of noise level. Consider the following ideas on dealing with noise.

Preparing some answers

The first tactic to be aware of is preparing answers to frequent objections. This is fine, but if you come across a set of frequent objections, also consider addressing them in both your initial communications with the prospect, before they become objections, and in your marketing material and perhaps your website (see Chapter 6 for an introduction to marketing matters). Heading off questions before they become objections is the easiest way to deal with them.

You can also adjust your sales approach — the way you address the positioning of the solution, for example — to preempt a number of common objections and stop them from ever being raised. For example, you can tell the prospect that

>> "Many people like to know that . . ."

>> "This can also be used to do . . ."

>> "We made it in this color because . . ."

>> "It's a good fit with . . . as a result of . . ."

Taking this approach helps correctly position your solution in the prospect's eyes and lets him know that you've considered some of the issues in designing the solution. It also can make him feel easier in hearing that he's not the first one to consider an issue.

TIP

Nothing is wrong with deliberately deciding to leave a common objection unaddressed in your standard opening approach. Let the prospect work it out for himself and raise it as an objection for you to quickly cover and move on. Doing so allows the prospect to begin the engagement process easily and, depending on his character, can make him feel happy to have found a "problem," albeit one that you have a ready answer for.

Returning to the issue

If you find yourself being interrupted in mid-flow or while you're discussing some key points, you can tell the prospect that you'll return to his issue later and fully address it, or suggest that you address it offline or out of the context of the current discussion and touch point. Give a reason for taking this approach, though, or you'll find that it doesn't get left alone. For example, tell your prospect that his question is a very valid one and that you'll answer it in context later, because it doesn't fit into the current discussion.

REMEMBER

When dealing with noise-level objections, you need to bring the focus back to the bigger picture. What is the prospect setting out to achieve? In the grand scheme of things, is the current topic something all that vital? If it isn't going to have an impact on the results, then you need to make this clear in addressing it.

Giving the trial close

When dealing with noise-level objections, especially those that won't go away after a couple of attempts at addressing them, consider using the trial close. For example, ask the prospect whether he'll give you the order if you can resolve this particular issue. This approach will hopefully focus the prospect's mind on exactly what you're both working to achieve, not on a side issue or one that's not paramount in solving the big picture. It's a gentle way of letting him know that he's going off track, while letting you clarify that the objection is in fact noise level and that you haven't missed something important.

TIP

As you handle noise-level objections, don't assume that just because you've answered a question that the objection has gone away. Clarify. Ask directly whether you've covered the point sufficiently, and if not, do it again, perhaps using a different approach rather than just repeating the same words.

Getting to the crux of the issue

A prospect usually doesn't raise objections to be awkward or to deliberately stop you from making a sale. If a prospect objects to something, it generally means that he's unsure of the way you're proposing to address his problem area. Keep in mind that the prospect has a very big stake in getting the correct solution. Getting his issue resolved is more important than you making a sale.

TIP

The real objection may not be immediately obvious if the prospect uses terms that are familiar to his industry and not necessarily to you, so you need to seek understanding to move forward. Don't be afraid of admitting that you're unsure of exactly what he's asking and that you need further clarification to understand and address the objection.

Fully understanding an objection may require a fair bit of digging. The stated objection may only hint at the underlying issue, and it's vital that you get to the real objection. You'll likely encounter situations where the prospect just won't tell you the real reason for raising an objection, which obviously makes resolving it a little difficult.

REMEMBER

Ask for help here. Let your prospect know that you're on his side and are working toward a solution that meets his needs, but don't be surprised if he's unwilling to open up. Some prospects are reserved by nature, and some see buying as a power game. There's no one-size-fits-all answer for you here. You need to use your powers of persuasion and observation as well as try to come at the problem from different angles, and then use a bit of lateral thinking to get to the crux of the issue.

After you understand the objection, determine whether you have a ready answer, and close it off if you do. For more complex issues, you first need to understand the severity of the problem and whether it's a deal breaker. If so, don't attempt to provide a stock, off-the-top-of-your-head answer that doesn't meet the needs. Take time to consider your response. Let your prospect know that you understand the issue and, if necessary, will come back to him with a considered response, after discussing with colleagues who perhaps are experts in that particular area. Agree on a timescale for doing this, and then move on with the call or meeting, covering the rest of the agenda. With this approach, you've dealt with the issue for the day and haven't left it as a festering issue clouding the rest of the contact.

TIP

In this situation, you should also agree on the priority for seeking a resolution. As well as demonstrating to your prospect that you're taking the matter seriously, the priority he assigns to it will give you a good indicator as to the relative importance of the objection.

You may discover a ready workaround to the problem or one that you can implement without too much of a compromise. Explore this workaround both internally and then, if it seems to fit, explore it with your prospect and get agreement that it resolves the issue and overcomes the objection.

WARNING

You need to recognize that some objections can't be overcome. In this case, either you agree to continue with the sales cycle with the understanding that this issue won't be addressed, or you end the sales cycle and walk away. The choice comes down to understanding whether the objection is surmountable by other means, and this feeds into what I call second-level qualification, which I cover later in this chapter.

Seeing opportunities rather than problems

As a mindset, you should treat objections not as problems getting in the way of a sale but as opportunities to restate your case and to demonstrate both your understanding of the issues and your determination to work toward a solution. Be a glass-half-full person and not a glass-half-empty one.

Depending on the severity of the problem or objection, you can proceed in a number of ways. If the objection can't be completely overcome or addressed in its own right, can you offer an alternative solution? Perhaps you can offer something that hasn't been previously discussed or an additional service or product that can augment the sale value further.

TIP

You can learn a lesson from the way politicians answer questions and handle objections. How many times have you heard a politician give a direct answer to a question that he doesn't want to answer? Generally, the way of proceeding here is to acknowledge the question with something like "I'm glad you raised that point," and then go on to talk about something else, preferably in a related area so you can at least pay lip service to the question but delve into an area that you're more comfortable with and that your solution addresses very well. If you can "answer" the question in this way and draw out your answer to several minutes, then chances are that you'll get away with it because the prospect will have forgotten the original gist of his question and will consider it to have been answered. You shouldn't, of course, do this with deal breakers or objections that are so fundamental as to cause your solution to be unworkable — but have you ever seen a politician let that get in the way?

REMEMBER

You need to remain positive and upbeat when addressing these types of problems-to-opportunities because you're the solution champion, the one offering to solve the original problem. You need to give the impression — true or otherwise — that you have a dedicated team behind you to work on the details of any problem area and will come back with a workable solution. It's always worth restating your key case and focusing on how your solution delivers the benefits sought by the original problem area that you're addressing.

Turning the tables

In overcoming objections, part of what you're doing is continuing to qualify the suitability of your solution to your prospect's needs but also qualifying him as a potential client. Does the company you're selling to meet your criteria to be a client?

Although winning a piece of new business is important, winning isn't the only consideration. You have to be sure that the deal is right for your business and that not only will your solution do a good job but also that you want that company as a client. You can think of it as you qualifying the buyer. Does the prospect meet your criteria?

I've been on the receiving end of reverse qualifications like this, and when it's done well, it can be a very effective way of making you want the solution even more, even to the point of ignoring some of your own objections.

To pull off this approach without looking like an idiot when your prospect pulls the plug on the deal, you need to make sure you know what you're doing and be good at it. It is, nonetheless, a helpful tool in your new business kit to be used as required.

Asking questions about how the prospect sees your solution fitting into his business and how he sees it helping with specific elements of his original problem area can be an effective means of getting him to overcome some of his own objections. Most people love to talk and to be perceived as an expert, so let your prospect talk himself into a deal, with a little prompting.

You need to own the entire sales process and be the one in the driver's seat, and this is no different when overcoming objections. Keep the initiative and steer the discussions where you want them to go. Establish the rules for how you're going to deal with any issues that arise, in advance of them happening, so that you can seamlessly deflect any difficult issues to handle them later.

In Chapter 3, I discuss using a contact report as a sales tool. This report enables you to document the decisions reached so far and can help you revisit those areas of agreement when objections arise that have either already been covered or are in areas similar to ones that you've already agreed on. Beware of allowing closed points to be reopened as you risk never closing the sale, and use the contact report to demonstrate that you've already discussed and agreed on points.

Earlier in this chapter, I touch on using a trial close as a means of overcoming noise-level objections. This technique can be appropriate as part of turning the table on a discussion, too. For example, saying, "Can we agree that the order is placed if I resolve this issue?" has a way of focusing the prospect's mind back to the important issues and, while it's unlikely to give you an immediate close, plays a part in getting discussions back on track and away from objections that may not be core to the solution being successfully implemented.

You'll have prospects who will appear to like raising objections, real or imagined, seemingly just for the sake of doing so. Take a hard line here. Ask some basic qualifying questions of your own and move on. If a prospect continues to object, then you need to question whether this prospect is serious or a time waster and to consider ending the contact early and not resuming until you've reexamined the qualification. Not every prospect you come into contact with is going to be a suitable customer, and many of them will fail your qualification criteria. This is fine and exactly what qualification is about: getting rid of the ones who won't buy from you and focusing on the real qualified prospects. The key part is doing the qualification before spending time working on a potential deal. I cover this in Chapter 19.

Dealing with Bias and Inequity

As your objection handling progresses, from time to time you'll come across some difficult issues that aren't always directly related to the problem and solution at hand, or at least not at first glance.

Issues of bias and inequity can arise in many different forms; some are quite innocent while others are deliberate attempts to discredit your solution and, bluntly, to get in the way of a successful outcome. I assume that you're not dealing with any subversive forms of bias, but if you are, then walking away is your only option. I discuss walking away and other methods for dealing with bias and inequity in the following sections.

REMEMBER

Your overriding objective is to maintain your professionalism and to handle whatever is thrown at you in a manner that builds up your status even more.

TIP

You can find historic data from your side in your CRM, of course, so make sure that you're up to speed on any historic data regarding a prospect who's showing bias. I introduce CRM systems in Chapter 9.

Being prepared to walk away

As a new business salesperson, you have the ultimate sanction — you can walk away and refuse to sell your prospect the solution that he's looking for. I've done this myself on occasions when faced with a prospect who, in my view, was going to be more trouble than it was worth. I now apply the following rule: If a prospect raises an objection to price after I've qualified affordability, then that's the end of the sales cycle for me. Experience has taught me that in my business, if prospects raise objections on price or affordability, then the chances are very high that we'll end up with a client who's driven by cost rather than results and will never perceive value for money. This is also why I never do "special deals" when asked by a prospect, because on every single occasion that I've previously agreed to do so, the client has been a problem one.

REMEMBER

Your new business mindset needs to be one of believing in your solution absolutely and understanding that the prospect needs you more than you need him. You can sell to other prospects, but he may not have other solutions that he can buy.

Another instance when you should walk away is if you discover that you're involved in a competitive sales situation and that you're just there to make up the numbers, with no realistic chance of winning the order, even if your solution is clearly the best one. If you discover that a prospect has made a decision or a shortlist in advance, then don't waste your time.

Qualification, as always, is the key. You should know in advance of getting involved in a sales cycle what the competitive situation is, and if you don't know or discover something different, then you're facing inequity. In my mind, that is grounds for walking away. I will do so every time. Thankfully, it doesn't happen very often, but that's a result from having solid qualification criteria that are rigorously enforced. (Flip to Chapters 9 and 19 for more about qualification.)

You shouldn't expect or accept being lied to, and you have a right to expect the same level of professionalism that you bring to the table. It's important to be true to yourself and live to fight another day and another sale where you're actually wanted. I discuss walking away from a deal in more detail later in this chapter.

Getting to a level playing field

Animal Farm, the George Orwell novel about equality, will have you believe that we are all equal except that some are more equal than others. And this almost sounds like an extract from a communist manifesto, too!

The point is that to deliver a successful new business campaign, you need to begin with a level playing field with none of your competitors holding an unfair advantage that you don't know about.

The following are two immediately obvious situations where this may not be the case, and one of your initial qualification jobs is to determine the lay of the land:

>> First is the case of an incumbent supplier. It may be naive of me, though I don't think so, but if you're bidding to supply a solution to a prospect who is already being served by another supplier who is also involved in the bidding, why would the prospect look to anyone else? He already uses the solution that the other supplier has and must be satisfied with it or the incumbent wouldn't have an opportunity to pitch again. So unless you (and I) are missing something glaringly obvious, who's going to win this sale?

>> The second immediately obvious situation is where a preferred solution has been found, perhaps after an exhaustive buying cycle, but the purchasing department has decided to invite different bids to be seen to justify their existence. You may gather from that last sentence that purchasing departments aren't high on my list of regarded functions! To understand this scenario, the prospect has gone through his buying criteria, had his objections overcome, and is ready to place the order. You, at the last minute, are invited to counterbid by a non-core member of the decision-making unit. You don't have to be a rocket scientist to see where this sale is heading, and in this type of situation, you really do need to walk away immediately.

Ensuring a level playing field, or even one that is biased toward your solution, is part of the role of qualification. Your initial qualification should have flushed out the type of problems outlined in the preceding list and should have ensured that you're dealing with a real, live project with a known budget, timescale, and need at an absolute minimum. I discuss the importance of qualification and how to go about it in Chapter 19, and you see in this chapter some examples of why it's so important in winning new business.

Asking your prospect to help you

There's something very powerful in a sales situation when you ask your prospect to help you. The dynamic changes, and you've temporarily given him control. This can have a profound effect because the prospect won't expect this behavior. Some sound selling reasons exist for why you may want to do this, as well as some human dynamics. It demonstrates the human touch, a measure of fallibility that you can turn to your advantage. *Help* is a powerful word and, when used carefully, can both deflect issues and open up opportunities.

For example, if you're facing a sales situation that is clearly biased against you, ask for help in understanding why that's the case. At the very least, doing so will stop your prospect in his tracks and cause him to consider the path he's heading down. There may have been a misunderstanding, for example, and in asking for help, you give your prospect an opportunity to take corrective action.

Unfortunately, some buyers like to play games, and this can especially be the case when dealing with inexperienced people. You need to establish exactly what you're dealing with and why you're facing some form of bias. It could be that your prospect had a bad experience with your solution previously, in which case you have to wonder why he's looking again, so ask him directly, and don't beat about the bush. A sanction that you have available to you in some cases is to refer back to another member of the decision-making unit (where there's more than a single decision maker) and get him to act as an honest broker and resolve the prospect's issues internally.

REMEMBER

When you ask for help in a biased environment and that help is neither forthcoming nor effective in changing the situation, then your prospect really has no cause to complain when you take the ultimate sanction and walk away. Keep in mind, too, that you can ask for help in any sales situation, not just one where you face bias or struggle to understand an objection and its impact.

TIP

In Chapter 5, I mention an old IBM sales technique of going over the prospect's head when a sale looks like it's being lost and telling his senior management that he wasn't doing his job correctly. This is the one situation where I actually advocate doing just that after you walk away from the sale. Remember, of course, to log everything in the CRM (see Chapter 9) so that other colleagues can learn from your experience in preparation for the next time that prospect appears on the radar.

Facing Objections Late in the Sales Cycle

Sometimes you can deal with objections fairly quickly and the sales cycle progresses; other times, it takes a little longer. Building a solid relationship with your prospect always helps get you through the objections.

Stumbling blocks do sometimes get in the way and cause delay, but when you have a prospect who's on board with the solution that you're proposing, it does make it easier to progress the deal. You need to take the time to understand what the stumbling blocks really are and why you haven't managed to clear them up along with other objections. The following sections help you overcome prospects' objections later in the sales cycle.

Again, it's always worth revisiting the original qualification to see what, if anything, has changed and how you can get the deal back on track. See Chapters 9 and 19 for more about qualification.

Using the referral upstairs

After you've answered solution-based objections, the only things remaining are usually contractual issues. You'll have covered budget and affordability early in the sales cycle as qualification criteria so they should be out of the way, leaving only obstacles that should be surmountable. Late in the sales cycle, no new issues should be introduced.

To help you resolve any remaining issues, you have a tool that I call the referral upstairs, where you seek to introduce a manager into the equation who plays the role of an honest broker, of course working for your company. He can side with your prospect on most of the issues and, while siding with you on the stumbling blocks, may have some insight or a solution that gets around any impasse, especially if it's contractual and beyond the details of the proposed solution's workings. In this way, should you need to offer some concessions, it's not you doing so but a manager so you maintain your credibility while easing the sale toward a close.

This is very different from bringing in a "closer," or high-pressure salesperson, which is an approach I never suggest. It's simply a way of utilizing a resource available to you with the prospect's perception of being in a more senior role and therefore overruling you in areas that aren't fundamental but still necessary to close the deal.

The referral upstairs has another impact, too, and that is to further build relationships between your company and the prospect's. This opportunity can also, if carefully planned, lead to opening other areas to explore beyond the original deal and bringing things like a future case study onto the table.

Performing second-level qualification

REMEMBER

Second-level qualification goes beyond some of the obvious criteria, such as affordability and ensuring that a real project exists (which you cover with your initial qualification early in the sales cycle; see Chapters 9 and 19). It goes into areas such as exactly how the solution is going to fit and ensuring that the prospect's organization has sufficient resources to deliver its part. You also need to dig to find and work around as necessary deeper and more complex qualifications, such as the following:

>> Existing or previous corporate-level relationships between your prospect and any of your competitors

>> Resistance somewhere in the decision-making unit

>> A relationship with a competitor's sales team

>> A weak relationship between you and the key prospect

>> Concern about the viability of your solution

>> Concern over the viability of your business

Any and all of these deeper issues can slow down or even derail your sale. You need to work on them as the sales cycle progresses to ensure that you have all the bases covered so no unpleasant surprises arise when it comes to getting the order signed.

TIP

You may need some help in getting to the bottom of some of these issues, but your job is to qualify against them and then look for solutions if you uncover problem areas. You can address viability issues, for example, by having a colleague in your finance department address them at a peer-to-peer level in the prospect's organization. New business sales can be a team game, and you should be free to call on the support of colleagues not directly involved in a sales role to play their part. The bottom line is that the relationship that you build with your prospect should be strong enough to enable these discussions to take place without either party being defensive about them.

Be sure you deal with any previously closed-off issues that arise, for example by using the contact reports that show the discussion and agreed resolution. That's the key reason for producing contact reports in the first place, even though you've more than likely positioned them as "just a record of what we have discussed." (Check out Chapter 3 for more about these reports.)

If second-level qualification highlights problem areas remaining, then you likely have a major problem — whether with capability, contract, or relationship — and you need to find a solution quickly. Often, going back to the very beginning and reexamining the need for your prospect to have a solution can provide the key. You need to be able to demonstrate that solving his stated business problem and delivering the benefits that have been discussed and agreed upon are more important than any side issues. If you're unable to do this, even with help, then the chances of your deal progressing to the order stage are practically zero. Second-level qualification is that important.

Help can come from unexpected sources, too. To illustrate this with a real example, I was once at the point of signing a new business deal when the managing director, with whom I had dealt through the entire sales process, decided that he had better get one of his non-executive directors to check it first. Subsequently, I met with the non-executive director, and he and I had a personality clash — we just didn't like each other. It was obvious to me that if this man was going to have any involvement in the implementation or any form of management role overseeing it, it wasn't going to work, and I wasn't prepared to enter into such an agreement. In this case, thankfully the managing director got similar feedback from his non-executive director and decided to keep the two of us apart. The deal concluded, and we worked well with the client for several years, without me ever meeting the non-executive director again. We were able to get into the contract only as a result of the relationship the key prospect and I had built before the third party became involved.

Letting the best solution rise to the surface

If you're confident that your proposed solution really is the best offer and truly delivers on the prospect's needs, and if you're comfortable with the qualification having been passed but you still can't get the deal over the finishing line, you can try backing off a little and let the prospect determine that you're offering the best solution without the pressure of trying to engineer a close to the deal.

Coming out on top in every area is not that important. You can let your prospect have his way on some of the less important objections and can even afford to be second to a competitor in some very minor considerations. Let the best solution rise to the top on its own, having sown the seed and left it to germinate a little without you pushing every inch of the way. No one likes to deal with a pushy new business salesperson, so don't be one. Stay professional and be prepared to be a little aloof after making your pitch, especially if you're truly confident in your solution and qualification.

If you're confident that your solution is the best option for your prospect, then you have won the battle, and your aim is to then win the war and get the order. Do this by remaining professional to the end. Accept that if the jacket fits, then you're almost there and getting the rest of the way just may require a little patience.

Exploring ways to make it work

After you've overcome the objections and are well placed to secure the order, you just need to get it over the line. This is the point at which a few hidden obstacles can get in the way, so beware of sudden changes to issues you've already agreed on. Use the contact reports that I outline earlier in this chapter and in Chapter 3 to stop this from gaining any traction.

Hidden obstacles that can get in the way of a new business sale can include such things as continued uncertainty about the right solution being chosen or your prospect having difficulty with selling the idea internally.

Keep in mind that your prospect has also been on this journey with you and will understand as well as you do what his alternatives are — at this stage, there shouldn't be any. The benefit of running a structured sales cycle is that you address qualification upfront and overcome objections as they arise.

Try to get an agreement in principal if the order isn't quite ready yet, and tie it into when the order will be placed, for example when the paperwork has been drawn up.

REMEMBER

This isn't the end of your sales cycle. It doesn't end until you have the signed order and arguably not until the solution is implemented and the new customer is happy, but that tends to depend on the size of your business and whether you've dedicated account managers or a similar role to take over from you. If that's the case, then your duty is to ensure that the new customer is completely comfortable with the new arrangements and to be at the handover meeting, whether your colleagues like it or not.

TIP

Before this stage, the deal structure has to be finalized, so don't take your eye off the ball because many deals that are in the bag can fall over at this late stage. Do you need to structure a phased approach, for example, to overcome any of the non-closed objections? Structuring a deal to involve commitment in the form of stage payments while parts of the solution are implemented can be a useful tool. I recommend this approach only with very large deals, because in any other way, it has the potential to water down the commitment to just the first phase, and any solution without total commitment has a much higher propensity to problems and failure.

REMEMBER

Any phased approach should solely be to overcome any inertia and push an order over the finish line and not be due to issues of affordability, which you'll have addressed during the very early qualification.

Walking Away from the Deal

Walking away from a deal and not getting involved in one to begin with are very different scenarios. In this section, I focus on walking away from one.

By way of summary, you shouldn't get involved in a sales cycle until it's qualified (see Chapters 9 and 19 for more on qualification). If it becomes clear during negotiations that you and the prospect are poles apart in basic areas, that's usually a sign that your qualification failed. So in addition to walking away at this stage, be sure to revisit your qualification to understand where it went wrong and to learn from any mistakes that were made. Of course, always keep your CRM up-to-date with everything (Chapter 9 has an introduction to CRM systems).

As a result of following a qualification-led sales approach, the number of times that you should have to walk away when you're in a sales cycle should be very few as you'll have already qualified out those prospects who fail to meet your criteria. The following sections explain how to walk away from a deal in a professional manner.

WARNING

Walking away from a deal that you've been working on and have qualified isn't something you should do lightly, not least because of the amount of effort you've already put into it and for no reward. Sometimes, however, it's the right thing to do, and other times you have no option but to do so. And then there'll be occasions when standing firm in negotiations and walking away will result in the prospect coming back to you and operating on your terms, although don't bank on it. When you walk away, don't go back because, if you do, you'll have zero credibility.

Managing your reputation

If you do ever have to walk away (and I'm sure that you will), then do it in a professional, civil, and courteous manner, allowing the prospect to save face. The prospect may come back to you on your terms, and he may not, but you'll have marked yourself as a new business salesperson with integrity, confidence, and courage, and that will only serve to enhance your reputation. You need to establish yourself as a top, ethical, and professional new business salesperson, and word will soon get around that you're not someone to be messed with. Reputation takes time to build up and can be easily damaged, so guard yours in all that you do.

When the time comes to walk away from a deal, you need to maintain your professionalism and allow your prospect to save face within his company. A good way of doing so is a letter or email thanking him for the time, effort, and commitment that he has put into the project but also saying that after careful consideration of all the points that have been raised, you have sadly concluded that your solution is not the best fit for him and that, accordingly, you won't be proceeding with the sales contract. Be sure to be courteous and to wish him every success as he seeks to have his original needs met elsewhere.

TIP

Reputation works both ways. If you discover that your prospect has pulled out of a sales cycle in the latter stages before, then you need to find out what happened and guard against it happening again to you this time.

WARNING

You may need to do some explaining internally as to why you walked away from a deal. But after you've explained and demonstrated that you acted in the best interests of your company, then you should be backed 100 percent. If not, it may be time to consider walking away again, in a different sense this time. I've only ever felt the need to issue a back-me-or-sack-me ultimatum once, and the managing director who I worked for at the time wisely, in my opinion, backed me after doing his own investigation. Unfortunately for him, the damage was done when he expressed any doubt, and I resigned very soon afterward but not before demonstrating that I was right in walking away from the deal.

Revisiting stated needs and dictating terms

If you find yourself in the unenviable position of having to consider walking away from a deal, then you need to understand how you got there. As you're following, or should be following, a qualification-led approach, then the qualification criteria should have guarded against you being in this situation. What went wrong? You need to revisit the qualification to find out and perhaps make changes to the qualification criteria to safeguard against this happening again in the future. When you can learn from mistakes, they're often not as difficult to swallow.

When walking away from a deal, you may want to spend a moment to consider how else your prospect is going to get his needs met and a solution delivered. If you really believe that your solution is the right one, you may find that before long he comes back and on your terms. If this happens and the prospect seeks to reopen the sales cycle, you have a one-shot opportunity to adequately address both the initial stumbling block and any other issues that you can see are contentious. Keep in mind that you're not negotiating here; you're dictating terms. Play it hard, because it's your only opportunity to do so.

REMEMBER

The prospect now needs you much more than you need him, and he has shown his hand. Use this to your advantage to ensure that you and your prospect have the best possible chance of going on to implement the best possible solution.

Stepping back if successful implementation is in doubt

Right from the outset of a sales cycle, through overcoming objections and onto delivering the solution, the overriding objective of both parties is to ensure a successful implementation. If at any point you feel that this result is in jeopardy, you need to address it quickly. It may be that your instinct is wrong, but trust it enough to give it the benefit of the doubt.

If you feel there's a chance your prospect won't be able or willing to commit the necessary time and resources to implement and drive your solution to deliver a successful result, then you need to question whether it's time to pull the plug and walk away from the deal. You and your company can't afford to have a failed implementation in your track record, and the importance of that should outweigh the cost of losing a single deal.

WARNING

The lost revenue from a single sale that you walk away from is nothing compared to the revenue that you'll lose in the future when news of a failed implementation becomes known, which it will. It won't matter in the archives of history that you sounded a warning note; you'll be associated with failure and all the inherent reputational damage that comes with it. If you go ahead and are proved right in your assessment of the likelihood of an unsuccessful implementation, other prospects will notice and it will likely cause you more lost deals.

Being committed to ensuring that your prospect, should he become a client, is successful in implementing your solution will also not go unnoticed, and both your company and principally you, as the new business salesperson responsible, will enhance your professional reputations, which will in turn help you with future sales campaigns.

Successful implementation without trust isn't going to happen, and for this reason you should walk away from a deal if trust breaks down, as the writing will already be on the wall. Trust, like reputation, is built up and established over time and can be destroyed in an instant.

WARNING

A deal at any price is not worth it. If you're being pushed on price, even after qualifying affordability upfront, or if price becomes the driving factor in a deal, then in my opinion something is wrong. You need to discover what the real issues are and either address them or walk away from the sale. In my experience, a deal structured around price after everything else has been painstakingly agreed on is simply a deal waiting to go wrong and is not worth the risk.

Chapter 11

Structuring the Deal

tructuring the deal — the topic of this chapter — is something you shouldn't leave for the end of the sales cycle after you've achieved the yes decision. Although the end is the time for formalizing the deal, setting up the deal structure is a natural part of the sales process, and elements of it will come into various discussions with your prospect along the journey.

REMEMBER

As the buying cycle progresses toward the deal structuring, you may find that the prospect's decision-making unit (see Chapters 9 and 19) expands to include purchasing or that the purchasing function comes to more prominence. It's important that you don't allow them to take over. It's your deal, and you need to be prepared to take a tough stance as you set the ground rules. If you fail to do this right from the start, then you run the risk of losing control at a vital stage and may end up being run ragged to someone else's agenda. It's also important that as a new business salesperson, you own this process on behalf of your company. Don't leave it for contracts administration or anyone else. Don't duck it. Leadership is required, and it's your responsibility to provide it.

Understanding that the Deal Isn't Always about Money

When structuring a deal that's going to deliver what both parties need, you have to take a lot of things into consideration, as I cover in this chapter. First, you need to recognize that a deal isn't always just about money. How much the deal will cost, whether you can apply a discount, whether the payment can be structured, and so on are all considerations you'll need to address (as you find out in the following sections), but structuring a deal is about much more than just that.

REMEMBER

Putting a winning deal together isn't simply an exercise in negotiating. In fact, it shouldn't be seen as negotiating at all from the new business salesperson's point of view. If you've driven a successful sales cycle, you should be able to smoothly conclude the deal structure component.

Asking questions about stumbling blocks

REMEMBER

A common perception that everything in sales deals comes down to money is simply wrong. A deal has to work for all parties involved, and some of the elements that you need to address are beyond the obvious. If you encounter stumbling blocks, you need to understand what they are and how they've arisen. Your role as a new business salesperson is to help your prospect buy from you; to achieve this, you need to understand what's behind any deal structure issues.

By this stage in the sales cycle, you should have built a strong relationship with your prospect and be able to directly ask what he needs to get the deal done. When you understand from his point of view what needs to happen, you're in a much stronger position to either deliver on that need or to find a way around it, diffusing the perception of need. In other words: Find the issue, act on it, and either resolve it or make use of the contact reports (see Chapter 3) to show that the issue has been addressed to the prospect's satisfaction and that there's no need to reopen it as an issue.

Take money out of the equation if necessary, and make sure that you've addressed all the issues. If the solution was free, would he go with it today? If the prospect says yes, then price is the overriding issue and at least you know and can revisit the qualification; if the prospect says no, then help him dig deeper to discover the real issues that are holding up progress. They may be something that is far from obvious, or they may be something you can resolve easily. The point is that unless you ask and dig for the answer, then you won't know and you allow control to slip away from you.

Use the contact reports to show that any old issues that arise have been covered and agreed on. If a new objection arises, then try to get it into context and ask why it has arisen at this stage. A good way of addressing new issues is to turn them around and ask your prospect how he would handle them. Ask how the prospect's company deals with whatever the issue is. This can often lead to some very revealing answers, and it isn't uncommon to hear that the prospect's company wouldn't tolerate whatever the objection is. Silence as a response here works well as your prospect contemplates what he's asking for in terms of his own company policy.

REMEMBER

Within the decision-making unit, or even above their heads at the signoff level, issues may exist that are outside your field of vision. The key prospect may have difficulty in selling your solution to management. Part of your role is to support him and provide the necessary ammunition for him to fight and win any internal battles that are needed.

Avoiding discounts

Discounts do drive sales in some circumstances. For example, how often do you see seasonal sales in retail shops? In fact, some seasons have come to be associated with deep discounting, such as Black Friday and New Year sales, and they're no doubt very effective in driving traffic to retail and online sales establishments, but there's little or no scope for this in business-to-business sales.

To inexperienced new business salespeople, offering discounts can seem like an easy way to sweeten the deal and get the order in through the quarter-end door, but this situation can quickly deteriorate and become the accepted norm. Don't let this happen. The following sections explain why you should avoid discounts and how to address requests for discounts.

Why you should avoid discounts

Your marketing department (see Chapter 6) will have carefully considered price as one of the key attributes of the solution, and they'll have set the pricing structure for strategic reasons. Your job is to understand this pricing background and why it's been set the way it has and then to run with it and implement it into your sales cycles. If the pricing strategy is right for the market, then discounts shouldn't be required.

Is your brand a premium one? Do you want to position it as a premium? If so, then you need to ensure that you don't give in to discount requests and are prepared to walk away rather than compromise your brand values by watering them down.

Attitude can make all the difference. I well remember the first time I went into a BMW dealership to look at new cars. My expectation was that, because this was an expensive purchase and it was in a retail environment, I was sure to get a couple of thousand dollars off the list price by just asking. When I asked about the pricing and what I could expect as the final price, the salesman replied, "BMWs are not discounted, sir" — and that told me! The attitude was

>> Our pricing is our pricing.

>> If you can't afford it, then you shouldn't be here.

>> Our brand sells itself; we don't need to discount.

>> This is a premium brand, and you're lucky if we consider you worthy of having one.

Although that type of sales attitude doesn't bode well in many situations, I did admire the way the salesman killed stone dead any idea in my mind about getting a discount off the list price. He also lost any chance of making a sale to me by his attitude and lack of any qualification or engagement, but that is outside the scope of this point.

In setting pricing structures for your solutions, profitability will have been a key consideration, and discounting from the list price will have an immediate impact on the level of profitability from a deal. Top-line sales revenue and bottom-line profitability are closely related, and changing one has a knock-on effect.

Consider it another way: What if your company recovered any discount you gave away directly from your salary? That may focus your mind a little more on selling on the value of your solution and not the list price.

How to handle requests for discounts

A request for a discount is essentially a pricing objection that should have been covered during the sales cycle before getting to the deal structure part. Regardless of where it crops up, though, you need to deal with it and don't let your prospect catch you off balance. You need to respond in a way that shows your professionalism and at the same time shows that you're not a pushover.

With a request for a discount, your prospect has put you on the spot and will expect a quick response to secure the deal. Take time to consider his request, clarify the issue, and check for any hidden agenda, and then offer a response.

To clarify, try restating his objection with a question to get to the crux of the issue, such as

>> "Could you be more specific when you say that our price is too high?"

>> "Could you help me understand why you consider the price too high?"

Look for clarification, and get your prospect to open up on what the issue really is or the drivers behind it with questions like these:

>> "What were your expectations on price?"

>> "Can you help me understand why price has become an issue for you?"

>> "Are you ready to commit if we can resolve this issue now?"

TIP

Something that I use often when asked about the pricing for solutions is to say that the pricing is "reassuringly expensive." This started as a throwaway line to deflect a pricing inquiry but has become a central theme to my business's pricing and positioning, showing that we acknowledge that others may provide something that costs less, while putting down a price and quality marker that we can fall back on at deal-structuring time. In other words, if you want the best, it will cost more than some of the others. That's life.

After you consider the prospect's request, clarify the issue, and check for any hidden agenda, you can respond to the discount request without giving away a discount by doing the following:

>> **Adding or subtracting aspects of the solution:** Work around discount requests by adding or subtracting elements of the solution that you've proposed. Tell your prospect that if he's concerned about the price, then you can either add some additional value to the solution — for example, additional support or training — and that you could provide this at cost or begin to take elements of the solution away. I've used this approach by asking "which part of the solution don't you want?"

TIP

This is a bit of a shock-and-awe tactic as it lets your prospect know that he can achieve a lower price only if some elements of the solution are removed. Ask the question sincerely, and then keep quiet and wait for a response. Use time and silence as tools in your kit.

>> **Restructuring some terms of the deal:** Restructuring some elements of the deal may work in some cases, perhaps by changing the billing cycle to match budget quarters.

You can assist with the perception of achieving a discount by offering to load the deal with added value items at a favorable price or even at cost price as long as you have good margins on the main solution, or you can even allow special deals for hitting specific implementation targets.

REMEMBER

Your objective is to protect your pricing strategy while securing the go-ahead for a deal, so packing the deal with added value can prove to be a good solution for both parties.

Do not, however, let your prospect lose face; allow him to have a little success on less important issues. A great example here comes from my own experience when structuring a deal with my very first consultancy client. He knew that I needed the business, but he also knew that he needed the solution and so the basic sale was fairly straightforward, and the price agreed on was fair to both parties. When the finance director was completing the standing order paperwork to enable automatic funds transfer on a weekly basis, as we had agreed, he looked me straight in the eye and rounded down the agreed figure to the nearest "sensible" amount. The fee was going to be something like $603.08, and he rounded it down to $600, daring me to object. I let him have his $3.08 victory, and we went on to work with that company for almost a decade, running up something in the order of $300,000 of fee income.

REMEMBER The moral here is to win the important battles, and don't focus on noise-level details; let the buyer have little victories to enable him to feel good.

Balancing risk and reward

In any new business sales situation, a deal is like a seesaw — it can be heavy on one side or the other, or it can be balanced just about equally, which is the optimal position in terms of balancing risk and reward. Too heavily biased in terms of either the buyer or the seller, and it stores up problems ahead. If you believe in your solution, why would you want to structure a deal that doesn't deliver value to your prospect?

WARNING This doesn't mean that you have to, or even should, agree to any terms that your prospect wants. Be wary of a buyer who wants everything in exchange for nothing, because he has clearly not understood either the value proposition or the sales and customer dynamics. This can be an early warning sign for future problems and should sound the alarm bells.

REMEMBER To strike the right balance for a successful deal, you need to understand your prospect's motivation — that is, what's driving him to want your solution and what his pressure points are in terms of doing a deal. You of course already know the budget and sign-off procedures because you qualified them early in the sales cycle (see Chapters 9 and 19 for more about qualification), but has some internal process got in the way? Ask questions that are designed to probe for the real reasons behind any objections (as I suggest earlier in this chapter), because when you understand what you're dealing with, it becomes much easier to build a balanced deal.

Here are a few methods you can consider to balance a deal:

>> Deals don't always hinge on money, but could you explore some sort of financing deal if that was appropriate? Depending on the size of your company, this may include offering to structure payments over a longer period in exchange for a price premium. My business does offer a pricing deal in this way, and I use it when faced with price issues, which usually go away when the prospect discovers how much more expensive the solution will be if he wants to do a price deal. (I return to payment terms later in this chapter.)

>> Trial periods can offer an answer to building a balanced deal, but your solution needs to be relevant for a trial, and all are not. My business sometimes offers a trial period, which we run as a separate project so it has sufficient focus but also to ensure that it has both an end date and a conversion plan to the full service. Trials need to be well defined and to be micromanaged in order to deliver the planned objectives quickly and move on. (I cover contracts for trials later in this chapter.)

>> You can try upping the reward element of a deal by introducing some upselling options, especially when faced with demands for more value or reduced cost. Keep the focus on increasing the value proposition, and don't be afraid to turn the tables and ask your prospect what his own policy is when his prospects ask for discounts. One example is to offer something like an extended warranty, which has a clear value, and include it at close to cost price. This delivers additional value to your prospect while maintaining your solution margin.

TIP

Do be a little wary of introducing upsells, though, because they're not always welcome, and you may find yourself under pressure to bundle them as part of the original solution price. When used with care and at the right time in structuring a deal, they can be nice profitable additions to a sale.

Using incentives

An incentive program is something that promotes or encourages specific actions or behavior. When used tactically, incentives can stimulate prospects to take the desired action, which should be to move a sale closer to completion or a deal closer to being fully agreed on and signed off. When putting an incentive program together, you need to consider whether the incentive you're offering does actually cause prospects to take that next step and that it's related to your solution.

An example of a poorly thought-out incentive program for business-to-business sales is offering a free iPod for salespeople to give to prospects. What would the objective of this be? Apart from giving it to children, what would your prospect do with it? Buying decisions would unlikely be affected, so it would be a waste of money and a wasted opportunity.

In coming up with an incentive program, consider how it could influence each stage of the buying cycle for your prospects and that it's linked to your solution. Anything outside that definition comes under hospitality, which is another topic entirely and not one I cover in this book.

REMEMBER

Your objective with incentives is to add value to the sales and buying cycles and to deliver something of intrinsic value to your prospect. If he can also use that something to further champion your cause internally, then that is an even better goal.

WARNING

In putting together an incentive, try to avoid being too clever. Your proposition should be clear and concise; otherwise, it risks just adding to the noise level or, worse still, confusing your prospect such that the sales cycle moves backward.

Do you regularly encounter the same type of concerns in structuring a deal? If so, this could be an interesting area to try to incentivize. Here are some examples of effective incentive programs:

>> Rewards program for which you perhaps partner with another supplier

>> Associated product or service free or heavily discounted

>> Extended maintenance or warranty period

>> Price freeze for a certain time

>> Volume discounts (the only type of discounts you should offer)

>> Leasing or other finance deal

>> Fast-start program with support to get early results

>> Trial periods (which I introduce in the preceding section)

With all these examples, the trick is to keep them as simple and straightforward as possible. If you can't explain your incentive on a single side of A4 paper or in less than a minute, then it's too complicated and you risk distracting from the bigger picture of structuring the deal.

WARNING

When it comes to incentives, you want to avoid artificial deal deadlines. By this, I mean things like "offer ends at 10 a.m. on Monday" unless you have a valid reason for having such a restriction. This is a little controversial because many experts will tell you that having a deadline for action is absolutely the right thing to do because it focuses attention and drives results. I don't believe it has anything like that effect in business-to-business sales. In fact, the effect can be the compete opposite, and unless you have a real, valid reason for a deadline, don't make one up because it will turn off a lot of people and irritate a lot more when you want them to be championing your cause internally, not spending time chasing artificial deadlines. If you really insist on having an artificial deadline, then don't extend it as it passes. You'll likely alienate lots of prospects with this type of action.

Looking to Establish a Win-Win

In the majority of business-to-business sales situations, you're not just looking to close a deal and move on because you'll likely have further opportunities with that prospect or, at the very least, with his network of contacts. This makes establishing a solid relationship important, and getting off on the right foot is key. If you can establish a win-win situation with your first sale to a prospect, then you're well positioned for long-term success.

WARNING

A win-win may not always be possible to achieve, but it should be your goal in structuring a deal. However, it won't work if either you or your prospect has a mindset of needing to beat the other and approach the deal structuring in an adversarial manner. (You'll often find this when faced with professional buying departments, which I cover in Chapter 13.)

Dealing with prospects who are inexperienced in structuring deals can also offer a bit of a challenge, and the relationship you've built with them can work to your advantage if you're in a position to drive the structuring process. You're a stakeholder in their successful implementation of your solution, so you need to not only get your deal concluded but also ensure that it's done in such a way as to maximize the chances of success.

REMEMBER

You may think that setting out to ensure that both parties win in a deal structuring to be a bit of an alien concept, but consider it this way: You need to make a sale to get paid and further your career, while your prospect needs to have a set of problems resolved. The deal is about fulfilling both of those objectives and doing so in a way that delivers the best possible agreement. If either you or your prospect are trying to gain a one-sided advantage or just trying to score points, you aren't striving for a win-win. You'll be able to conduct a deal structure that delivers the best possible mutual agreement only if both parties share the same goal.

The following sections provide pointers on how to establish a win-win as you structure a deal.

Being creative

To structure a solid deal as a win-win, you need an open and sharing mindset, and you need to understand your prospect's position before you can really begin to get anything substantial in place. You should of course have already covered all the key issues as part of your ongoing qualification (see Chapters 9 and 19) and should have no nasty surprises in store.

Being in a position as a new business salesperson where you need to close a deal puts you at a major disadvantage. It often leads to you not securing the best deal and is unlikely to even get you to a win-win position if your desperation is obvious to your prospect.

TIP

Breaking a deal down into its component parts is a good way to move forward in negotiations. Tick off the items you agree on, and park them as dealt with. To establish a win-win deal, you need to have built trust during the sales cycle and discussed limitations, objectives, and needs along with how to collaboratively reach them. By parking the elements as they're agreed on, you also protect yourself against a change as the discussions continue.

Be prepared to be creative within the bounds of your authority as you look to build a final solution. Some time ago, I was well into final discussions with a prospect who was well qualified so I understood the real needs and understood budgetary limitations, which were fine for my solution, but I couldn't get to an agreement to proceed. I was prepared to walk away rather than push for a reluctant deal, but before doing so I asked what it would take to get it to work. It transpired that the prospect was afraid of failure, which was perhaps why he needed our help in the first place, and the thought of committing to what was a sizeable deal for him was holding him back. Having understood the issue, I offered to structure the deal a different way — to introduce a support package so that he had a higher level of support available and to build in monthly reviews with me personally as long as we could do them remotely using Skype or FaceTime. This was going to cost us a bit of money and time, but it wasn't a big problem for me.

As a final attempt to help, I suggested that we structure the deal as a rolling trial period, one that never really came out of trial so that his maximum commitment at any stage was only one month. This clinched the deal, but in reality all I did was creatively address the issue in another way because our standard contract has a one-month termination clause anyway, so the "clincher" was nothing that wasn't already there.

That particular prospect went on to be a long-term client, and all his future deals were structured as rolling trials as far as he was concerned. We achieved a win-win solution.

Building a long-term relationship

Some sales cycles are very quick, transaction-oriented ones where little or no opportunity exists to build a relationship, but the majority of business-to-business sales and all complex ones take more time to progress through a sales cycle. In this case, the outcome is often more than a single sales transaction at a moment in time and will result in repeat business over a long period of time, often many years, so time invested in building a relationship with the prospect or client is time well spent.

REMEMBER

In addition to putting you in the driver's seat as far as future new business is concerned, your relationship also ensures a much smoother path through accounts and a variety of other functions in the client's organization that you're expected to cover.

You have an opportunity at the beginning of a relationship to set precedent and then expect that it moves forward in the same way. By doing this, you save time on future deal structures and don't have to reinvent the wheel each time. Establish the way that you expect things to be done and be clear about any implications of actions slipping. Building a long-term relationship enables general issues to be dealt with just once; it also leads to future sales being easier and quicker to conclude as both parties understand the basics and can concentrate on specifics in the future, ensuring that the chances of a win-win solution are enhanced.

TIP

You can help both yourself and your new client by documenting steps taken or creating forms and processes to monitor each stage, flagging exceptions for you to work on. This creates added value for your client because it makes his role easier while further cementing your relationship. Done with some care and forethought, something like this can quickly become an accepted norm in your client's business, meaning that whenever a need arises in that area, you automatically get the order.

In building a long-term relationship, you need to remember that it's about both give and take and not a one-way street. Cement the relationship further with the perception of more and more added value; things like these can play an important role:

>> Loss leaders

>> Early access to information

>> End-of-life product offers or giveaways

>> Additional months on support coverage

Strive to make your relationship more of a partnership of equals rather than a client and supplier agreement. Give your client access to people and information in your company and in your wider network who can provide added value.

REMEMBER

Make a point of going the extra mile as a matter of routine. Your goal should be to make yourself invaluable as a trusted partner, and then why would he even consider going elsewhere for solutions that you provide? In addition, when you need to deliver bad news or when a measure of negotiation is required, if you've built up sufficient goodwill, it will be a softer blow. Tasks like this should be approached as exercises in engagement rather than bargaining.

Continuing solid reporting and communications

From the very early stages of the sales cycle, you'll have been producing contact reports, as I outline in Chapter 3, so you have established a clear precedent for doing this. By the time your sales cycle reaches the deal-structuring stage, your prospect will have come to expect and, to a certain extent, rely on them.

As the sales cycle reaches its conclusion and you hopefully move into the implementation phase, your company needs to continue to deliver the same type of documentary audit trail. The information needed will obviously change and will likely be produced by someone else, but as a new business salesperson, you've set the bar and your colleagues need to commit to carry through on this.

Proving clear communications throughout both the sales cycle and the implementation phase helps to establish credibility and demonstrates that you're acting in your prospect's best interest, which will in turn help to further the relationship into a win-win solution.

All notes and reports are of course documented and stored in the CRM system (see Chapter 9) and are available to colleagues as the project moves forward, ensuring that everyone has access to all the relevant information and that nothing is forgotten about.

REMEMBER

The importance of solid and dependable reporting comes to light when a solution contains outsourced work or anything of a creative nature because you often need to provide solid evidence for an audit trail. For example, if you've delegated an activity and it hasn't gone according to plan, you have clear evidence of the lines of responsibility and accountability as you seek to get the issues resolved.

The start of an implementation phase is when new business sales hands over client responsibility to an account manager or a project manager. Your role as the company lead in the deal comes to an end, but having worked hard to establish that you can be relied on to produce solid and accurate reports, you need to ensure that this accountability continues. Your sales responsibility will always be present with the new client, and although you may lose ownership of the day-to-day activities, you need to maintain accountability as you'll most likely be involved in securing another contract from the client in the future.

Communication is as important as reporting, and as a new business salesperson, at handover time, your responsibility is to ensure that both the new client and your colleagues are all connected at the appropriate level, with the correct introductions made between parties in your prospect's organization and yours. That way, everyone knows who is responsible for what activities, and regular communication plans, such as email updates and phone updates, are in place before your handover is complete.

TIP

Make sure the new client knows that you're in the loop and are available to discuss any issues as you're the one who built the relationship and trust. Account managers sometimes resist sales "interference," but my view is that they'll have to live with it if it's my sale, and they'll have to report to and be accountable to me in the event of any problem. Account managers need to be copied on correspondence, of course, but your objective of securing additional business and their objective of running a project have the potential to be at odds with one another, so ensure that intracompany issues are dealt with out of the new client's sight.

Making referrals as part of your terms

Referrals work so well as a prospecting tool because they're backed by personal recommendation and come with inbuilt credibility and inherent trust from a peer. I cover prospecting in detail in Chapter 9, but one of the most effective ways of gaining new prospects is through the power of a referral from an existing client. When you're structuring the deal is a good time to introduce the fact that you thrive on doing a good job for clients and rely on recommendations to their peers. Don't be timid in raising this request, and let it be known that it's something that you'd not only like but expect to be provided with.

REMEMBER

Reverse referrals are also an effective way of building a client relationship, where you, from your vast array of contacts due to the very nature of your job, refer people you know to your client. Providing referrals for each other is definitely a win-win deal.

When seeking referrals, you need to be as specific as possible to get the best results, so don't ask broad questions. Narrow the focus and even have a list of targets that you can ask about being introduced to. Be specific in your request, and accept that if you don't ask, then you more than likely won't get. A lot of books cover how to ask for and get referrals, so I won't go into the techniques here, but do let your new customer know that he should help you in this way. There is no problem with asking a straightforward question like "Who do you know that might benefit from this type of solution, and could you introduce me, please?"

In some cases, a new client may not be comfortable with giving referrals by nature of his personality. Respect this and find another, less direct way that he can be of assistance to you. For example, ask whether he'd be prepared to give a case study or even a client reference. In this case, feed that information back into your marketing department and make sure they follow up on it. (Flip to Chapter 6 for more about marketing matters.)

Some people advocate setting up a referral commission scheme so that anyone providing you with a referral that goes on to result in a sale receives a payment of some kind. This is fine in consumer sales, but I don't recommend it in a business-to-business environment because it's too fraught with danger and open to accusations of illegal inducement.

Recognizing that "Guarantee" Is a Big, Powerful Word

The word *guarantee* in a new business sales environment carries a lot of weight with it. And as long as you're able to clearly spell out what you mean and back that up with a real documented program, then guaranteeing that your solution will deliver for your prospect can really set you apart; otherwise, it's just an empty word. The following sections help you work with guarantees.

A guarantee helps build trust. Your prospects will think that if you're guaranteeing your solution, then it must be good because otherwise you wouldn't do it.

Be aware of the provisions of the Sale of Goods Act in the United Kingdom or its equivalent in other countries. This legislation protects the buyer when something goes wrong, so don't fall foul of statutory regulations with your guarantee.

Structuring a guarantee

When deciding how to structure a guarantee, you need to consider exactly what you're setting out to achieve, because if you don't understand that, then you may as well try to guarantee the weather. You next need to consider how you can structure your guarantee. Consider the do's and don'ts I discuss in this section.

First, the don'ts:

>> Avoid any form of money-back guarantee because this has the effect of telling your prospects that it doesn't really matter whether the solution works. It encourages them to try your solution but without any real commitment. A deal to implement a solution without full commitment from a prospect is almost certainly going to fail, and so a guarantee of this type sets you up for failure.

>> If you can't do it, then don't commit to it. For example, you may guarantee that the solution is so simple to implement that if the prospect can't do it, then you'll pay for a third party to do it on his behalf. Something like this risks opening a whole can of worms, and before you know it you'll have both an unsuccessful implementation and a big bill.

>> Stay away from easy-to-deliver guarantees that perhaps don't hold as much weight in terms of contractual impact. For example, saying things like "I'll work with you personally" and "I'll manage our resources to make sure we deliver" aren't real guarantees and have little real meaning.

REMEMBER

Some types of guarantees aren't worth the paper they're written on, so if you're going to guarantee your solution, make the guarantee something that's worthwhile and that addresses a real and potentially deal–breaking concern. When structuring a guarantee program, make sure it's realistic, sensible, and achievable.

My business guarantees performance, which helps move deals to completion. The guarantee is simple to understand, realistic, sensible, and achievable and works like this: We guarantee that over a rolling 13-week period, clients will achieve "xyz" results from us. If we fail to deliver those results in that time frame, then we'll continue working on the project at our cost until the shortfall is made up, and only at that point will we begin charging again. This guarantee is subject to all payments being up–to–date and to clients doing what they're meant to do, which is specified in the guarantee. Do we ever have to deliver on the guarantee? Yes, on occasion we do, and it's never a problem because the terms are simple to under–stand and fair to both parties.

Here are some more do's:

>> Consider what level of buy-in and commitment you need your prospect to commit to. Offering a guarantee of successful implementation is no good if your prospect doesn't commit any resources to it because it will always end in failure.

>> Consider whether the guarantee needs to be conditional or if it's more binary in nature. To do this, you need to assess the impact to your business of both the likelihood of the guarantee being called on and the effect of delivering on the guarantee.

Knowing that guarantees work both ways

The role of a guarantee in structuring a deal is to help you get to the end game as quickly as possible by taking one or more obstacles out of the equation. Whether the prospect needs a guarantee doesn't really matter; your confidence in providing it is more important and much more powerful.

REMEMBER

Guarantees are designed to reduce the perception of risk in the structure of a deal, but it's important that you understand the risk of the guarantee being called on and that you don't leave yourself open to any possible abuse of it.

TIP

Don't allow the fact that the prospect has a guarantee from you to mean that he doesn't need to be fully committed and engaged with the solution implementation, because he does, and guarantees work both ways. Get your prospect to match your guarantee with one of his own. The idea is to work as a partnership and to reduce the perception of risk, not just pass it on.

For example, you may guarantee that a certain level of individual, usually named, will lead the project for your company and be responsible for ensuring success. You should strive to have an individual in your new client's company named as being accountable for ensuring that all of the client's obligations are also met.

Maximizing chances of success

To make sure you maximize the chances of success and build a partnership between yourself and the prospect, you need to gain commitment from all the stakeholders. Just having this type of discussion with your prospect can help build bonds of trust, and sometimes you may discover that it alleviates the need to actually formulate a guarantee.

TIP

Consider implementing a trial as I outline in the earlier section "Balancing risk and reward." Trials can be effective if you follow some simple ground rules. Another element to introduce at the guarantee stage is whether you should provide a premium level of support and, if so, whether it's at your cost or the prospect's.

Creating Unambiguous Contracts

Many deals turn sour because the new business salesperson fails to adequately address the contractual and paperwork side of the job. Understanding the importance of orders and making them crystal clear is a necessity in sales. The following sections provide contract help.

TIP

Make sure you understand the nature of any of your client's systems and processes and whether they'll have an impact — for example, if your client does payment runs only on Tuesdays, structure this into the contract, and don't expect payment on Monday.

Written terms

Contracts offer mutual protection, and their role is a vital one in business. You need to have, at the very least, a simple written and signed agreement. Contracts should be written in natural language and should avoid jargon. Don't rely on verbal contracts, which are acceptable in a legal sense but nearly impossible to either challenge or defend should the need arise.

REMEMBER

You don't need to go over the top in terms of order or contract length in the vast majority of cases, as long as all the bases are covered. In most cases, a degree of common sense and a basic understanding of contract law are all that you need to form an order and contract that is clear and unambiguous.

Include a schedule of deliverables and dates or milestones. In other words, set out the individual stages of the solution and attach dates to each stage so that it's clear when actions are required and expected to be achieved.

Even trial periods need contracts, because they are vital in outlining what's to be achieved, by whom, and by when and in defining what the scope of the trial is intended to do, along with what happens at the end.

REMEMBER

Wherever possible, you should use your contract and not one provided by your prospect. Own and drive this process to completion with the same zeal that won you the business in the first place.

Processes for dealing with changes

The objective here is no surprises. Be aware that changes do occur once an implementation is underway, but you can't always anticipate what they'll be. Contractually, you should cover who's responsible for sorting out the impact of any changes and who's responsible for the cost of doing so.

For example, you may want to include a clause setting out that any changes to the agreed-on specification that occur after the contract is signed will be charged at a standard hourly rate.

Don't allow yourself to be bullied into accepting changes made to the contract, either. Be aware of buyer games, especially professional buyers (see Chapter 13), and be prepared to act accordingly.

Absolutely clear payment terms

The number-one reason for failure of business relationships is frustration over payments. Cover payment terms in simple, clear language and have all parties agree to it so there can be no scope for later misunderstanding.

A good mindset to adopt, and one that I do all the time, is one of "we are not a bank." If the client can't afford you, then you should have qualified him out long ago, and it's not your problem to solve. While you're structuring the deal isn't the time to be sorting payment schedules because this should have already been agreed on; your role now is to get it implemented.

If you can achieve direct payments on the due dates, then that is the best possible option; if not, then you need to avoid any form of monthly manual sign-off on invoices because this will always eventually lead to delays in payment and the associated frustrations they cause.

Have terms for dealing with late payments and be prepared to enforce them every time. In my business, we operate a three-strikes-and-you're-out rule. If you mess with payments three times, then you're now an ex-client. It may be viewed as tough and uncompromising, but as I say earlier, we are not a bank.

Payment in advance or at least in advance for each stage of the implementation is a good target to aim for and should usually be achievable. If the prospect wants the solution, then why would he delay paying for it?

Chapter **12**

Having the Confidence to Say No

New business salespeople love to hear prospects say yes to them. A lot of teachings focus on how to ask the types of questions that can result only in positive, or yes, answers early in the sales cycle, so, as the theory goes, your prospect gets into the habit of saying yes to you. Excuse me, but we're in the 21st century here, and prospects are as equally sophisticated as salespeople. So don't try to patronize them with things like this because it will more than likely end with you getting the relationship off on the wrong foot, and as I discuss in Chapter 3, first impressions set the scene for the entire relationship.

REMEMBER

Don't risk being labeled as a pushy salesperson at the very beginning (or ever, in fact), and use your experience and common sense at all times. Forget the tricks or old-school techniques to try to manipulate your prospect; you're building a business relationship of equals.

New business sales is also not about you saying yes to everything you're asked for; building a client-supplier relationship is about give and take, even from the initial exchanges. Of course, you don't ever go into a sales situation wanting to or expecting to say no to your prospect, but the reality is that it's going to happen, sometimes frequently, during a sales cycle, and although *no* can be a massively powerful word, as I discuss in this chapter, the way you say it is as important as the words you use.

Understanding When, Why, and How to Say No

It can easily, and wrongly, be assumed that your job, in a new business sales role, is to just agree with everything that your prospect asks for, but nothing could be further from the truth. You represent your company and have a duty to secure the best deal that you can, and on occasion this means taking a hard line and pushing back on your prospect when he wants to do a lot of taking and not much giving. In this section, I look at when and why this may be the case and how to say no.

When you may need to say no

Sales cycles rarely if ever run to their conclusion with all parties in total agreement all the way through. In fact, at many points in a typical sales cycle, such as the following, the salesperson is in a position of having to reject a request:

>> During qualification (see Chapters 9 and 19)

>> When handling objections (see Chapter 10)

>> During negotiations (see Chapters 16 and 20)

>> During deal structuring (see Chapter 11)

As the sales cycle moves through each of these stages, the impact of saying no increases, as does the likelihood of it becoming an issue that needs to be addressed.

Why you may need to say no

In this section, I explore both clearly defined and hazier reasons why a no may be necessary as your sales cycle progresses.

>> **Clear reasons:** Clearly defined reasons for saying no to a prospect include the following:

- Failure of some qualification criteria (see Chapters 9 and 19) may be a reason either for not taking a sale any further or for asking some searching questions. Be upfront in this case. I've told prospects that they don't meet our criteria and so we can't work with them at this stage, but if these two things change, then I would be delighted to look again.

This type of no message leaves the door open while sometimes making your solution even more attractive to the prospect because he can't have it. It's called taking away and, used with care, can leave you in a stronger position in the sales cycle.

- A clear case of needing a no message is where a specific request for a function as part of your solution just can't be done or can't be done without making significant changes.

- Another clear no case is where a request is unreasonable or contrary to company policy. In Chapter 11, I tell a true story of my first attempt at buying a BMW, which resulted in a failed purchase by me and a failed sale by the salesman due initially to my request for a discount being contrary to company policy.

For details on handling discounts or requests for them, see Chapter 11. When turning down a request like this, be sure to get your message across clearly but professionally.

>> **Hazier reasons:** Less clear reasons for saying no to a prospect may include things like the request could be met but wouldn't be cost effective to provide it, or it wouldn't add long-term value to your solution, or it took your proposed solution in what you consider to be the wrong direction. I address this type of situation in the later section "Sometimes it's not meant to be."

How to say no

Saying no to a prospect doesn't necessarily mean saying the actual word *no*; it's about disagreeing with a point of view or turning down a request. I rarely advocate using the literal word *no* because it's too closed of a word and can convey that a dead end has been reached, when more likely than not what you actually want to convey is a "no, but . . ." meaning.

Find phrases that allow you to turn down a request without using the word *no*, and practice your delivery, for example:

>> "There may be a better way to achieve this."

>> "Have you considered looking at it this way?"

>> "I'm not sure that's the best way to approach this."

>> "Can you help me find an alternative?"

REMEMBER

Of course, sometimes a simple "I'm sorry, but I can't do that" is the clearest message to deliver, and in that case, don't delay in delivering the message clearly and concisely but also professionally and positively. Don't ever gloat at saying no. As a new business salesperson, you're likely to hear no more often than yes as you progress through your career, so consider how being on the receiving end of a no makes you feel — dejected, disappointed, and frustrated are some adjectives you may apply in times like these. So when you need to deliver a negative message to your prospect, bear that in mind and be professional, courteous, and solution-oriented in your delivery.

Saying No Doesn't Mean that a Deal Isn't Possible

Sometimes no doesn't mean "no, and that's the end of the matter." A no can be any number of things. Life would be so much simpler if we all just said what we really mean!

Even a significant no offers opportunities to a new business salesperson, and it's not the same as walking away from a deal. In Chapter 10, I cover the issues associated with walking away, but here you need to understand that saying no is an opportunity rather than an obstacle, and opportunities should be the lifeblood of a top new business salesperson. The following sections cover two important considerations:

>> The first thing to consider is whether the need for the solution is still there or whether the obstacle negated the need, which seems unlikely if your qualification (see Chapters 9 and 19) was accurate. Assuming that the initial need still exists, you need to find a way around the obstacle before it becomes immovable. Strike here as soon as the issue raises its head, and be sure to cover the obstacle and its solution in a contact report (which I introduce in Chapter 3). You want to avoid fixing an issue only for it to return later, so you need to demonstrate that it has been addressed and then the sales cycle can move forward.

>> Go back to basics and give yourself permission to think outside the box when faced with a no situation from either party. How can you present the issue in another light to shift the focus from the sticking point? If the prospect's need is real, and you'll know this only if you've correctly qualified, then there'll always be a way to work around issues that result in a no.

Using no as a negotiating point

Consider whether the issue that has presented itself is a real one that needs to be taken seriously or a negotiating position that's being established. Look beyond the obvious, and find the real issue that needs to be addressed. If you're hitting an objection that has already been covered, then use the contact reports to demonstrate that it is no longer a real issue. Any new issues that are raised need to be dealt with, but if they are anything substantial, then ask why the problem has only just arisen and was not part of the stated need. If you don't get a sensible reply, then you can let your prospect know that you consider him to be playing games that you won't entertain.

There is nothing wrong with taking a hard line to time wasting or posturing, but you do need to handle it with care and allow your prospect to back down gracefully without being seen to lose face. Take the sting out of a no by focusing on the positive aspects of achieving the goals in the ways you have shown him.

TIP

If you find that you've come up against a negotiating point, then you have a wider range of options besides just saying no, even in the nicest way. If your prospect is playing hard to get and you don't believe that the issue is a real one or a deal breaker, then let him sweat it out for a while by using the power of silence. See whether he changes his position or backs down completely when you don't respond. Some prospects will just try to see what they can get away with, so don't feel the need to defend your decision not to run around after them if you encounter a prospect who introduces issues for the sake of them.

Giving yourself permission to change the rules

Sometimes getting to a no position on an issue can be refreshing because it gives you permission to change the rules to work on a solution that addresses the objection or stumbling block. In changing the rules, you have an opportunity to reengage with your prospect, building a deeper relationship in the process, and work with him to help redefine the question together, seeking a solution that has a feeling of joint ownership.

REMEMBER

At some points during a sales cycle, you have permission to easily introduce a step change in either your solution, perhaps extending the scope of it, or in the way the deal is structured (see Chapter 11). One of those points arrives naturally when you get to a no question, something that's to be acceptable to either party with the status quo. This, almost of necessity, requires a bit of rethinking and gives the opportunity to introduce a step change as a means to an end (in other words, getting past the no). Getting to a position where it becomes "our" solution is a major milestone in a sales cycle, and the prospect will then feel ownership and is much more likely to champion your cause internally.

Protecting Your Interests

Being confident enough to say no is sometimes necessary to protect your interests, either personally for the new business salesperson not wanting to be seen as a pushover or for the company to, for example, protect profit margins.

Don't allow yourself to be backed into a corner with demand after demand for concessions; as you find out in the following sections, saying no is a powerful weapon that you have at your disposal, so be prepared to use it tactically when necessary. You need to be able to justify your actions whenever you say no to a prospect, and the decision is likely to be reviewed at internal sales meetings, so be sure in your actions and be ready to justify them to colleagues.

REMEMBER

Dealing with professional buyers can be a challenging time, especially for less experienced new business salespeople (see Chapter 13 for the full scoop on this topic). Having the ability to say no to counter unreasonable demands thrown at you is powerful as long as you use it professionally and with integrity.

A deal at any cost isn't your aim

You should never get yourself into a position of needing a sale so desperately that you'll give anything away to secure it. Something has gone badly wrong if you get to this stage and you need to get support from colleagues to rescue you.

WARNING

Every concession you make needs to be funded in some way. Rarely can you get something for nothing, and all funding actions result in an impact on bottom-line profitability. Company reputation needs to be safeguarded, too, because giving away concessions will quickly spread in your industry and soon all your prospects will be after the same thing, with devastating effects on your bottom line.

Sometimes it's not meant to be

There's such a thing as trying too hard. You're not going to win every sale, regardless of how well you qualify it, because life doesn't work that way. So accept that you can and will increase your win percentage, maybe as high as 80 percent or more, but be realistic in your expectations of 100 percent because it's not going to be sustainable.

REMEMBER

Pick the battles you can win when it comes to being prepared to say no. Some are more important than others, and some are more winnable than others. Every new business deal has two sides, and your prospect will also be looking for some wins, especially if he has a management chain to report to. So pick your battles with care, and focus on the big picture, not the nitty-gritty detail where you could give ground without too much difficulty.

For example, don't spend time and energy trying to win every point if they don't really matter in the long run. You may want to concede on some implementation timescales more easily than a copyright issue. Timescales can be adapted to meet needs, but copyright is fundamental. Spend your time on the things that really matter.

Chapter **13**

Asking for the Order

When your sales cycle reaches a natural conclusion, hopefully aligned to your prospect's buying cycle, the time to ask for the order arrives. This needs to be a smooth and natural progression of the sales cycle and not some momentous event that you build up in your head. Asking for the order — the topic of this chapter — generally marks the end of the sales cycle and the beginning of the implementation phase, and you need to make it as seamless as possible.

Don't forget, though, that you do need to ask for the order, or you risk never getting it or at least delaying it. Surprisingly, many new business salespeople trip over on this one simple point and build it up into a huge obstacle. But if you've done your qualification correctly (see Chapters 9 and 19), it's a simple step to achieve.

As the sales cycle has moved through the stages and you've been qualifying all along, you understand the criteria that your prospect is buying against, and you have an in-depth understanding of both his problem area and of your solution. You've discussed and overcome any objections, you've clearly defined the budgets and made sure they're in line with your proposal, and you've met and covered the decision-making unit (see Chapter 19). The order is yours, and all you need to do is conclude it. Check that your prospect is happy, shake his hand, and get on with the paperwork and then implementing the solution.

Both parties are exactly the same as they have been throughout the sales cycle, and you have long ago set the standard and ground rules for the way you work, so asking for the order is no different. You're simply following through to a natural conclusion.

Being Professional and Straightforward

During the sales cycle, you built a relationship with your prospect that's based on professionalism and established a position of trust with him (see Chapter 3 for details on how to perform these tasks). This relationship needs to continue right through to the order being placed and beyond because it's based on reality and not an act that you've been presenting. Anything short of that standard and you'll have failed yourself and will be seen as shallow and unprofessional, with all the untold damage that comes with it.

As the deal reaches its climax, guard against a sudden switch into salesperson mode, and continue to be yourself. If you fail to do so, you're doing yourself and your prospect an injustice, and you risk the deal collapsing at the last minute. Inappropriate closing techniques, sudden changes in attitude, and a breakdown of professionalism can do damage to your credibility and the trust you've built and ultimately put the deal at risk.

Some ways of asking for the order are better than others, and you need to find your own style, making sure it's still you — the new business sales professional who drove the deal to reach this stage and not some new, strange closing machine that scares your prospect away.

Of course, you have a right to expect the same professionalism from your prospect as the sale enters its final stage; he should continue to behave in the same manner and not switch into some form of tough buyer mode.

The following sections provide basic guidelines on how to ask for the order in a straightforward, professional manner that avoids mind games.

Professionalism works both ways, and you and your prospect have the right to expect it of each other. It's how you got to the order stage in the sales cycle because the deal would have likely been killed off before this stage if a lack of trust or transparency on either side had occurred.

Asking whether you're the solution of choice

When it comes to buying options, choice isn't always a good thing for your prospect because it can lead to confusion and delay. How many times have you pondered an ice-cream menu or a wine list and been indecisive as the waiter or shopkeeper stood ready to take your order? The same principle applies in winning new business. Your prospect needs help narrowing down his choices, and that's part of what the buying cycle is about. Your role is to assist him in making the choice, ensuring that your solution is the one that rises to the top.

How do you know when your solution has become the preferred one? Your qualification should go a long way to confirming this. And having built real trust and interaction with your prospect over time, you can ask where your solution fits in his plans and how he sees it fitting into his workflow.

REMEMBER

Your prospect is looking for a solution that meets a business need, and that need may not have been clearly defined, even in his own mind, at the beginning of the process. Having guided him through the options and demonstrated how and why your solution fits the need, you're in a strong position be able to ask searching questions aimed at establishing when the time is right to ask for the order. The response to a question such as "How do we progress this to get started?" will quickly show you where you are in the preferred solution hierarchy, and if at the right place, press on and get the deal done.

TIP

Your contact reports will confirm for you that everything has been covered and that the choices facing your prospect have been eliminated, one by one. (Check out Chapter 3 for a sample contact report.)

Ask your prospect whether he has any reason not to proceed. A simple question should result in a straightforward answer. For example, I'm currently in a buying cycle with a potential supplier. I've been qualified, which I always find a little amusing — that is, being on the receiving end — and if it's any good, the qualification should show that the time is right to ask for the order because they should know that their solution is the one of choice. I haven't yet been asked for the order, but they've attempted a soft close by offering a discount for a decision before month's end. I was actually a little disappointed by the way that soft close was tried, via email almost as a throwaway line. Maybe I'm not a typical buyer, but I'm not playing games with them and genuinely want the solution. However, it's not at the top of my priority list to do right at this moment; if they were to ask, I would tell them. To be clear, I'm a serious buyer and will buy the solution, but they have not really qualified properly in terms of timescale, and it would be fascinating to see what their qualification and forecast are.

Is winning new business an art form or a science? It has elements of both really — art in terms of how you structure a sales cycle and how you present a solution, and science because you have predictable paths and predictable outcomes to situations. It's not formula-driven as such, but winning new business needs to follow a structure or methodology to deliver sustainable success over a long period.

Planning for implementation and resource commitment

Getting a deal over the line and converted to an order generally results in a chain reaction from your company as your colleagues gear up to implement the solution and hence deliver the benefits that resolve your prospect's initial problem areas. This involves resource planning and is why your forecasting is so important, as I outline in Chapter 21.

You can turn resource planning to your advantage in seeking to close the deal by sharing the issues with your prospect, which should help get him involved with the solution before the deal is signed and therefore make it easier to get to the final close. Share with your prospect the resource planning that's taking place in your company, and remember that his company also needs to supply resources. Discuss where the resources are coming from, when they'll be ready to go at each stage, and any knock-on effects that you'll have to mitigate against.

Getting your prospect engaged in the solution changes the language of the solution from "your proposal" to "our project." Doing it as part of the lead-up to the deal being signed off makes sense from a planning perspective, but that is only part of the reason for doing so. The main driver is to get your prospect involved and committed, which will make getting the final yes so much easier.

Getting a letter of intent or an order in principal can help with locking in your prospect to your solution and can be a good interim step if you're not able to secure a final order. Although not binding, a letter of intent is exactly that — an indication that you'll be given the order at a certain point in time on successful completion of set milestones, which should be given in as much detail as possible. When these milestones are met, the order becomes final and binding. A letter of intent can be especially useful when dealing with bureaucratic organizations that have prescribed ways of doing things and place orders, for example, only once a month. A letter of intent also serves as notice that your solution is formally the preferred one and that any remaining competition has been eliminated. Figure 13-1 shows the structure of a letter of intent.

Dear [Name of Recipient],

[Short introduction paragraph — indicate you are submitting this letter with the intent to do a specific action (purchase, partner, acquire, license, and so on). Indicate that the intent is based on the following conditions.]

[Define the specifics about the item behind the intent, listing all pertinent variations of the item or supporting material. Provide indication or your intent with respects to the liabilities.]

[Considerations — propose what you are willing to provide as compensation or other as consideration for the specifics listed previously. Be sure to define amounts, timing.]

[Provide conditions for the transaction. This may include conditions on due diligence, limitations on further seeking other interested parties, or confidentiality.]

[Indicate that this letter is not an official offer and that all details would need to be negotiated and executed through a formal purchase (or other) agreement.]

[Indicate your expected timing for the transaction to take place assuming you were selected.]

Sincerely,

[Name]

[Position]

FIGURE 13-1:
A letter of intent can help you ask for the order.

WARNING

A letter of intent is not legally binding, but it significantly increases the likelihood of a deal being done in the near future and can be a useful tool in getting over the line as well as planning resource commitments. Be aware, however, that getting a letter of intent signed can take as much effort as getting the deal closed, so use it with care. If you have the option, always go straight for the full order, but bear in mind the letter of intent approach and have it as a tool in your new business kit.

Cutting to the chase

So much noise can surround the closing of a deal, and most of it isn't really all that relevant. Keep your focus on the details, and don't let peripheral issues side-track you.

Taking a consultative approach to the sale all along puts you in a strong position to call it as it is. You'll have been, and have been seen to be, more concerned about meeting your prospect's needs than getting a sale. A natural progression is to continue in this vein and tell your prospect that the solution is the right one and that all the elements are now in place and it's time to sort out the order. Push back if you get any resistance, and call it as it is.

Having received a buying decision from your prospect but not quite an order from him, you can keep on the front foot and get the order paperwork completed while the moment is right. Don't delay or agree to do this offline; get it done while you're sitting in front of him and the yes decision is still firmly in his mind, because delay can lose the moment and the decision if you're not careful.

REMEMBER

A presumptive close is in order when you've run a consultative sales cycle. With this type of close, you don't have to fear rejection because you've always had your prospect's best interest in mind, and now is no different. Why should he suddenly switch tack and reject your solution? He still has to have his original problem addressed, and your stance should be one of moving things forward. The right deal is on the table, it meets the original need, the sales and buying cycles have run their course, so the next step is to ask whether your prospect is happy, shake hands to confirm the deal, and get on to the paperwork. Don't make a huge thing of it; your mindset should be as though prospects buy your solutions every day and, having got the correct deal in place, it's natural to close it and get on with the implementation phase.

Avoiding the order-for-discount game

Getting a deal signed off now in exchange for a discount is something that all new business salespeople have to face all too often. Affordability has already been qualified so you know that in absolute terms the solution price is right. And if the procurement department isn't involved (as I describe later in this chapter), then you don't have its games to contend with. That just leaves your primary prospect trying to score some last-minute points. With this type of request, my standing answer is always to ask which part of the solution he no longer requires and how he's going to cover it.

TIP

Don't feel the need to elaborate on this question or to defend it. Keep silent, and let him see that it's a serious question in response to his own and let him squirm for a while before he retracts it.

Of course, he may not retract it and in fact be really fishing for a discount late in the game. In this case, consider the facts:

>> Affordability has been qualified.

>> The price has been known for some time.

>> You can demonstrate both of these facts with your contact reports.

>> Yours is the solution of choice.

>> Value has been consistently demonstrated through the sales cycle.

>> How else is he going to address the initial problem?

You'll see that you have all the cards stacked in your favor, so you don't need to go rushing around trying to arrange a discount. In fact, you don't even need to try; just say no to the request, politely but firmly. If the issue doesn't go away, check what you have missed in qualification and postpone the close for another day. Don't allow yourself to be put on the spot for a decision right then, even if pen is poised over contract. (Chapter 11 has more information on structuring the deal.)

Working with Professional Buyers

Professional buyers, or procurement departments, are the bane of many new business salespeople's lives, and the majority of salespeople would be happy if they never had to deal with buyers again. The reality is that, depending on the nature of your solutions and your prospect base, you'll likely have to deal with them at some point. Some new business salespeople have to get every deal past them, so be thankful if you're not in that category.

First, you have to understand the role of the professional buyer. Procurement departments exist as a service within mainly large companies and aim to secure the best possible commercial terms for their internal clients. They're often seen as an obstacle even within their own organizations, but they have a significant amount of power and, as far as new business salespeople are concerned, need to be addressed head on. There's nothing to be gained in trying to circumvent them in a deal.

WARNING

Procurements will actively try to get the best deal for their internal customer — your prospect — and will more than likely be driven by one single element: price. The value proposition that you've worked so hard to build up with your prospect will be ignored as irrelevant. They'll want you to reduce the price — that's the bottom line. Unfortunately, they can wreck a deal at worst and at best delay it considerably.

In dealing with procurements, you need to recognize that they have a valid role to play but so do you. You need to find a way to work with them and not against them; the following sections can help.

Engaging professional buyers early on

As part of your qualification, you understand that procurement departments have a role to play in the deal and that they're therefore part of the decision-making unit. With that knowledge, you need to engage with them as part of covering the bases and not just wait for them to pop up at the end and try to change your terms. Bring them on board as part of the discussions you have with your prospect; invite them to attend meetings to enable them to understand the nature of the problem and proposed solution, and to give any input that they consider necessary. This will enable them to feel like they're adding value and protecting their internal client's interests and thereby have a sense of control over the buying process.

You may be able to help procurements position themselves as internal consultants on the deal to advise your prospect. Feed procurements case studies and solution- and industry-specific information and encourage them to play an active part in the decision-making unit. (Flip to Chapter 2 for details on case studies and other evidence.)

REMEMBER

By proactively engaging with procurements, you make them part of the team and part of the solution. This makes them less likely to cause you problems as you get into the details of the final deal and ensures that you have a positive and proactive relationship with them throughout the sales cycle. Put your relationship-building skills to good use.

When the deal structure time arrives and procurements take an active role, don't allow yourself to be bullied or have the initiative taken from you. Hold firm to your deal, and reject any attempt to sideline your value-added proposition. Keep returning the focus to the solution and how as a team you're all going to be involved in achieving it.

TIP

I've often been told that, in order to proceed, I'll need to take 20 percent off the prices, and my standard reply is always to ask which 20 percent of the solution they don't want to implement and how they'll fill the gap. I always say this with a serious face and a serious tone of voice, and it's always followed by silence. I will not, nor should any new business salesperson, allow myself be pushed around.

REMEMBER

If your pricing structure is fair and your solution is the one of choice, then you're in a strong position to rebuff any attempt at blanket game playing by procurements. In Chapter 10, I discuss how to walk away from a deal, and you do need to be prepared to do that when faced with a procurements blockage. If the deal is real and your qualification is accurate, your prospect will sort out some internal battles and come back to you.

Putting everything in writing

As I introduce in Chapter 3, contact reports are a valuable resource to have, and you should make a habit of writing them. Contact reports are also an important tool in dealing with procurement departments, because any dealings will result in a contact report that you'll routinely send both to them and to your prospect. This gives your prospect ammunition to fight your corner internally. Your contact reports should specifically cover any issues that procurements have raised along with your responses, regardless of how off topic you considered them to be. This is necessary as procurements will often try to trip you up with seemingly small issues that, if not dealt with, may cause delay further down the line. Cut off their ammunition supply by addressing and documenting everything as it arises.

REMEMBER

You need to maintain an image of professionalism at all times and not be distracted by anything thrown at you. If it becomes known that everything will be sent back in a contact report, then you may find that attitudes change quickly, so use this weapon in your new business sales armory. You can also use contact reports to build people up, so be aware of this when writing them for general meetings that also involve procurements. This minimizes the later impact that procurements can bring about to damage your deal.

Having everything confirmed in writing also provides you with the necessary ammunition should you find that the procurements become an unreasonably immovable object. Take a lesson from the old IBM sales book and go over their heads, suggesting that they're standing in the way of having the original requirement met and that the quantifiable cost of that happening is $x.

WARNING

Engagement and interaction are the preferred routes (as I explain in the preceding section) and going over their heads is a sales solution of the last resort, but you do need to be prepared to act on it. Although doing so won't win you any friends in procurements, it will demonstrate to everyone that you're a professional who isn't prepared to be messed about with.

Involving the end user at each stage

When you're dealing with professional buyers, the end user is your prospect, the linchpin in the decision-making unit and ultimately the person who has responsibility for the problems that you're attempting to resolve. The end user is your internal champion, buying in to your solution, understanding the benefits, and doing all that he can to get it signed off quickly.

You need to involve your prospect in all interactions that you have with the procurement department and be able to support him with any information that he needs to progress the deal internally. Don't assume that he understands all elements of the solution; provide him with anything and everything that he needs, spoon-feeding sound bites as necessary.

If your solution is technology based, for example, procurements may not realize the impact of a relational database over a flat file structure, so don't assume that they will accept what you say if it had a higher price point. Spell out the requirement to them, and explain and document why there is a higher price element that's required to make the solution work. Be seen as the expert but also as someone who cares about getting the correct solution for the end user.

TIP

On some occasions, your prospect will act as a buffer between you and procurement. Although this isn't ideal (because you should be leading the way), it's important to keep your prospect on message. For example, make sure that he knows about the importance of a relational database over a flat file structure and why it has a higher price point. Ensure that your prospect understands your solution and how it will fit with his needs, and ensure that he is able to articulate that message. Write him a script to remember if necessary.

Sticking to the original objectives

Dealing with procurement departments is really no different to the rest of your sales cycle. They have the power to try to dictate or amend terms but only if you allow them to have permission. In all other respects, they're a normal member of a decision-making unit, and as such you should cover them during the qualification process and learn then of any potential pitfalls that may await you. You should, of course, document everything in contact reports so they don't try to spring something on you late in the day.

You need to understand the procurement department's motivation and processes, and it also need to understand yours. This company is likely not the first one you've ever sold to, and when all the branding is stripped away, it's no different from any other business and you therefore instinctively know how to sell to it.

REMEMBER

Stick to and revisit the original deal objectives as often as necessary. What is the company setting out to achieve with your solution, and how is your solution going to meet these needs? These are the only issues up for debate, so don't allow procurements to attempt to introduce any new elements into the deal. If the original solution didn't specify pricing parameters, then make sure that you cover price as part of qualifying; and if this was satisfactorily dealt with, don't allow procurements to reopen it now. Refer to the contact reports to demonstrate that this has been addressed.

REMEMBER

Establishing a relationship with procurements (in exactly the same way as with every other member of the decision-making unit) as early in the sales cycle as possible is key to heading off any last-minute rebellions. Give every opportunity for objections to be raised as you progress through the sales cycle, meeting and heading them off as appropriate, and then document them and move on.

Chapter **14**

Understanding That "Selling Hard" Isn't the Answer

O ld-school selling was about closing the deal, and companies — especially in consumer sales — employed specialist closers to get deals over the line. I remember being on the receiving end of this a few times, and it didn't make buying a pleasant experience. I'm thankful that old-school selling is a thing of the past and certainly has no room in business-to-business sales.

Hard selling or pressure selling appealed to buyers' insecurity or vanity to justify making a quick buying decision that wasn't necessarily in their best interest, with the sole purpose being to enable the salesperson to secure a sale. You need to avoid this or even the perception of it if you are to succeed in business-to-business sales and establish a solid reputation as a good person to do business with. Otherwise, it will harm your career.

Today's buyers are much more sophisticated than they've ever been and empowered with information at their fingertips on your solution and your competitors. Internet-savvy and results-focused prospects have led to the need for new business salespeople to take a much more professional approach and build sales relationships with prospects, as you find out in this chapter.

In some cases, playing the hard-line sales game may progress the odd sale, but you can be sure that it won't help you in the long run, and your sales reputation will suffer as word spreads among target companies and prospects that they should avoid dealing with you. You can also be sure that any short-term gain you manage to achieve does you nothing but harm in the long term.

Recognizing That People Prefer to Be Buyers

The world has many more buyers, and therefore prospects, than it does sales-people. Although selling is a traditional profession that brings lots of accolades to people doing that job, the majority of people still prefer to be buying a solution rather than selling one, and that also applies to salespeople themselves. Person-ally, I really enjoy running a sales cycle, and I love being in front of prospects with my solution. But however much I like that, I still prefer the experience of buying something, even though I don't much enjoy being sold to.

Your prospects will likely fall into this same category of enjoying buying but not enjoying being sold to. Bear this in mind when you're running a sales cycle and especially when engaged at touch points with your prospects. (A *touch point* is any occasion when you have contact with your prospect and can occur face to face, via email, or via phone call.)

Buyers and sellers do actually have the same need when they come together in that they seek a solution to a problem. Although the two face different pressures resulting from their own side of the process, the basic need remains. And to bring the sale to a satisfactory solution, they need to work together.

The Internet has changed selling forever. Before Internet buying came into play, the only real way that a prospect could find any meaningful information about a solution or about how to address his needs was to speak to a salesperson. This put the salesperson at a real advantage because he had the knowledge and the answers to those questions. Fast-forward to today, and asking a salesperson about a solu-tion is just about the last thing a prospect will do. First, he looks at your website, reviews, and competing solutions before you even have him on your prospecting radar. So if information is power, then the power has shifted to buyers, and they're much more knowledgeable. The sales role has shifted from providing information to really being about understanding needs and fulfilling them with tailored solutions.

In the following sections, I describe a few methods that will help your prospects enjoy buying — especially from you.

TIP

I like to tell prospects that I've never sold anything to anyone in my life but that I'm fortunate in that sometimes people will buy from me. It started as a throw-away line to take away any perception of pressure of closing a deal, but I quickly realized that it was mainly true. I find that it's a mindset. Yes, I want the deal as much as anyone else, but I don't want it at any price. If the time is not right now for the prospect, I want to leave the door open for him to return in the future.

Creating a pleasant buying experience

Why wouldn't you want to make buying from you a pleasant experience for your prospects? If your approach is anything but this, then you may need to consider whether you're in the right job.

Prospects demand higher levels of service than ever and want to deal with some-one who they trust to deliver the solution and who takes the time to understand their unique (to them) needs. Today's prospects are also going to give you refer-rals to future business and provide case and reference studies for you, so it's in your interest to make the buying experience as pain-free and helpful as you can. This does not, however, mean rolling over and submitting to every whim.

Be human and engage with your prospects, but do so genuinely. If you ask ques-tions, then ask them sincerely and actually listen to the answers. Avoid clichés like "How are you today?" You're not looking to build a friendship or find a best buddy for fishing trips, so keep it professional (but nothing's wrong with adding a bit of human touch, either). You can take an interest in your prospect as a person and pick up on clues that may be visible, such as sports photos, but make sure that anything you comment on is done sincerely and not as a glib comment in passing. For some reason that I have never really figured out, a lot of my prospects are soc-cer fans and so I make a point of keeping up-to-date with headline soccer news so I can have a real conversation about it should the need arise.

You also need to care about, and be seen to care about, the issues that individual prospects seek to address with your solution. You may have seen these issues hun-dreds of times and already know what they're going to say, but let them tell you the problems, listen carefully, and engage with a positive answer that's tailored to each individual prospect's needs and not some off-pat response that you always say at this stage. For example, I was once involved in selling campaign tracking software solutions and could almost guarantee that I knew what questions would arise and in what order, because I had heard them so many times. Every time I was in front of a prospect, though, the questions were treated with respect and answered with explanations as if the prospect were the first ever to ask.

TIP

The process of managing expectations is an important one in new business sales, and you should use it, among other things, to make the buying process pleasant so your prospects always know where you are and what you've achieved (because you tell them). Use contact reports (as I introduce in Chapter 3) as a tool to assist you here.

Fostering long-term buying opportunities

Not all sales cycles conclude as quickly as you'd like them to, even when there seems to be little reason why your prospect can't move ahead. Other sales cycles are, by their very nature, always elongated, especially in high-value capital goods or services such as buildings or other infrastructure projects with multimillion-dollar price tags.

REMEMBER

When conducting longer-term sales cycles, be patient, especially when you can't see the reason for slower-than-expected progress. As long as you're covering the bases and qualifying continually (see Chapter 19 for details), you're in the right place. You need to gain an understanding of the buying cycle from your prospect's perspective, which will give you the required insight.

In longer-term sales cycles, the relationship always comes before the sale, and how you conduct it will help you get over the finish line in first place. As I was writing this chapter, I received an email from a potential supplier. I'm the prospect in this instance for a business-to-business tool that will assist in the daily operation of my business. We had some discussions several weeks ago, and then both the salesperson and I were away so we scheduled a touch point for this week, which she duly confirmed in an email as her type of contact report, along with the decisions we had already agreed on. For reasons that she likely won't feel especially relevant for a delay, I don't plan to move forward into a sale just yet, although the qualification shows that I'm ready. I'm actually going to be traveling over the next few weeks and want to wait until I return because I'm on the critical path for the implementation, or so I believe.

She'll get the sale because the solution fits, although other solutions could also do the job, but she built a relationship with me, and I'm confident that she'll ensure that our implementation succeeds. The only way she can lose the sale now is if she makes a mess of the longer-than-expected sales cycle.

You likely won't be able to do much to speed up the buying cycle if you feel a mismatch with your sales cycle. For example, the email I received today offered a 10 percent discount for a close this month. Although a discount would be welcome, this is a strategic purchase that isn't driven by cost.

Building your reputation for buyers

Your reputation as a new business salesperson goes before you and is something that you need to build on and protect. In addition to making prospects like and want to deal with you, your reputation opens the door to many new opportunities as you're more likely to get good, solid referrals. Prospects will begin to seek you out and ask to deal with you.

TIP

Among the ways to build a reputation with people yet to interact with you are to use social media and speaking opportunities, and you can find many great books and articles on these topics. To provide a quick overview, you can enhance your social media reputation building by

>> Writing articles and posting them on LinkedIn and Twitter

>> Posting value-added comments on existing posts on LinkedIn and Twitter

>> Engaging in discussions on both those platforms and on Facebook business pages

Post on a regular basis, and you'll both build up followers and enhance your reputation. (For more information, have a look at *LinkedIn For Dummies,* 4th Edition, by Joel Elad and *Social Media Marketing For Dummies,* 3rd Edition, by Shiv Singh and Stephanie Diamond; both are published by Wiley.)

TIP

Getting involved in speaking opportunities with local business groups or chambers of commerce is often as easy as just asking because they're usually desperate for good speakers. Breakfast meetings are another good opportunity to both build your reputation and practice speaking because they often include a roundtable 60-second slot as well as a main speaker at each meeting. These are excellent opportunities both to talk about your product or solution and to position yourself as an expert in your field — someone audience members can remember the next time they have a requirement in that area.

REMEMBER

The bottom line in terms of reputation building is to have prospects seek you out as someone they want to deal with, which is exactly the effect that you want to create and couldn't be further away from the hard-selling environment. (And note that after you build a positive reputation, you need to maintain it; I explain how to do so later in this chapter.)

Knowing That People Buy People First

It may be an old adage, but it's still true: People buy people first before whatever they're selling. Build trust with your prospects, and you'll be surprised how far this takes you. Follow these tips and the ones in the following sections to become a person that others buy:

>> Focus on understanding and then meeting their needs and present your solution as aligned to those needs. If you just use active listening (see Chapter 2) when your prospects speak, you'll get all the clues you need.

>> Adopt a consultative selling approach (see Chapter 5) rather than pushing a product or service for its own sake. Position yourself as a sales consultant and make it known that your role is that of a problem solver. Concentrate your efforts and your attention on helping your prospects solve their problem and meet their needs. Do this, and sales success will follow.

>> Be enthusiastic about how your solution meets your prospects' objectives and solves their needs (see Chapter 3). Let your enthusiasm shine through and be infectious, but back it with solid business logic.

REMEMBER

Don't forget to ask for the order when you judge the time is right. It is said that two difficult problems occur in new business sales: saying no, which I cover in Chapter 12, and asking for the order, which I cover in Chapter 13. Align these skills along with covering all the bases, and your career in new business sales will go far, without ever going near a hard sell.

Enhancing your credibility

When you initially meet a new prospect, chances are that he won't know a lot about you, but if he's on the ball, he'll have done some background checking. One of your first jobs subconsciously is to enhance your credibility in your prospect's eyes so that he sees you as a partner who can help achieve his objectives and not some sales guy who wants to take the money and run.

TIP

Enhance your credibility as you win new business by doing the following:

>> **Listen more than you talk.** Practice active listening as I cover in Chapter 2, and be sure to use your mouth and ears in proportion — two ears and one mouth should be a clue! Don't attempt to sell to prospects, especially in the early touch points. Take the time to listen and understand what they're trying to achieve, and then in a consultative manner you can guide them to your solution as the best fit.

- » **Observe body language.** What prospects do is often as important as what they say. If you see that you're losing your prospect's attention — perhaps he's looking around and not focusing on you — then stop talking. Use the power of silence to refocus his attention. If the words you're hearing aren't consistent with the body language you're observing, then challenge and requalify his real need. If the need is genuine and the prospect has the authority, then he should be engaging with you; if you aren't getting this engagement, ask whether this is a good time and suggest rescheduling when he can give you the necessary attention. If you're seen as being focused and professional, then your prospect should reflect that.

- » **When you ask questions, make them open ended to give an opportunity for your prospects to tell you what you need to know.** Try to avoid questions that can result in yes or no answers and get them to elaborate on key points. Ask questions such as "How does this . . .?", "What do you think about this . . .?", and "Why do you think that this . . .?" — questions that are intended to encourage your prospect to open up to you and engage in a meaningful conversation that will help you with both qualification and moving the sales cycle forward.

Maintaining your reputation

After you've enhanced your credibility as being seen as a partner in a consultative approach to the prospect's problem, you need to begin to deliver to maintain your reputation. Stay in contact between touch points. And be sure you do as you say you will and document it in contact reports.

TIP

When you don't win a sale or when the sales opportunity goes away for circumstances beyond your control, you maintain your reputation and credibility with the way that you handle these types of situations. If you implement these golden rules, you'll live to fight another day:

- » **Stay in touch.** Staying in touch doesn't mean pestering or phoning frequently to see whether your prospect has changed his mind; instead, schedule quarterly emails or brief messages just to let your prospect know that you're still available if needed. A good way of doing this in a positive and nonobtrusive manner is to send news or information snippets that are relevant to your prospect's situation and maybe ask questions like "Does this have an impact on you?" or "How are you solving this issue?"

>> **Thank the prospect for the opportunity.** Thanking someone for the opportunity is just as it sounds. When a sales cycle ends without a deal being struck, send a thank-you note saying that you appreciate being given the opportunity to discuss a potential solution and wish him every success with whichever path he selects, even if it's with a competitor. You want to be seen as a good guy and one who your prospect can return to if the first choice goes wrong, so never burn bridges. You may, of course, encounter him later in another role or another company, and this will give you a head start.

>> **Walk away professionally.** Walking away professionally involves accepting defeat gracefully and not sniping at either your prospect or his chosen path. Shake hands if in person, or if email, give a "best wishes" note, and don't attempt to interfere with his selected solution. See Chapter 20 for more information on walking away.

Ensuring That You Don't Force a Solution

At times, a solution may look like a good fit for your prospect in the early stages, but after a more detailed investigation, you discover that it's not really right for him. What should you do? Acknowledge the situation, and if the solution isn't right or isn't going to deliver the required results, then walk away without trying to force something onto your prospect that's setting him up to fail.

TIP

Here are some guidelines for gracefully dealing with this situation:

>> Don't attempt to oversell your solution. Make your pitch, position your solution relative to the problem it's addressing, handle objections (see Chapter 10 for details), and answer questions. Don't embellish the capabilities of the solution, and don't force something that you know isn't going to serve its purpose.

>> Avoid being seen as desperate to make a sale because that will not only be obvious to your prospect but also sound alarm bells with him, which won't do you any favors.

>> Don't tell lies. This may sound obvious, but it does happen. Don't fall into this trap and expect to escape with any credibility left.

>> If your solution isn't quite right, consider whether you can tailor it for your prospect's needs. Or determine whether the terms of reference on the problem you're addressing can shift slightly without compromising the chances of a successful implementation. If so, then great; continue with the sales cycle. But if not, then don't attempt to force a square peg into a round hole because it will break at some point.

REMEMBER

One of my early mentors was a man called Ken Olsen. Ken is known to many people as the founder of Digital Equipment Corporation; he's one of my all-time heroes, and I've tried to build my business by following his mantra of "Do the right thing." This doesn't mean always say yes to your customers and prospects; it means considering all the angles and taking the correct course of action even if it appears to harm your short-term opportunities. Even if you lose a sale, if you do the right thing, then you'll have won.

Chapter **15**

Taking Action Today

Taking action today is one of the most important mindsets that a new business salesperson can have, because only by taking action can you reach your goals and hit your targets. The *today* part is especially important because you have to start sometime, or nothing will ever happen. Sales can be a lonely place, but it can also be the most rewarding of places. Because a lot of the time you're plowing a lonely furrow, you can easily hide and keep your head down, but you need to avoid falling into this syndrome.

Today is the best time to start taking action to put yourself in control; nobody is going to do it for you, and in new business sales, you need to, and be seen to, lead from the front. In this chapter, you find out the importance of setting goals, build-ing momentum, and having a structured plan as you take action every day.

REMEMBER

Your mantra needs to be "don't do tomorrow what you should do today." Or to use a sporting analogy: You've got to want the ball, demand the ball, and, when you get it, use the ball to maximum advantage. Lead the line.

Recognizing the Power of Taking Action and Setting Goals

New business sales is perhaps the only role within a company where you need to define for yourself how you're going to set about achieving your goals, and you have a real responsibility to deliver against those goals. Nobody else is going to do it for you; the buck stops with you.

You may not necessarily *like* taking action today, but you just have to do it until it becomes an instinct or second nature to you. If action is required, then why put it off if you're to be seen as a leader? Create a sense of urgency around everything that you do, both internally and in front of prospects, and this sense of urgency will become infectious. It gets things done and sets the ground rules that you're action oriented. After creating that sense of urgency, you need to maintain it and make it the norm for the way you operate; you're a doer and an achiever.

In the following sections, I explain how action overcomes inertia and describe the importance of setting goals and having a peer or mentor review your goals.

REMEMBER

If you make only one change to the way you operate, then make it this one: Take action immediately — today — in everything that you do. This is one of the most important changes that you can make in your approach to winning new business.

Knowing that action overcomes inertia

In taking positive, decisive action today, you need to overcome the inertia that may be holding you back, and only you can make this change. You need to do so to provide the correct mindset for new business sales success. As you find out throughout this chapter, you can do a number of things to proactively make the change to being action oriented.

TIP

The first thing to do is to actually get moving, because physical action stimulates your brain to respond and follow. Get up from your desk or wherever you find yourself and get into a place where you can take action. If you're procrastinating about a phone call, for example, then pick up the phone and dial the number; don't think about it, just do it. This works for me every time when I'm delaying making a call. I just force myself to get on with it, and my action overcomes my inertia. Don't allow procrastination to rule you; use today's action to win the battle.

Sometimes the biggest changes come from the smallest beginnings. If you have 20 or 50 or 100 calls to make, just pick up the phone and make the first one. After that, continue with the next, and it becomes easier. Make it a habit, for example, to not have your first coffee of the day, or even to sit at your desk, until you've made the first five calls, and this will become a pattern quickly, giving you a victory over inertia.

REMEMBER

Understand that sometimes you'll have less motivation than at other times, so don't beat yourself up about it. It happens. Action and results drive motivation, so focus on the small victories until the bigger ones come along, but keep taking positive action to win new business.

You need energy to overcome inertia, and you need to supply energy in the new business sales role. Lead from the front, not letting inertia hold you back. Just get on and do what you need to do but in a deliberate and focused way, and inertia will soon be consigned to history. For example, I didn't want to write this particular subsection of the book at the moment and was trying to convince myself that I could do it later. Guess what? I just sat down at the keyboard and began typing; I let my actions overcome my inertia.

Improving your focus by setting and writing down goals

When I was in my early thirties, at the beginning of my move into a full winning new business role, I was told about the importance of goal setting and specifically about the importance of writing down your goals. To say that I rebelled would be an understatement. Of course, I knew better, or so I thought. Writing down goals was plain stupid and a total waste of time, which is what I told anyone who would listen. I had a sales mentor at the time who decided it would be a wise move to stay away from the subject when discussing new business planning with me. That was probably the right move for him from a self-preservation point of view but the wrong move when it came to helping me with winning new business. Single-handedly, this probably cost me two years of lack of correct focus, but it was only later that I had an aha moment and realized just how important both setting goals and writing them down really are.

REMEMBER

If, like me, you have some form of resistance to establishing, committing to, and writing down your new business goals, then please don't wait two years for your own aha moment to maybe arrive — just do it (to borrow a phrase). Genuinely, this is one of the real cornerstones to success in winning new business. Laser-sharp focus is a natural follow-on and an essential part of your winning new business tool kit, but without a committed, directed, written set of goals to train that focus, you're seriously weakening your sales arsenal.

TECHNICAL STUFF

So why is goal setting so important? You can find a ton of academic research on this, but it all boils down to training your brain to focus on what really matters, and having written goals sets off a series of subliminal actions. It's not a new concept; it's a tried and tested element to successfully achieving a set of goals. Napoleon Hill was one of the early authors to expound this theory, and I recommend reading his master class *Think and Grow Rich*. Although it was written in 1937, it'd take a braver man than me to dismiss its relevance in winning new business today.

Goal setting is vital, but it also comes with a word of warning that I pick up on elsewhere in this book; don't spend all your time setting and revising goals. Do it once and review it according to a regular schedule that you define — and then get on with the job of winning new business. Don't overplan or hide behind revising the plan as an excuse for inaction. Don't be someone who's so busy being busy that you don't have time to be busy — that doesn't allow you time for the tasks and actions that deliver success.

So what type of goals should you set, and how should you do it? The following sections explain.

An example of setting headline goals and filling the pipeline

Headline goals are the top-level goals that you need to hit in order to deliver the sales performance that's expected of you. In defining your headline goals, think of the big picture, not the underlying details. Here are some examples of headline goals:

>> $500,000 new business revenue this year

>> 20 new business wins this year

>> Increased profitability of new business projects by 15%

You then need to break these headline goals into stages that form part of your routine action and activity planning; you may choose to do so by quarters. So, for example:

>> $125,000 new business revenue by the end of Q1

- $30,000 in Month 1

- $40,000 in Month 2

- $55,000 in Month 3

>> 5 new business wins by the end of Q1

- 1 new business win worth $30,000 in Month 1

- 1 new business win worth $15,000 in Month 2

- 1 new business win worth $25,000 in Month 2

- 1 new business win worth $30,000 in Month 3

- 1 new business win worth $25,000 in Month 3

Regardless of your average project value and monthly revenue targets, your goals need to include enough pipeline-filling activity to ensure that you have enough qualified prospects at each stage of the sales cycle to give you the best opportunity of achieving each monthly goal (see Chapters 9 and 19 for more on prospecting and qualifying). Your initial focus each month needs to be at the IDMC, SDMC, MCPQ, and RPBT levels, with all your actions focused on hitting these goals, which will in turn lead to the achievement of the revenue goals (flip to Chapter 22 for details on these metrics; I also discuss them in the later sidebar "Qualification terminology for goal setting"). So, for example, each month may have these types of goals:

>> 20 initial decision maker contacts (IDMC)

>> All outstanding contacts moved to at least subsequent decision maker contact (SDMC)

>> 10 prospects moved to MCPQ (qualification key stage three)

>> 10 prospects moved to RPBT (qualification key stage four)

You can, of course, split each of the preceding stages to show how you're going to, for example, deliver 20 IDMCs during the month, but I suggest that you don't set your goals at such a micro level to avoid the potential of spending all day planning and having no time left for actually taking the necessary actions. You need to apply a measure of common sense here. Goal setting is an aid to achieving your objectives, not an objective in itself.

Customizing and reviewing your goals

Your unique situation will lend itself to a specific set of goals that are necessary to meet your winning new business objectives. The example in the preceding section serves as a good starting point, but you need to make your goals just that — *your goals* — rather than simply following a prescribed procedure. So split your objectives into time-related parts, and define the goals that you need to achieve along with the necessary tasks at a macro level that you need to deliver against. These then become *your* goals.

Writing down each of your custom goals reinforces its importance. These goals become a contract with yourself; you know you'll deliver on them, and they're not optional to be done if and when you feel like it. You need to focus each working day and each working hour on the steps you need to take right now to achieve those written goals. If you don't write them down and keep them in full view in your workspace, then you're giving yourself a built-in excuse to not deliver against them. As you see elsewhere in this book, technology can help when it comes to tracking goals and progress, but nothing takes away the importance or responsibility on you to take the necessary actions to deliver against your written, committed, contracted goals.

QUALIFICATION TERMINOLOGY FOR GOAL SETTING

Depending on the sales methodology you use, you should be tracking a number of key milestones to ensure that your prospect pipeline has sufficient leads at each of the stages and that you keep filling up the front end. The TLG (Targeted Lead Generation) methodology that I developed almost 20 years ago tracks four key stages, which I refer to in this chapter and also in Chapter 22.

Along with demographics, which aren't measured in the same way, the following are the key qualification metrics that you need to measure, along with any company-specific ones that you need to add for yourself. Setting goals for the number of prospects at each of these stages and how quickly you can move prospects along within them is key to successfully taking action today toward meeting them.

- **IDMC:** This basic but very important metric ensures that the early pipeline stages are stacked as they should be. IDMC stands for initial decision maker contact and refers to the first time that you actually have an interaction with the identified decision maker in your target prospect's organization. At this point, you're not tracking contacts elsewhere in the organization, who may be further down the food chain, but only at the decision maker level. You likely won't achieve IDMC before you've had several other, lower-level contacts within the target organization. The TLG metrics don't track these early contacts because they're not considered key milestones.

- **SDMC:** This metric helps measure progress within the sales cycle by tracking when and how often subsequent decision maker contacts (SDMC) occur. Only with subsequent contacts do you begin to establish a relationship with your prospect, so they're an important metric to have as a goal and to be able to track.

- **MCPQ:** The original meaning of MCPQ was meeting, confirmation, proposal, and qualified, but this developed over a few versions of the methodology to become the measurement of whether a sales cycle had moved forward in terms of qualification. The basis of MCPQ now is tracking when and how the qualification has made a step forward. In Chapter 22, I refer to this as qualification stage 3.

- **RPBT:** This metric tracks and measures how and when four of the key qualification stages are reached. (In Chapter 22, I refer to RPBT as qualification stage 4.)

  Identify the *role* in the decision-making unit of your key prospect and ensure that his role carries sufficient authority to be able to drive the purchase internally.

  Identify the *project* that's being discussed and ensure that it's a real, live one, and discover the needs that the proposed solution will have to address.

Identify the *budget* for the project and ensure that it's in line with both the prospect expectations of a solution as well as being of sufficient size to justify the amount of resources that you'll need to commit to the sales cycle.

Identify the *timescale* for both a buying decision to be made and for the implementation schedule and ensure that these are reasonable and achievable in terms of your solution. Understanding the timescale can be a major factor in determining when you commit to really driving the sales cycle as opposed to just keeping in touch until the time is right.

TIP

Review your goals on a regular basis to make sure you're delivering on them, and then also have a peer or mentor review them (as I examine in the next section). While you should review and revisit your goals at least monthly, be wary of changing current-year goals to reflect changes in circumstances. If you have committed to a set of numbers, then it's your responsibility to deliver them, regardless of circumstances.

Considering a peer or mentor review

Having goals to achieve is a significant factor in driving you to take action today, but they're more effective when you share them with a peer or mentor review. Knowing that you need to report back on progress toward hitting your goals prevents you from backsliding on them. For example, changing the due date on a goal is all too easy if you don't feel like committing the time to it today and have no one to keep you accountable. Of course, doing this is cheating only yourself.

On the other hand, if you have to discuss progress on your goals with a peer or mentor on a regular basis, then you'll likely think twice before just changing a date or skipping some action because you don't feel like doing it. Be accountable in your review and see it as a positive force to keep you on track. Try to make sure that you have a review weekly, and remember that it doesn't need to be formal or time-consuming; in fact, it shouldn't be time-consuming at all if you work it into your normal daily routine.

TIP

There's no point in reviewing your goals with your boss or someone further up the management chain for the simple reason that as a new business salesperson, you know how to package a message in the way that they want to hear it. Having an informal support network, such as sales colleagues, is far more effective, and it doesn't necessarily need to be in the same company — they don't need to understand the details, just be able to ask you how many "x" you've hit each week. Being honest and knowing that this question is coming and that you'll have to justify missing the goal is usually enough to keep you focused on hitting the goals. It works for me. Give it a try for yourself and find the power of the peer or mentor review.

Building Momentum Every Day

In new business sales, momentum is everything. Building and sustaining a sense of momentum is one of the key differentiators that separate the top new business salespeople from the also-rans.

Taking action by making an immediate start each day, with no room for procrastinating, sets the right tone. As you arrive at your desk, you need to already know your action plan and just get on with it. Maintain your focus on the task at hand, and don't attempt to spread yourself too thinly by taking on peripheral tasks. Concentrate your effort on building, maintaining, and qualifying your pipeline, and the momentum will build.

REMEMBER

Two key metrics to watch with regard to momentum, to ensure that your focus is correct and leading you in the right direction, are

>> **Volume of leads at each pipeline stage:** The volume of leads that both enter and progress through each stage of your pipeline shows you the overall picture of the health of your new business funnel. Understanding these numbers and the ratios as prospects progress through the sales cycle is important. Make sure that you invest sufficient time to managing your pipeline and have systems in place to track this metric. Any loss of momentum here can have a serious domino effect as time progresses.

>> **Conversion ratios:** You need to track and understand the ratios of sales progressing through each sales cycle stage and to be able to accurately predict the number of new IDMC hits that you need to achieve the required sales volume. Resources also play a part here, so it's not just a simple case of feeding more leads into the sales funnel to generate more revenue at the other end, and you need to understand the impact of any changes planned to the ratios.

In Chapter 22, I discuss these metrics and their place in the role of winning new business, but as far as momentum is concerned, you need to be aware of them and be able to track your activity in relation to them. The following sections describe the importance of building momentum and explain how qualifying and planning help.

Seeing that success leads to more success

One of the reasons for building sales momentum is that success really does lead to more success. Lecturing about systems and processes and expecting people to take it on board is all well and good. They may remember 50 percent of the information and act on half of that. By rolling up your sleeves and getting on with the job rather than just talking about it, you make all the necessary difference to results; early success is quickly followed by further success, and the pattern repeats, all because you build and sustain momentum. It really is that important in winning new business.

When I begin a new client project, I always tell the client that my role is to help him build and maintain momentum and to do all that I can to ensure early sales success, which will lead to a step change in his approach to winning new business.

Subconscious programming of the mind is one of the reasons behind this reality, and you can read about it as much as you like, but only by doing and implementing it can you realize the power behind it.

When discussing momentum, the first thing that generally comes to mind is that it's a positive thing; momentum drives you forward and toward your goals. You need to be aware, however, that negative momentum prevents you from achieving success just as effectively.

Negative momentum is a dangerous trap that a new business salesperson can easily fall into. You decide to take a day off making calls because you don't feel like it. A day turns into two days, and two days turns into a week. You can't get that time back or reverse those decisions, however hard you try to convince yourself otherwise. This always has an impact further down the line as new opportunities that you've missed out on are no longer in your pipeline and you struggle to hit your metrics and ultimately your sales numbers.

Some years ago, a respected psychologist proposed a three-step model for changing momentum in individuals, and it's relevant today in new business sales:

>> A form of disruption or unfreezing of mindset is needed.

>> Change takes place as a result of the disruption.

>> Refreezing of the new state takes place.

This may sound a little dramatic, but if you think about it for a few minutes, you'll see the logic as applied to new business sales. The disruption required can be your wake-up call to change perhaps a realization that you've fallen into a negative momentum spiral.

Momentum, positive or negative, by its very nature takes a little time to produce an impact, but when you decide to really hit the ground running and make those calls today, tomorrow, and every day, you'll find that real and sustainable sales results follow. Your pipeline fills, your deals stack up, and you achieve your numbers.

Another way that success leads to success is through association. This is among the reasons sales conferences generally lead to an upturn in sales results. Take a group of new business salespeople and expose them to high energy, positive energy, and people, and they have newfound motivation to succeed. Surround yourself with positive, can-do achievers, and avoid associating with negative influences, and then measure the results after six months. It may surprise you.

Always be qualifying

Old-school sales training taught people to always be closing, and to an extent, this remains valid for some consumer sales, such as the more irrational or left-brain purchases like clothing, cars, and maybe even real estate. It has no valid role in business-to-business sales, however, where today's buyers are sophisticated and market savvy. A much more realistic approach in business-to-business sales is to always be *qualifying.*

Qualifying is a continual state done throughout a sales cycle, not just once at the beginning. You have to accept that prospects change their minds sometimes, that needs change, that new internal and external influences come to bear, and that priorities change. Just because you qualified last week doesn't mean that qualification will still be valid tomorrow, so make sure that you keep on top of events.

I'd go so far as to say that qualifying is the single most important part of a new business salesperson's job. I rate it as being more important than prospecting, presenting, handling objections, and structuring the deal, all of which are vital components in the new business salesperson's role, but qualifying is right at the top of the pile. By continually qualifying, you continue to build momentum in your sales cycles as you're always forward thinking and always looking for the next reason to move quickly.

The bottom line with the importance of prospecting is that you need to keep your pipeline full and to understand how your prospects are developing. If you never take your eye off the ball, changing events won't catch you by surprise. Qualifying is one of the best practice principles of winning new business. Flip to Chapters 9 and 19 for more about qualification.

Planning for tomorrow

In building and maintaining a sense of momentum, you need to make every minute of your working day count. So, for example, don't arrive at your desk in the morning and spend the first half-hour wondering what you should do. Being able to get your working day off to a fast start just takes a bit of organization and a lot of willpower to avoid the usual distractions, but achieving it can set you up for a winning start to the day, which can then propel you forward.

TIP

Consider the following ideas:

>> Make a habit of checking your schedule the previous night, and at the end of each working day, arrange your calls for the morning so that you really can hit the ground running.

>> Depending on your role and your sector, you may not be able to ignore early morning emails, but try to look for anything important while getting ready to leave home so that when you arrive at the office, you can get straight down to productive work and leave email catch-ups for later in the day.

Technology also has a role to play here in getting you organized. (I cover the role of technology in Chapter 4.) Consider how you can make some significant gains to time, especially first thing in the morning, by taking advantage of the help available to you with technology. Anything that makes the job of a new business salesperson easier to plan and execute has to be worth exploring.

Acting with a Structured Approach

You can achieve individual sales success easily enough with a haphazard approach, but it won't deliver sustained success over the long term. The only surefire way of delivering a consistent flow of profitable new business is to follow a structured process or methodology.

If you search the Internet for sales processes, you find many, often conflicting, systems, but the common theme is that a winning sales process needs to be repeatable and scalable. In my opinion, it doesn't matter in an absolute sense which process or methodology you follow, as long as you have and follow one that works for you.

Don't jump between methodologies, though; select the one that works best for you, and implement it, taking the time to understand the methodology and why it leads you down a particular path. Most methodologies teach you to keep the bases loaded — that is, have numbers of prospects at each stage of the sales cycle to keep the pipeline fueled.

The following sections go into more detail on having a structured, active approach to winning new business.

Avoiding headless chicken syndrome

The last thing you need to be doing is running around chasing every potential prospect that rears his head, regardless of qualification, in a desperate attempt to pull in some business. I've seen this happen too often, and without exception, it's a sign of a process that's either nonexistent or out of control.

Two things that help you take action here are planning and focus:

>> **Planning:** If you fail to plan, then, as the saying goes, you plan to fail. Look at any successful salesperson, and you'll see a definite pattern: He's organized, follows a system or methodology, and plans consistently. He may not realize that he's following a methodology because his actions and processes are second nature, but each sales cycle he runs is based on replicable processes, which is the very essence of a successful methodology.

>> **Focus:** Successful salespeople are driven in pursuit of a goal, and you can guarantee that they've written the goal down and review it frequently, allowing nothing to get in the way of achieving it. (I talk about setting and writing down goals earlier in this chapter.)

Giving yourself the best chance of success

Success in sales isn't by accident; it's the result of very deliberate focus and planning. Sales in the 21st century is a solid profession, and one that you should be proud to be engaged in. I am.

As in any profession or occupation, you need to give yourself the best chance of success by consistently learning and applying best practices. Don't accept second best. Nobody said that you have to play fair against competitors as long as you play ethically. Nothing is wrong with seeking to give yourself an unfair advantage by playing to your specific strengths. Don't be pushed into playing by someone else's rules; set the agenda for yourself. If your approach or solution lends itself to a particular approach, then load the dice in your favor and focus on this as the key attribute in the sale, and then get everyone else playing to your tune.

For example, if you discover that a competitor is focusing on a specific feature of a solution that you're perhaps not a leader in, then turn the attention to something else. Find a reason to draw the prospect's attention away from where you don't want it to be and onto where you do want it. Use a case study, for example, or use an industry statistic to reinforce your message today and to keep the discussion where you want it to be. Learn a lesson from politicians here; observe how they deflect questions back to areas that they want to discuss.

Using replicable processes

If winning new business sales has a single absolutely key attribute, it's making use of a replicable sales process or methodology that guides you through the prospecting and qualification steps in a coherent and consistent way, giving you a clear competitive advantage. Don't try to reinvent the wheel with every sales cycle; go with a tried and tested system that's designed for your situation.

REMEMBER

The clue to delivering sustainable new business sales performance is to work smart, not just hard. Of course, you should work hard to justify your position and salary, but working hard in the traditional sense of long hours of labor won't lead to sales success unless it's aligned to the way you work, too. Smart working is the key. Understand the nature of your prospects, solutions, and processes, and use your sales methodology to guide you as to where to make the effort.

REMEMBER

Take note of the following best practice principles, and apply them to your hard work to become a smarter worker:

>> **Qualifying:** Nothing comes even close to being as important as the role of qualifying potential new business. You don't have time to chase everything that moves, and you need to know where to invest your time for maximum return. By always qualifying your prospects, you get a much better understanding of how the sales cycle is developing and avoid any nasty surprises as the deal reaches its climax. (See Chapters 9 and 19 for more information.)

>> **Prospecting:** You need to invest significant time and resources into adding prospects to your pipeline. Dedicate time every day to work on this or risk running out of potential new business somewhere down the line. You can automate many of the prospecting tasks, but you still need to drive the process. (See Chapter 9 for details.)

>> **Building relationships:** Face time or telephone time with your prospects is of vital importance. This is where you handle objections and drive the sales cycle toward completion. (Find an introduction to making a good first impression in Chapter 3.)

>> **Structuring deals:** In business-to-business sales, no two deals are generally exactly the same, and you need to be able to understand the requirements of all members of the decision-making unit to structure a deal that delivers a win-win solution. (Check out Chapter 11 for the full scoop.)

>> **Being solution oriented:** This is as much a mindset as a physical attribute. You need to approach each sales cycle with an attitude of finding a solution to a need rather than looking for a quick order and moving on. Not many obstacles stand in the way of having a solution-oriented approach. (Flip to Chapter 5 for more information.)

I once had a new salesperson join my team who had been promoted internally from a more technical sales support role, and he had a penchant for working hard. He was in the office early and stayed until late most days, and he learned the ins and outs of the set of products that he was given responsibility for and got immersed in detail. His client-facing skills were nonexistent, but that would come with training and support. But he would just not take on board any feedback about how to focus on the things that mattered instead of drowning in detail at a product level. After months of coaching, he wasn't getting any better, and eventually we had to conclude that he wasn't cut out for a new business sales role.

Had he worked with a sales methodology and used replicable processes, like everyone else did, he could have been a success, but he "knew better" and was determined to do it his way. Sadly, his way was a one-way street out of a sales role.

4

Rainmaking: Developing a Constant Stream of New Business

Chapter **16**

Reaching a Win-Win Solution

I n Chapter 11, I introduce the importance of establishing a win-win as you structure a deal, and in this chapter I provide additional guidance. A win-win is the Holy Grail in sales negotiation, but it shouldn't be as hard to achieve as the Holy Grail has been to find.

Achieving a win-win solution requires both you and your prospect to have the right mindset as the discussions and deal progress. If you've achieved this from the beginning of the sales cycle, then you have a good chance of carrying it through to completion. If you both can keep all cards on the table throughout the sales cycle, you have a good chance of securing a win-win solution. Avoiding an adversarial sales cycle is usually in everyone's best interest, so if you and your prospect can keep this philosophy in mind, there is almost no limit to the benefits that you can gain.

WARNING

If one of you is seeking to beat the other, your chances of reaching a win-win are zero; you can't enter discussions with a selfish mindset, because this creates a negative buying experience for your prospect. In this case, you're unlikely to win a deal at all, let alone a win-win. Equally, you need to avoid any attempt by your prospect to take you to the cleaners — that is, winning every possible concession from you and leaving you wondering what happened.

Defining a Win-Win Solution and Its Benefits

You achieve a win-win solution when both parties — you and your prospect — consider that all the needs have been met with a little give and take but that neither of you have had to back down on any major points, dealing with any obstacles encountered along the way in a professional, solution-oriented manner. (Flip to Chapter 10 for more about overcoming objections.) You both have a good feeling about the solution and are happy to act as a reference for the other. No feelings of buyer's remorse exist, and the sales team feels no euphoria for having won a deal and scored some points in the process.

Simply stated, with a win-win solution, both you and your prospect have mutual gain; both of you have achieved your primary objectives without feeling that you had to make unreasonable or unnecessary sacrifices to get it.

The following sections explore the benefits of a win-win from two viewpoints: your company's and your customer's.

TIP

One way to look at a win-win solution is to consider slices of a cake: If you each have equal portions, then you've achieved a win-win. But if one party has more or wants more of the cake, then the solution is out of balance, and a win-win has not been achieved.

From your company's viewpoint

Your company will benefit significantly if you're able to get a prospect into a win-win situation, for a number of reasons:

>> **Happy client:** Having a happy client makes life much easier for your finance and administration functions as well as for your colleagues who are tasked with implementing the solution. A spirit of cooperation and ownership of the solution should prevail and make it easier to get implementation-specific decisions made and signed off faster.

>> **Margins maintained:** A win-win solution will have protected your profit margins, so you'll be a hero with your finance department. (Well, hero may be overstating it a little, but they'll be quietly pleased and relieved that you haven't given away the company silver because their view of sales tends to be when margins are under threat.)

>> **Referenceable:** Having a referenceable client is great news for marketing who can get straight to work on case studies and arranging for press coverage as well as having a new reference site for you and your new business sales colleagues to make use of.

>> **Conflict eliminated:** Perhaps the biggest gain for your company from a win-win solution is that it eliminates conflict right from the very beginning of a client-supplier relationship, giving the best opportunity for a smooth implementation and making life easier and more pleasant for all your colleagues who come in contact with the new client.

From the buyer's viewpoint

As far as your prospect is concerned, as long as he's been open and honest with you through the sales cycle, seeking a win–win solution can only be good news. However, you need to be a little cautious until you're certain that no game playing is going on first. (Have a look at Chapter 13 for details.)

A win–win solution for your prospect becoming a client delivers some real benefits:

>> **Needs met:** Having his needs met is fairly obvious as a benefit, but getting to that stage as part of a win-win solution sets up the implementation phase to be much easier to cope with as he already knows that you are on his side and will do whatever is needed to make the project successful.

>> **Comfortable price point:** As part of achieving a win-win solution, by definition, the price point at which your prospect bought into your solution is one that sits comfortably with him. He doesn't feel that he's been fleeced, and he should generally accept that he's getting value for his money. (If you encounter issues, though, see the next section.)

>> **Some concessions gained:** Inevitably, the new client will have gained some concessions from you in reaching a win-win solution.

>> **Avoiding buyer's remorse:** Buyer's remorse is a widely accepted cognitive reaction after making an expensive purchase and is associated with fear of having made the wrong choice and a suspicion over having been unduly influenced by the salesperson. Helping your new client achieve a win-win solution will dramatically cut down and may completely eliminate this reaction.

Addressing Price as You Seek a Win-Win

Any number of factors will ultimately make up the components of a win-win solution, and price, although just one of them, is generally seen as the big stumbling block. The reality here is that if the price point that either you or your prospect needs to hit is really nonnegotiable and if price is a real issue, then the chances of achieving a win-win are next to nonexistent.

You can avoid getting into this position in the first place by addressing price and affordability as part of the qualifying process early in the sales cycle (see Chapters 9 and 19 for more details). If you do, you'll know whether price is an issue and should be able to position the deal around that sticking point or be prepared to walk away (as explained in Chapters 10 and 20), knowing that the deal can't happen.

If you still get into a situation where price is a sticking point as you seek to put the deal in place, then the only option you have left is compromise (see Chapter 11 for guidance). At this point, you need a degree of transparency on both sides. If neither party feels manipulated into a deal, then you can resolve the situation, and a win-win is still possible; otherwise, it will only lead to resentment. And although a deal may be done, the relationship has been damaged, which will lead to further issues as time progresses.

REMEMBER

As a new business salesperson, your focus shouldn't be on getting a deal at any cost, which I address in Chapter 11. Even the most novice of prospects can spot a desperate new business salesperson, and if you're willing to give up anything to achieve a sale, expect to be taken to the cleaners. In this case, the chances of a win-win are nonexistent, and the chances of a deal actually happening are also remote. You always have the option of walking away. If the need is real and your solution really is the best, then the chances are high that your prospect will return to the table and find a way past his issues. If not, then your qualification was faulty.

This reminds me of a situation I faced a few years ago when a key prospect was giving all the correct buying signals, and I had qualified need, affordability, decision-making authority, demographics — in fact, all the qualification was fine — and a deal looked likely, until the prospect decided to ask for another opinion from a "business friend" who worked in a different sector and knew nothing about my solution. I wasn't even able to speak to him and only ever knew his first name. The friend, no doubt trying to be helpful, insisted on some key changes to our contract, specifically payment terms, if the deal was to go ahead. This change became of paramount importance to my prospect and got in the way not only of a win-win but of the entire deal. I walked away, half expecting him to ditch the friend's advice and come back, but he didn't, and no deal was ever reached. I tell this story to illustrate that things don't always go according to plan, but as affordability had become an issue, this prospect failed the qualification anyway, and I wouldn't have signed a contract under those circumstances.

As you can see, a win-win solution isn't always possible, and you need to recognize that fact. This doesn't mean that no deal is possible, however. The nature of your solution may exclude any chance of a win-win if it's a must-have solution, for example, or on occasion when dealing with professional buyers who have their own agenda. I cover this in Chapter 13 in more detail.

REMEMBER

To achieve a win-win, both you and your prospect must want to do so, and if you're selling to a business where the prospect is just going through the buying motions with no real engagement in the solution, then you're likely wasting your time even trying to get a win-win, so just close the deal on the best terms that you can.

Securing and Extending Your Client's Buy-in with Support

You've presented your solution and demonstrated how it meets the stated needs that your prospect defined, you've dealt with any objections and qualified all the way through the sales cycle, and you're now ready to get the order. Sometimes your prospect may surprise you by saying he's ready to sign the order, but most of the time you'll need to assertively and politely ask for it (I provide pointers on how to do so in Chapter 13).

The first step to asking for the order is to understand where your prospect is in terms of his company hierarchy and understand the pressures that he's under to deliver a working solution to the problem. Your job is to be on his team and to act as a resource in helping him address any issues, physical or political, that stand between you and a win-win solution. Your new client will be much more motivated to help you achieve a win-win if you're there for him to provide support and guidance and to troubleshoot where necessary.

REMEMBER

Your prospect has a big investment in your solution if he's recommended it internally and can't afford to be seen to have any doubts and certainly not to fail to deliver. Although you'll likely hand over day-to-day control at the implementation phase to a colleague, you need to retain ownership of the solution and be available to your new client as the project progresses for two distinct reasons:

>> **To act as a member of his support team, always being available to discuss any issues and to provide support to him:** In building the relationship with your prospect, you're not looking to become best buddies with him,

but you are seeking to build a solid, trusting, and professional relationship where you can assist each other both now and in the future.

>> **To always be on the lookout for additional sales opportunities, both from your new client and from his professional network:** Your new client is the most important contact you have at the moment a sale concludes, and you need to take the necessary time to build him up in his own eyes and his colleagues' eyes. Time invested wisely after the deal closes will return dividends in the form of additional business and referrals, almost without exception. Your client is your internal champion and can be the gatekeeper to additional sales opportunities both within his company and within his wider network.

You don't need to be, nor should you be, subservient, and the relationship you've built doesn't change; it just moves to a new level of mutual support. Your client is never wrong but may occasionally be misguided, and your role is to keep him on track and on message.

Enjoying Longer-Term Success

The essence of reaching a win-win solution is much more than getting a deal over the line, booking the revenue against target, and collecting a nice commission check. Achieving a win-win solution with your new client is the starting point to a longer-term relationship both with you and with your company. Your initial job is to bring in the business in terms of a sale on the optimal terms and to ensure that your company is well positioned to take advantage of other opportunities, but as you find out in the following sections, you need to build on that professional relationship to ensure longer-term success in sales for yourself. In addition, retaining a client is significantly less expensive for your company than winning a new one, and that responsibility is one you share with colleagues in other functions.

REMEMBER

The new business sales role is not just about securing a single deal. In this book, I discuss the need to always be qualifying and on the lookout for new business opportunities. The biggest cost in sales is in winning a new client. So if you can secure a win-win solution, then you're part of the way to getting a payback on that initial investment, safe in the knowledge that as long as you and your colleagues deliver the solution, then additional business should follow.

Focusing on the bigger picture

In your focus on the bigger picture, you obviously need to consider the size and market position of your prospect: Is he in a position now, or could he be in the future, to need more of your services over time? The answer is always yes because you don't know what may happen further down the line in terms of mergers, acquisitions, or organic growth.

One of the first new business deals I concluded was with a small business with a turnover of less than $500,000 and a staff of around six to eight people, including some part-time staff. Over 15 years, it grew organically to become a sector leader with a turnover of approaching $10 million and a head count of more than 100 people. My original solution worked well for this company, and I was quickly seen as an integral part of its business and the first port of call when anything new was needed. An initial contract worth around $500 grew over the years into a million-dollar account.

Did I know that would happen? No. If I hadn't built a solid relationship and ensured a successful implementation, would I have been able to win a massive amount of business from this company over a 15-year period? No. Does this happen all the time? Sadly no, but you never know when it may, so keep an eye on the bigger picture.

You need to consider not only the revenue and profit from the deal you're working on but also the cost of client acquisition and the lifetime value of a client.

Losing the battle but winning the war

In the dark days of the Second World War, General De Gaulle, future president of the French Republic, was quoted on propaganda posters that appeared around the country as saying, *"La France a perdu une bataille! Mais la France n'a pas perdu la guerre!"* which is literally translated as "France has lost a battle! But France has not lost the war!" New business sales isn't in the same league by any stretch of the imagination, but the sentiment is important to take on board.

You can't expect to win every deal that you chase, and you can't expect to win every objection or every negotiation within a sales cycle. There's another party to consider — your prospect, whom you're building a relationship with — so you do need to let some things go if they're not significant enough to impact the overall deal or compromise the solution. Stick to your principles on major points, and don't concede on these, but on issues that don't have a great impact on your solution or getting the deal done, you can concede without fear of compromising the end result. (Have a look at Chapters 3, 7, 10, and 11 for more information.)

Just as a war is made up of many battles, a sales cycle is made up of many head-to-head issues, and you may need to concede a few to secure the end result of winning the deal. Nobody likes a smart aleck who insists on being right all the time, so eat a bit of humble pie occasionally and let your prospect enjoy his victory.

WARNING

You don't want to be seen as someone who steamrolls his prospects and gains a *Pyrrhic victory* — a victory that inflicts such a heavy toll that it's tantamount to defeat for you in that you never win anything else from him or his network of contacts as the price of dealing with you is too heavy. Do this even once, and you're finished in new business sales.

A PYRRHIC VICTORY

The term *Pyrrhic victory* is named after Pyrrhus, King of Epirus, whose army suffered irreplaceable losses and causalities in defeating the Roman Armies in battles at Heraclea in 280 BC and at Asculum in 279 BC during the Pyrrhic War.

Today, it has come to symbolize a victory that inflicts such a devastating toll on the victor that it's tantamount to a defeat. Someone who wins a Pyrrhic victory has been victorious in some way; however, the heavy toll negates any sense of achievement or profit. It has become synonymous with a business analogy to describe struggles that end up ruining the victory.

Chapter **17**

Networking Effectively

B usiness networking is a modern socioeconomic activity that has grown in importance over the last 20 years as a way of putting some structure into a centuries-old tradition of building mutually beneficial business relation-ships. Most people have heard the term "old boys' network" in relation to making use of contacts or getting information that's not common knowledge, and it's also been associated with cronyism and a degree of cynicism from those who don't understand its power.

Business networking makes use of the same fundamental principles of who you know and who they know but puts it into a modern-day business environment, and it has become a powerful tool in the new business salesperson's toolkit. However, networking is only one thread, although an important one. It hasn't suddenly become a new business panacea, replacing other forms of prospecting for new business. Networking is a key tool, and getting its use right, as I cover in this chapter, can give you a real new business sales advantage.

REMEMBER

You don't have to go out of your way to become involved in networking, and you don't have to attend any events. What you do have to do in new business sales, though, is build relationships, and in essence that's what business networking is about. The principles I discuss in this chapter are equally relevant whether you're an avid networker or just someone who needs to build business relationships to succeed in new business sales.

As you get involved in any form of networking, one of the challenges you face is how to allocate and manage the time and resources that it can eat up, and you'll need to carefully consider this as you work it into your business day. It's not just about new business sales relationships, either, because networking effectively can open new job opportunities for you, too, putting you in the frame for possible future career moves without getting involved in the traditional recruitment cycle.

WARNING

You can see networking as giving you the opportunity to build an advantage over competitors in business, but be aware that they'll also likely be doing the same thing, so don't rely solely on networking as your primary prospecting tool. Networking has an important place, but it won't deliver success in isolation. I'd be wary of employing a new business salesperson who relied on networking as his primary prospecting tool.

Seeking, Selecting, and Timing Networking Opportunities

Years ago, many people, especially sales management, viewed networking as "trading favors with strangers," and they didn't give it any importance; in fact, many frowned upon networking for taking up valuable time. Nothing could be further from the truth today, but you do have to approach networking with a plan and an objective, or it will eat up vast amounts of time and resources for questionable gain.

As a new business salesperson, if you're going to use networking as a successful prospecting tool (because that's exactly what it is), you need to be selective in the type of networking you engage in. The opportunities are almost boundless, but you can't spend all your time on this activity. However, you also need to recognize that networking isn't a flash-in-the-pan, quick solution to finding more business. It requires sustained effort and time commitment over a long period to produce real results for you.

REMEMBER

The challenge becomes one of identifying what will deliver results and not just about finding the opportunities to network that you enjoy the most. Networking can consume an enormous amount of time if you let it, so you need to manage it accordingly and treat it as one of your many prospecting tools.

You may, of course, get lucky and identify a prospect who quickly becomes a client. This does happen, but you shouldn't expect or rely on it. Personally, I've had a lot of success with finding new clients through networking, but I've also wasted a lot of time and energy pursuing opportunities that have led to nowhere.

What networking gives you is face time with people who may have a need or, perhaps more importantly, whose contacts may have a need, but it takes time to develop these relationships based on building trust initially. If a total stranger asked you whether you knew and could introduce him to a senior decision maker in a company, how would you react? You likely wouldn't give him the time of day, let alone an introduction with your credibility to someone you knew. However, after getting to know the person and after establishing his credentials, you may feel differently and be able to assist him. Establishing this takes time and effort.

So is networking "real work," or is it an excuse to avoid some of the more difficult sales tasks? Networking, approached correctly and as part of a structured sales plan, is indeed real work, but in isolation it won't deliver sustained benefits over the long term.

In this section, I explore how to seek, select, and take maximum advantage of different networking opportunities, and you also see how some can fit into your environment, aiding your prospecting efforts. (For the full scoop on prospecting, see Chapter 9.)

Qualifying opportunities

Over the last few years, many new networking opportunities have sprung up all over the place, online and offline, as people seek to both open new avenues for collaboration and make a quick profit from something that's in vogue.

REMEMBER

One school of thought is that there's never a bad opportunity, just one that isn't taken. If you subscribe to this view, you risk watering down your networking efforts by spreading yourself too thin. Instead of chasing everything that moves, apply some sales logic and qualify the networking opportunity, starting with the following questions:

>> Is it right for you?

>> What is the profile of the others involved?

>> Who is behind it, and what is their track record?

>> Does it involve a sector that is of interest to you?

>> Does it cover areas that are unique?

>> How else could you access those contacts?

How would you react if a prospect invited you to meet with him just to pass a couple of hours when you had nothing relevant to discuss in terms of moving the sales cycle forward? I'd feel that it had been a waste of my time, even if it meant building the relationship further. Keep in mind that you want to build relationships for business purposes and not for seeking new best buddies. So in the same vein, why would you spend a couple of hours at a networking event that you hadn't qualified as being worthwhile? The same logic applies in both cases, and using your time wisely is your biggest asset in new business sales.

REMEMBER

You may have to acknowledge that you won't really know whether a networking initiative is right for you unless you try it, and that is where you should do some basic qualifying first. If the initiative fails your qualification, then you really shouldn't get involved, even for a taster session. Just because a new networking initiative comes across your desk doesn't mean you have to be involved in it. Value your time and invest it where you're going to achieve the best return.

Success in networking isn't just about numbers, and he who gets involved in the most initiatives won't necessarily get the best outcome. Challenge rather than accept when it comes to reasons to get involved in something new. Keep your eye on the end game; you're seeking new business contacts to meet today's and tomorrow's sales objectives, not just to build up the number of contacts you have.

WARNING

To use LinkedIn as an example, when you have more than a certain number of connections, the system stops showing an absolute number and reverts to "over 500," or whatever the number currently is. This isn't a badge of honor because these contacts are meaningless unless they result in new businesses. Don't get hung up on networking numbers, LinkedIn connections, number of offline events you attend, or any other measure of success other than real, live prospects resulting in real live sales.

TIP

Many networking opportunities also have a membership cost associated with them, which is justified in a myriad of ways that don't matter for the purposes of this book. Be aware of the amount of money you commit, and look at your return on investment both financially and with regard to your time commitment.

Identifying creative opportunities

Before jumping headlong into the exciting and time-consuming world of networking, you need to understand what's likely to give you the best return on your time investment. (Qualifying opportunities is crucial, as you find out in the preceding section.) Look beyond the obvious, too; for example, if you're invited to an event on urban regeneration in your business neighborhood but your territory is further afield, don't automatically turn it down. Consider who else will be attending and whether any of them are likely to be in positions of influence, or know people who are, within your wider territory. You need to do some out-of-the box thinking when selecting networking opportunities, and this should come as second nature to new business salespeople, giving you a distinct advantage.

Look at, and ask, what your colleagues do about networking opportunities and how they find their effectiveness. You can save yourself a lot of time and effort by learning from the experiences of those you work with. Equally, look at the types of events that your peers get involved in. It'd be rare for a networking event not to be known about by someone in your sphere.

Not that long ago, the mainstay of networking events involved chamber of commerce meetings, often as breakfast meetings. Although I've personally done fairly well with business from them in the past, I now avoid them at almost any cost because the same people, or at least the same profile, are present all the time. Accountants, solicitors, stationery supply companies, the local florist, and a handful of other similar people were at each meeting. Although all of them were nice enough people, this type of event became a bit stale. It was the "same old" without any new blood, and even after returning to such an event after a year away, nothing changed. Avoid falling into the trap of "Steve always attends," and consider each event on its merits in terms of how it's going to help you reach your overall objective of reaching your winning new business sales target.

Here are additional effective networking opportunities to think about:

>> Consider starting your own event as a way of generating a fresh approach, perhaps in conjunction with some noncompeting businesses in your area. Don't do this for the glory of running an event or because you expect to make money from it. Do it to stimulate opportunities for you and others, and if it becomes established, then get someone else to organize it to free up your time.

>> Depending on your type of business, you may consider holding a networking event for your clients. Invite them along, and let them meet one another. This event holds a lot of potential, although it can represent a bit of a risk. If it's successful, you may consider inviting some key prospects to attend, too. The success of this event depends on how good you and your business are at looking after clients and implementing solutions. I've considered running this type of networking event because I can see a myriad of opportunities coming from it, not only for me but also for clients. Of course, if it helped with converting a few prospects, then that would be all the better!

Keeping an eye on your networking time

Networking can become all-consuming if you aren't careful. Keep your eye on the real objective of winning new business, and plan your time accordingly. Set some time parameters on networking, whether online or offline. A salesperson I once worked with spent countless hours at breakfast meetings, lunch meetings, coffee afternoons, and then was on LinkedIn and Facebook when occasionally in the office. She once remarked, in all seriousness, that she didn't have enough time to write a proposal so it would have to wait.

REMEMBER

When you're networking, the people you're speaking to aren't the only ones of interest to you — so are the people that they can introduce you to. Connecting with contacts of contacts is the most powerful attribute of networking. When you introduce someone to a contact of yours, your reputation is on the line, and the same applies the other way around. Never lose sight of this, and always respect introductions as the powerful tools they are.

Getting introductions into someone else's network, especially when it's to people you've been specifically targeting, is an immensely powerful prospecting tool, and in terms of time efficiency, it can save you countless hours of trying to get past a gatekeeper (an assistant or someone else who guards access to your prospect). Your networking objectives should include securing this type of personal introduction, and keep in mind that an investment in networking time is a good payoff for the right introductions.

TIP

You get the right kind of introduction only if people know what you're looking for, so you need to make this known but not in an in-your-face way. Introductions work both ways, of course, so if you meet someone you trust and think that contacts of yours could benefit from meeting him, then ask whether he'd like to get a referral and introduction from you. Don't wait to be asked; be proactive when you consider the opportunity to be right. In this way, your reputation as an effective networker expands, along with other opportunities, making your investment in networking time very cost effective.

For example, I once presented outsourced new business solutions to a graphic design company. My solution was probably what the company needed, but they failed some of my qualification criteria, so I wasn't going to follow up. From our conversation, though, I remembered that the company needed a good freelance designer. I happen to know a very good freelance designer who had some spare capacity, and so I was able to put the two of them in contact with each other. As far as I know, they still work together.

REMEMBER

Success with networking is as much about who you know as what you know. You're seeking access to networks of contacts, and they're looking for the same from you. Be prepared to help other people without expecting something in return; that's the mark of a true networker. Let your help be irrespective of how high in seniority your contact is, and go out of your way to help and give pointers to more inexperienced people.

Structuring Your Networking Approach

Networking clearly offers lots of potential to interact with and discover new prospects, but as I note earlier in this chapter, it can also be a time-consuming task. Your challenge is to attain the maximum advantage from a reasonable time investment, and that requires you to have a plan. If anyone attending networking events should be good at planning for success, it is a new business salesperson.

In addition to planning which events to get involved with, you need to plan your approach and how you're going to be memorable enough to make a positive impression. In Chapter 3, I cover the importance of making a good first impression and give some tips on how to go about it. Networking events are one of the situations where making a positive first impression is important, especially because you'll be in a room full of people all with the same objective as you — or at least those who have considered why they're there.

REMEMBER

Having a plan for the events that you attend helps you to retain focus and to remember why you're there. The purpose isn't to socialize but to build contacts and look for prospecting opportunities. The name of the game is building business relationships, not making new buddies.

Networking, of course, doesn't have to be event focused, and even if it's based around an event, it can be an online experience almost as frequently as offline these days. Similar structure rules apply to online networking, especially the amount of time you commit and the need to qualify before getting involved. You can easily build up lots of online contacts, but you have to consider whether you're getting value from that. I explore this topic in detail later in this chapter.

In planning your networking activity and approach, consider how you're perceived. You need to be seen as positive, because negative vibes are a big turnoff for anyone and there's no room for that in new business sales. Always have something to say. Networking is a good opportunity to use your elevator pitch, and you should have a networking version of your pitch at the ready (see Chapter 8 for more info). You need to bear in mind that everyone is looking for opportunities, so be sure to listen as well as speak. Be interesting, and be interested. Take note of what people say, engage with them, and ask questions. Your turn will come.

TIP

In a room full of people with similar objectives, being memorable can be difficult, so try to be a little different from run-of-the-mill in your approach. Think outside the box but remain positive and professional. At networking events where everyone gets to present for 60 seconds or so, try to be different. I don't tell the audience that I run a new business consultancy, for example, but I do tell an apocryphal story that lends itself to new business. That way I know I'll be remembered by anyone who's interested in what I have to say, and I'll be a bit different from everyone else in the room.

REMEMBER

Integrity is important, as is being seen to act with integrity, so pass up any opportunity for gain that's associated with dubious means because it will only muddy your reputation, which is a price you can't afford to pay. For example, you may come across a company desperate for help in an area where you know a little but are not an expert. Avoid trying to position yourself as the one who can solve the company's problems if that is really not your field of expertise, however easy a sale may seem to be. It'll be far better all around, and especially for your reputation, if you can introduce them to the right contact for their situation, with no gain for yourself.

Distinguishing Types of Networking Events

Today, you face a bewildering array of networking opportunities: online and offline events, breakfast meetings, golf days, black tie dinners, chamber of commerce events, and so on. It's important to note what opportunities are available to you, but it's equally important to select the ones that are right for you rather than risk spreading yourself too thinly by attending everything.

TIP

Should you get involved with networking events that cost money or stick to free ones? This is a personal choice. Generally, more of the right types of people engage at paid events for business reasons, not just for free food and drink. The answer to this once again comes down to qualifying the event (as I describe earlier in this chapter), and you can often get an advance guest list just by asking for it.

Offline networking events

Offline networking is the traditional form, based around a specific event, such as a breakfast meeting or a conference. This is where business networking grew up, with lead sharing clubs, chamber of commerce meetings, trade events, and other similar functions. Offline networking is as important today as it has ever been, even with the advent of online resources that I explore in the next section. Here are a few typical offline events to consider:

>> **Breakfast meetings:** These have exploded onto the scene in recent years. Although they've been around since the mid-1980s, new organizations and clubs are springing up everywhere these days, and you only have to do a Google search in your local area to see how well covered you are. They take various forms, but the essence is that the same group of people meets on a regular basis, and you share leads with one another. This approach has both positives and negatives, and it's up to you to decide whether it's right for you,

but a word of caution: Don't take at face value the figures that are claimed; research for yourself, and, as in all things, qualify hard before committing to anything.

TIP

You can usually manage to get an invitation to go along to a taster session before making any commitment to join, but take the time to understand what you're being asked to commit to. Remember, they're new business salespeople, too!

>> **Local trade events:** These are often sponsored by either a chamber of commerce or a bank and aim to bring the local business community together around a theme. They're intended primarily as a sales tool for the sponsor, however they're pitched, and networking opportunities at them are as good as individuals make them. The point is that at these types of events, you have to go out of your way to network, but it's often worth doing so.

  I attended a local trade recently on the theme of protecting intellectual property. The event was sponsored by a bank, hosted by a local major company, and attracted about 50 businesspeople from around the region. Although I didn't gain any new prospects at this event, I became a prospect for a couple of companies that I'm likely to do business with in the future. This is an example of networking that resulted in a buying rather that a selling opportunity.

>> **Golf day:** This is another increasingly popular event, but it first relies on attendees being golfers and is a massive time commitment because a round of golf takes three to four hours. The good part of that is that you have a captive audience for a long time. Personally, I've used golf a lot as a networking tool and have struck a few big deals on the golf course.

>> **Speed networking events:** These are usually held as part of a conference or exhibition and mimic speed dating in that you have about one minute to make an impression. Personally, I consider them a waste of time, and they'd never pass my qualification criteria, but you have to make up your own mind because it may work for you and your specific needs.

>> **Trade shows and conferences:** These are good opportunities for networking because people who attend are generally receptive to new messages; that's why they're there.

REMEMBER

Whatever form of offline networking you get involved in, the guidance in this chapter is intended to help you prepare and attain the best value for yourself as a new business salesperson. Check what's available in your area and what your colleagues and peers do, and, above all, qualify the event before committing to anything (as I explain earlier in this chapter).

Online networking without time-wasting dead ends

When asked about online networking, most people tell you about LinkedIn, but other platforms exist, most notably Facebook, which you should also consider as a networking tool due to the success of business pages. (LinkedIn and Facebook are particularly great as research tools, with a goldmine of information that I cover in Chapter 23.)

WARNING

You can find books and courses on how to master prospecting and networking with LinkedIn and Facebook, but using these tools should come with a health warning. Gaining new followers is easy, but it's not necessarily the best way to proceed with these platforms, especially LinkedIn, because you may find that you're suddenly swamped with requests from all quarters, and the value can be questionable at best. Beware of accepting requests from unknown contacts that can take up time, and, as always, the golden rule is to qualify before committing resources to them (see Chapter 19 for details). You need to invest a lot of time and effort to make much progress that you can measure in monetary terms, and as a new business salesperson that has to be your focus.

I've had real business close from blind requests on social media, so it can work. As with everything, my advice is to qualify and you'll find the answer there. I find the most effective qualification for online networking is fee based, making it clear that you can do whatever is required but that there's a cost associated with it. That will quickly lose the majority of time-wasters. I once had a request on LinkedIn from the Far East, from a man who claimed to be the CEO of a technology company and wanted help in breaking into the U.K. market. I spent an hour on the phone with him, getting some basic information and qualifying him, and then wrote a short proposal, which made it clear that there was a fee involved in going to the next stage. Strangely enough, he disappeared, and all it cost me was an hour or so of time. The same man came back to me about a year later with a new venture that he wanted to discuss. I gave him a time slot to call me, out of mainstream hours, and I'm still awaiting the call some months later. He won't get a third chance.

With online networking, don't get hung up on the quantity of followers or connections that you have because that's irrelevant. The only true measurement of effectiveness is the quality of the connections you have and how you interact with them. You need to be strict about how you filter connections to maintain the integrity of your contact database. As I write this, I realize that I need to take my own advice here!

TIP

Online networking is a good follow-up tool after meeting a new contact at an offline event and a good way to keep in contact without appearing to be too pushy. After you've exchanged business cards, there is nothing to prevent you from connecting on social media and then waiting for the right opportunity to present itself before taking the contact any further. Having connected with your potential prospect, you can then send him case studies or any relevant industry or background information, seeking to establish yourself, in his eyes, as an industry or solution expert that he can come back to with questions.

Following Up

In effective networking, you can take all the lessons on board, build great networks of contacts, and be introduced to all sorts of useful people, but if you fail to follow up, then it will all have been a waste of time. Following up — the topic of this section — is the single most important part of networking, and you simply have to get it right if you're going to use networking as a tool in your new business sales life.

It's important not to expect to see immediate results from your efforts, so don't be disheartened if your results take longer than you hoped for. Keep in mind that networking is just one of your prospecting tools, so don't use it in isolation. Equally, you need to be prepared to make things happen in order to drive the process. You're a new business salesperson, so you have a methodology to follow. Wherever your prospects come from, you need to get them into your CRM system and drive the sales opportunity.

TIP

Take the time to thank people for their networking assistance and for providing any introduction for you. Make it a habit to welcome new contacts with an email. Maintain communication with contacts you meet through networking (as I state earlier in this chapter, LinkedIn is a good tool for assisting with this). You can also use your CRM system to schedule regular keep-in-touch actions to ensure that they don't forget about you. (Flip to Chapter 9 for an introduction on CRM systems.)

Knowing the basics of following up

Following up should be an obvious task in new business sales, but we can all be a bit lazy at times. Don't fall into that trap and risk losing valuable contacts that you've worked hard to get. Here are three basic rules to following up on networking opportunities:

>> **Strike while the iron is hot.** A lead or opportunity is at its greatest shortly after you've uncovered it and will go cold remarkably quickly. A good rule is never to let more than 24 business hours pass without being in contact with a thank-you note at the very least (I provide more timing pointers later in this chapter).

Everyone is busy, and all have full email inboxes, so you can acknowledge this fact with a short email saying that you understand they're busy but wanted to remind them of "x, y, and z" and that you'll be in touch within the next few days. And make sure you keep to whatever time frame you commit to. You find out more about creating a good first impression in Chapter 3, and this is very relevant here.

WARNING

>> **Don't blanket follow up.** Blanket follow-up is an email to everyone who attended an event (usually getting the list from the organizer of the event), saying how good it was to meet with them and that you'll call next week to arrange a meeting. The only problem with this is that you didn't speak to even half of the people you're sending the email to, and some of them weren't even there. So you have just shot your credibility in the foot and can't expect to be taken seriously.

I've been on the receiving end of lots of these messages, and the lack of professionalism it portrays makes me cringe. I don't think I've ever actually taken the follow-up call when it eventually comes in.

REMEMBER

>> **If you say it, then do it.** This should go without saying really, but if you tell a new contact that you'll send something, then make sure you follow through and send it. Establish yourself as someone who delivers and can be relied on.

Checking out follow-up methods

You should have collected business cards from your new contacts and so should have their contact details on hand. Agreeing to a follow-up action while at the networking event is completely acceptable, but be sure to set expectations as to how and when you'll be in touch, and of course make sure that you deliver on your commitment. Add it to your CRM to ensure that you don't forget.

Next, you need to decide how you're going to follow up. On occasions where the contact becomes a hot lead immediately, following up on the phone to confirm some of the details is probably appropriate. Generally, unless it's a really hot lead, I recommend not phoning initially so as not to be perceived as too pushy, or worse still, desperate.

Both email and social media are fine as follow-up methods, and your choice, to a large extent, depends on how you assess the qualification you do. For anyone you consider to be on the path to qualification, then email is a better choice because it's more personal and more time critical. Earlier in this chapter, I discuss how social media can be used as a follow-up mechanism. The ultimate choice is yours to make, but it should depend on both your workflow rules and your assessment of opportunity. The key thing is to remember to include the details of the follow-up and any subsequent plans in your CRM.

Your new contacts are networking, too, so expect them to follow up with you, and treat each of them with the professionalism that you expect yourself, regardless of whether you have an interest in connecting further with them at that stage.

One of the keys to successful networking is to give before you gain, so be aware of the needs of others, and, if you can, help someone or make a connection. Use that as your primary follow-up rather than a blander "nice to meet you" type of message.

Looking at timing tips

Waiting some weeks or months to follow up with a new contact for the first time is no use, because he'll have either forgotten you or considered you to be rude and unprofessional for waiting so long. Make it a solid rule that you instigate some form of follow-up within 24 business hours of meeting a new contact. It doesn't have to be in great detail, and probably shouldn't be at that stage, but sending a short note saying "good to meet you" and confirming the next follow-up is a good idea.

Another key rule with follow-up is not to waste anyone's time. You don't need to follow up with every single person you come into contact with, just those you actively engaged with; otherwise, you risk being perceived as a time-wasting nuisance, which defeats the whole objective of networking.

Consider whether you can automate some of your follow-up activity. You will of course add the contact details into your CRM, so you could prepare welcome templates and select one of those, or if possible, give this task to your assistant (if you have one) to take it off your workload.

At a minimum, have a workflow, and make sure that you include your networking follow-ups so you don't forget them. You need to act on anything that may turn into an opportunity and don't leave it for another time. You can discover how to do good and not-so-good follow-ups by observing how other people follow up with you. Take the best of these and adapt them to your own style, while avoiding the mistakes highlighted by the worst examples.

You're still seeking to make a good first impression, as I cover in Chapter 3, so be sure to make your initial follow-ups both professional and friendly.

Chapter **18**

Managing the Perception of Risk

I n this chapter, I discuss the role of risk and its mitigation in a new business sales environment, specifically how to mitigate risk in a business solutions context. Risk management is a complex topic, and many books are dedicated to the subject alone. Here, I just try to highlight the issue and give some pointers on what you can do to allay the fear of risk. I don't intend this discussion to be chapter and verse on dealing with risk because it's far too complex a topic to cover in a single chapter.

Nothing is without some form of risk, and nothing worth achieving is ever done without an element of risk. I define managing the perception of risk simply as understanding the issues and taking steps to reducing adverse effects.

Some people are risk averse, and if you come across prospects who fall into this category, then your sales efforts won't be as straightforward as they otherwise may have been. It's also worth remembering that from the prospect's point of view, doing nothing to address his business needs means that he's also taking a risk. You may need to point that out and address the complexities and fallouts with him.

Defining Risk for Different Groups

According to the International Organization for Standardization (ISO), risk is the "effect of uncertainty on objectives," and the effect of it is a deviation in either a positive or negative sense from what's expected. In plain English, this means that the potential for anything other than a straightforward solution is, in reality, risk.

All of us take and are exposed to risk every single day, but generally we never give it a second thought because our inbuilt safety mechanisms help us to mitigate or avoid it; for example, crossing a busy road could be perceived as a risky venture, but we don't avoid doing so, even though our brains recognize it as a risk. Therefore, you shouldn't get hung up on the idea of risk being introduced as a sales objection; it's just one of those things you have to work with.

REMEMBER

You can't avoid risk; it's inherent in everything. As part of the new business sales team, your job is to manage your prospect's perception of risk in regard to your solution. Almost all cases have an element of risk — that's just human nature. Keep risk in context and recognize that although a sales decision can be seen as a risk, making no decision at all is generally a bigger risk. Because you can't avoid risk in a new business sales environment, the key becomes how you manage it. Mark Zuckerberg, the founder of Facebook, has been quoted as saying, "The biggest risk is not taking any risk," and I think this statement sums it up perfectly.

In this section, I explore the ways in which buying your solution may represent risk to your prospect. Keep in mind that risk works both ways, and part of your new business sales role is to protect your company from any unreasonable risk that's associated in dealing with your prospects.

For your prospect

When dealing with the perception of risk in a business solution that you're proposing, you need to consider what the elements of risk are to your prospect, which can be broken down into four major areas:

>> **May not work:** The fear that the solution you're proposing meets the prospect's needs but may not work (or may not work correctly) may be a reasonable one to harbor at the beginning of the sales cycle as far as your prospect is concerned, but the sales cycle progresses as if nothing is wrong.

REMEMBER

Beyond the very early stages, this fear should diminish. If it hasn't, then you're probably not doing your job correctly. A fear that the proposed solution may not work isn't a valid risk if your prospect continues with his buying cycle beyond the initial stages.

>> **May not do the job:** The perception of risk that your solution may not do the job for your prospect's needs can be taken back to the original requirement specification. You can reasonably assert that your solution meets the stated needs and is a good fit for the job as defined to you.

If this risk is raised as the sales cycle progresses, then push back on your prospect and tell him that as long as the need requirement was done correctly, then he has nothing to fear because, as he'll have seen for himself, your proposed solution more than adequately meets the stated needs.

>> **May be the wrong choice:** The perception that your solution may be the wrong choice for your prospect is an area that you need to cover in some detail as part of objection handling (see Chapter 10) and qualifying real need (see Chapters 9 and 19). The essence of the new business sales role is about handling and overcoming such objections and ensuring that they don't become perceived as risks.

>> **May be a bad decision:** The perception of risk here is a tell-tale sign of an inexperienced or nervous buyer. You should have identified this as part of the qualification processes when getting to know the key members of the decision-making unit. And if you perceive the problem at that stage, that is when you should take action to perhaps ensure that another member of the decision-making unit is kept fully in the loop.

The last thing you want to do as a new business salesperson is to get to the end of the sales cycle only to discover something you should have covered has reared its head and risks, at best, a delay or, at worst, cancellation of a project.

If your prospect begins to talk about risk in the early stages of the sales cycle, you need to qualify exactly what he means and take any necessary steps to ensure that it isn't going to be a deal breaker as you get to the latter stages of the sales cycle. If he tells you that he's risk averse or if it becomes apparent, the sooner you get the issues into the open to address them, the better the situation will be. Acknowledge any fears and don't play them down as unimportant, but point out to your prospect that perhaps the biggest risk he faces is not addressing his fundamental need. Bearing in mind that he must be in a reasonably senior position to conduct the buying cycle with you, he wouldn't have gotten into that position if his approach to risk was in any way going to cause a negative impact to his company.

For your company

By far the biggest risk your company faces in winning new business is one of delay or cancellation of the order, owing to circumstances that you haven't seen or adequately covered — for example, a company takeover, your key prospect leaving his job, or simply you as the new business salesperson failing to correctly qualify the opportunity in the first place.

Beyond that, five separate areas have the potential for some risk. You need to understand these risks and be able to mitigate against them (I discuss dealing with risk later in this chapter):

» **May not get paid:** This is a genuine risk and will be your accounts department's number-one fear. It falls under the pricing and affordability area, which you should have covered during your prospect qualification. Note that different companies have different processes on credit control checking, and you need to be aware of your company's requirements regarding any needed deposits.

» **May damage reputation:** A deal that doesn't go according to plan is one that can do untold damage to your company's reputation, irrespective of who was at fault. It doesn't matter whether the sale didn't close when it should have or the implementation failed to go smoothly or indeed just failed. Of course, any deal represents a form of risk, and one of your roles as the new business salesperson is to guard against this.

» **May overstretch resources:** If a new business deal is larger than expected, is more complex than expected, or just comes in when it's not expected, then it will have a serious impact on your company's ability to deliver the ideal solution in the timescale required.

   In Chapter 13, I cover the impact of resources on a deal, which as an element of risk is important to note, but if the deal doesn't match the expectations that have been set, it could cause a problem.

» **May be a client from hell:** We've all heard of them, and some have experienced dealing with them firsthand. The client from hell is one who really isn't worth having, and you'll be much better off just walking away from such a deal (see Chapter 20 for help). Unfortunately, sometimes the nature of the client doesn't become apparent until it's too late to do anything about it.

   Some warning signs are specific to your sector, but some are generic — for example, the prospect who wants special treatment or a special deal just for him and feels that his needs are so unique that a standard approach just wouldn't be suitable, regardless of how many times your company has implemented the solution in the past. Another generic warning sign is when the prospect wants a pricing deal. Be aware of the risk of taking on a client from hell and consider whether it's truly worth it.

» **May lack commitment:** A prospect who appears to want your solution but isn't really committed to it can be worse than losing a sale in the first place. In many instances — indeed, the majority of the time — closing the sale is just the beginning, and if you perceive a lack of commitment from your prospect, then this truly does represent a risk that will only increase as time goes by.

Putting your neck on the block is an excellent way of securing commitment. If you have a lot to lose, you're going to go out of your way to ensure that whatever the risk is, it's not standing in the way of success. Entrepreneurs understand this very well and indeed thrive on risk.

REMEMBER

Keep all these potential risks in mind when progressing a sale so you can see that the burden of risk is shared between buyer and seller. Consider these different risks when your prospect is talking about the risk that he faces.

Dealing with Risk

Dealing with risk can be broken down into six actions, and one of them is likely to provide a solution that you're looking for. Here are the options available to you as you protect your prospect and your company from risk (the topics of this section):

>> **Accept.** You need to acknowledge the existence of a particular risk and decide to accept the risk without making any special efforts to control it. This is a perfectly valid solution, especially when the perceived risk is low level.

>> **Avoid.** Change what you're doing, change the parameters, or change the rules to eliminate potential for a particular risk. Don't be afraid to challenge the norm; it's part of the new business salesperson's role.

>> **Limit.** Take steps to minimize the impact of a risk. Seek to take control and define the agenda in a different way to take focus away from whatever you're seeking to limit exposure to.

>> **Transfer.** Don't just accept the possibility of risk yourself; find out whether another stakeholder, either within the decision-making unit at your prospect's company or indeed your own company, is better equipped to handle the impact of perceived risk, and then engage with him and involve him in the process, thereby minimizing or sharing the element of risk on your prospect.

>> **Exploit.** If the perceived risk is a positive one, such as your company's resources are needed for different projects that are yet to be agreed on, the risk is that the last one to sign up may have to wait for implementation. You can exploit the perception of risk to try to pull forward your order, which then allows your prospect to take a higher priority in the implementation cycle.

> » **Mitigate.** Mitigating against the possibility of risk is perhaps the most commonly used risk management strategy. Mitigation limits the impact of the risk so that, if it occurs, the impact it creates is smaller than it otherwise would be and therefore easier to fix. You need to understand the potential risk and take agreed, documented steps to ensure that the processes and procedures are in place to minimize the impact.
>
> *Note:* Limiting and mitigating may seem similar, so to be clear about my meaning, *limiting* is taking steps to reduce the likelihood of adverse impact associated with risk, and *mitigating* is taking steps to ensure that any impact is understood in advance and has actions in place that are ready to provide some form of correctional activity in the event of the risk happening.

REMEMBER

You can't avoid risk in new business sales, so learn to live with it and turn the management and mitigation of risk to your advantage. I'm talking here about sensible risk, not irrational risk, and there's a huge difference. (For example, a sensible risk may consist of hoping that a contact stays in his job during the sales cycle when it's known that he is seeking new opportunities, whereas an irrational risk may be planning for someone who could stop your sale to leave his role when there are no signs of it even being thought about.) If a carefully calculated risk resulted in a problem, it likely wouldn't cost you your job; on the other hand, if you took an irrational risk, you'd be out of the door before your feet hit the ground, almost regardless of whether it succeeded or failed. Calculated risk can also be an adrenaline rush, and you'll find prospects and new business salespeople who thrive on this, but it's by no means the norm, and you need to understand your prospect's view of risk. If he is risk averse, stay well away from even a calculated risk for fear of alienating him.

Protecting your prospect

Sometimes you may need to actively encourage your prospect to take a risk. For example, you may need to remind him that not taking action has negative consequences, too, and that his original needs or problem won't be addressed if he doesn't take at least a little risk. Or you may need to gently push him in the right direction and remind him of why you're involved in discussions. Your job is to help him understand the reality and potential consequences of not taking certain risks.

If no one ever took risks, then nothing would ever get done. The world of business and commerce sees people taking risks every day, and the majority of them are relatively low-level ones that lead to progress. New business sales don't usually incur high levels of risk in absolute terms, and sometimes you need to make your prospect get on board with this fact. Ultimately, your role is to get your deal over the finish line by mitigating the impact of any potential risk and not getting hung up by it.

If your prospect fears exposure to a perceived risk, then part of your role is to protect him from that exposure and guide the solution past the risk. To do this, you first need to understand what the real issue is; however trivial it may seem to you, if it's a real issue for your prospect, don't underestimate its impact on your deal.

REMEMBER

Set your prospect's expectations from the outset. You're not offering to save the world from all ails. Your solution addresses a set of specific problems and does so in a unique way, but it may also have some side effects that your prospect needs to know about. Discuss and agree on how to fit your solution into your prospect's business in realistic terms, not promising the world but showing how you'll solve problems. Having a realistic set of expectations will help mitigate his perception of risk.

For example, if your solution is going to address your prospect's fundamental problem successfully but do nothing about addressing a secondary problem, you need to set these expectations accordingly at the outset of the sales cycle so that perceived failure to address the secondary problem isn't an issue that comes back to bite you.

TIP

Leveraging the power of qualitative data and third-party endorsements is a powerful tool at your disposal. This can be in the form of research papers or case studies involving your solution as implemented by other clients. A combination of articles from different sources, within and outside of your company, is ideal. (Flip to Chapter 2 for more details on case studies and other similar materials.)

User references are a powerful sales tool, but you do need to be careful how you use them because you have no real control over what people say. Your top customers are good reference sources, but so are some of your newest customers because they'll be better able to identify with the risks that your prospect is facing, having recently come through the buying experience themselves.

TIP

External documents, such as press coverage and analyst or expert reviews, are worth their weight in gold. Showing your prospect that he's not alone or being a pioneer will go a long way toward alleviating many fears. This creates a safer environment for him to operate in. If you have user groups, then that's perhaps the safest environment of all to introduce him to so that he can see firsthand that he's not operating in isolation. User groups, while primarily for the mutual benefit of your customers, are in fact a brilliant sales tool if you're able to leverage them successfully.

Take the time to engage with as many stakeholders as possible. This is especially important if they form part of the identified decision-making unit. Don't leave your prospect isolated if an issue of risk needs to be addressed. Direct engagement with stakeholders helps protect your prospect from side issues that he may not be immediately aware of. If you can head these off before they become issues, then you'll be both protecting your prospect while also moving the sales cycle forward.

REMEMBER

There's absolutely no point in trying to hide any negative issues that are in the public domain, as social media and savvy prospects are sure to uncover them anyway. Be transparent in dealing with any negative issues; address them openly and move on, acknowledging that they exist and giving your spin on them before your prospect finds them anyway.

Protecting your company

One of your duties as a new business salesperson is to ensure that not only is your prospect protected against the perception of risk but also your company.

One thing I've come across fairly often in dealing with the perception of risk is that prospects want it all one-sided — that is, they're interested in protecting only themselves. I'm quite open about this and tell prospects that I'm willing to take steps to share some of the risk but that I'm not going to carry all the risk. Push back if you get into this situation because it can be an early warning that all is not right.

I've encountered this situation a few times when selling services. The prospect wants every form of guarantee possible in order to protect himself and wants me to take all the risk; in other words, if anything however remotely connected to the project doesn't go according to plan, then the prospect wants me to resolve it and will accept no responsibility, even if the issue comes as a result of his actions. I always push back on this and try to demonstrate reasonably that his expectations are unrealistic. This is one situation where I will walk away from a deal rather than have risk be too one-sided. (Look at Chapters 12 and 20 for more on walking away from a deal.)

WARNING

Sharing a risk is fine in new business sales because it shows belief in your solution, but transferring all the risk onto yourself isn't a smart move and is usually linked to a lack of commitment on behalf of your prospect. Lack of commitment is a surefire sign of a deal or implementation that has trouble stored up for you.

You may need to address compliance issues as part of a deal. My business quite often faces this when clients provide us with data to work with. We need to ensure that the relevant data compliance regulations are correctly dealt with, and, although we're happy to sort this out, we do charge for it and are upfront about this. We also won't proceed with a deal unless this is agreed on because we're not prepared to take all the compliance risks. I turn these issues into sales benefits by suggesting that the prospect may like to consider how our competitors who don't insist on compliance are going to handle it and who will have the ultimate exposure. Being open, honest, and upfront about it positions us well in the prospect's mind as a company that will protect him, even though there's an extra cost for doing so.

REMEMBER

Credit risk — the risk of not being paid for your work — is a big risk that you need to mitigate against. Ultimately, you can only go on proven past performance and can credit check this, and you should do so. Tell your prospects that they need to pass a credit check before you sign them up for a deal, and if you encounter a problem, then get them to pay in advance. Do be prepared to stand your ground here. I tell prospects that we're not a bank and we're not going to fund the work.

Product liability can be an issue at times, and you can insure against this. If your solution falls into this category, you should have a suitable insurance policy in place to protect you in the event of a problem. You need to discuss liability insurance with your senior managers and insurance company.

Avoiding the Death of a Deal by Managing Risk

As in most things with new business sales, it's best to handle the perception of risk during the early stages of the sales cycle in such a way as to ensure that it doesn't destroy a deal. You do this through qualification (a process I discuss in Chapters 9 and 19).

Recognize that some prospect types thrive on the possibility of risk and love the adrenaline rush that it provides. They're typically pioneers in terms of adoption cycles, and you need to manage them in a different way from the majority of prospects that you're likely to deal with. Pioneers and early adopters won't be put off by the perception of risk and will often actively seek the more complex solutions on offer, pushing the boundaries.

The majority of prospects that you'll deal with won't fall into this category, however, and you need to carefully manage the perception of risk so the deal doesn't fall apart. I provide pointers in the following sections.

REMEMBER

If you uncover risk as a qualification issue, this in turn becomes a risk to your sale, and your time may be better invested elsewhere. Dropping a potential deal at the early stages is easier and less disruptive than waiting until after you've invested time and energy into it. Also, if you're seen to be distancing yourself from a sale, this can have a sobering effect on your prospect, and you may find that his perception of risk changes to your benefit and that you can conduct the sales cycle much easier after that.

If, in the early stages of the sales cycle, it becomes apparent that your prospect has an adverse attitude to the perception of risk, you may be better off thanking him for his time and walking away from any potential deal, because the requirements on your time and patience are likely to be stretched. You're not going to win every opportunity that you uncover, and you need to manage your time carefully.

Addressing risk during qualification

As a successful new business salesperson, your prospect's perception of risk should never come as a late surprise because you'll have dealt with it during early qualification (covered in Chapters 9 and 19).

You need to gain an understanding of what the problem is and of the real risk your prospect may be hiding behind something else. What exactly is the problem or potential stumbling block? You of course can address only issues that you know about, so make it clear that you can probably help but only if you know what you're facing. For some reason that has never been satisfactorily explained, prospects don't always tell you the truth and will hide behind something else almost as a smoke screen. You need to penetrate the smoke screen to uncover the real underlying issue so that you can address it and move the sales cycle on.

REMEMBER

Handle risks in the same why you do objections (see Chapter 10) because, in effect, that is what they are. As you would with objections, document everything in contact reports, which are vital in showing that you've already closed off issues. After you've dealt with an issue, risk, or objection, then that door is closed, and you need to adopt a strict regime in keeping it closed. Documenting everything in contact reports (introduced in Chapter 3) gives you an audit trail of issues that you've already addressed.

When dealing with the perception of risk during qualification, don't just accept it as a real issue; push back, seek to understand the details and why a risk is perceived, look for an immediate solution to head off an issue, and document it in a contact report.

REMEMBER

If the perceived risk is noise level to any reasonable observer, then confront it and be prepared to walk away if common sense doesn't prevail. Accept that you can't fix everything and that your primary focus is on selling a solution that fits a business need and not pampering to unreasonable demands. Your prospect still needs to have his original business need addressed and may have lost sight of that, so a sobering action on your behalf may result in him returning his focus to the main issue of solving the business need rather than worrying about some side issue.

Understanding the importance of relationships

As with many areas of winning new business, I can't overstate the importance of building a solid business relationship with your prospect. The strength of this relationship will frequently guide your prospect beyond the perception of risk and toward a deal. (I explain how to start with making a good impression in Chapter 3.)

REMEMBER

Wherever possible, you should take a consultative approach to selling, positioning yourself as an industry expert whose role is to guide your prospect toward making the right decision, while protecting his interests and helping him to mitigate against any risk (as I explain earlier in this chapter). A solid, supportive sales relationship keeps you in good stead when it comes to dealing with some of the more difficult aspects of risk.

If your prospect allows you to guide him, using the benefit of your experience in selling and implementing solutions similar to his requirement, then you're well positioned to act as his champion and to lead him around any obstacle that stands in the way.

REMEMBER

Bear in mind that some prospects do thrive on being trailblazers, and if you have a prospect like this, your role is to support him. The likelihood is that the opposite will be true in the majority of situations, so don't set out to make your prospects be trailblazers unless that is their intention. It comes down to understanding where they are in the adoption cycle and understanding their attitude toward risk. If you successfully cover these two issues, then you'll be well positioned to successfully guide them to a mutually beneficial conclusion of the deal.

Revisiting the deal structure

If you can mitigate the perception of risk by revisiting the structure of the financial aspects of a deal, then this may be a worthwhile exercise to conduct. (Chapter 11 has full details on structuring deals.)

As I discuss in the earlier section "Protecting your company," any movement toward restructuring a deal is on the basis of sharing the risk and not passing the risk entirely to your company. Taking on the entire risk of the project is a poor business deal, whereas sharing risk is often a sensible move that can assist in driving the deal toward a successful conclusion.

Structuring the deal in terms of stages with associated stage payments is often a sensible approach. Bear in mind, however, that this arrangement can have a negative impact on your company's finances if your normal terms are payments in advance. One way you can alleviate this payment risk is by being prepared to load costs — in other words, accept stage payments — but increase the overall cost to compensate for the delayed revenue. This is something that I do as a matter of routine when prospects request stage payments. Sometimes this leads to objections, but it then becomes a matter of discussing sharing the risk instead of one party carrying it all. If no deal is possible here, then you need to consider whether this is a client you really want to work with.

WARNING

Another way of dealing with the financial element, and one that's related to stage payments, is to consider an escrow agreement, where a proportion of funds is held in reserve pending a predetermined set of events that lead to its release. This tends to be rather complex and should never be entered into lightly, although it can be a good solution for large, complex deals.

In Chapter 11, I discuss guarantees and offer some advice on how to work with them. Guarantees also play a role when the perception of risk is an issue, and providing a structured guarantee can be a good way forward and around any impasse. Be aware, however, of exactly what you're guaranteeing, and make sure there's no room for ambiguity, with everything clearly defined in writing.

One of my first consulting clients demanded a personal guarantee as his way of mitigating against risk. Undoubtedly, this cost him business and was seen by many as an over-the-top reaction that was very one-sided in its implementation. I could never recommend this as a solution, even though I did sign such an agreement once as a new supplier to this client, who did on one occasion threaten to implement the personal guarantee and that proved to be the kiss of death to that business relationship. The phrase "having your cake and eating it, too" seems most appropriate here.

Chapter **19**

Qualifying Potential Business

You have a finite amount of time in your role of winning new business, which means you can't endlessly chase every bit of potential new business. Although that may sound contrary to the job, it's one of the keys to being successful in your role. Think about the most successful salespeople you know. Are they constantly chasing their tail trying to keep all the balls in the air? Or are they more measured in their approach, taking the necessary time to cultivate the right opportunities?

You need to have a set of criteria to help you decide which bits of new business are worth spending your time and effort on and to help you to manage the sales process to maximize your chance of getting to the yes decision as quickly as possible. You also need criteria to help you figure out the new business opportunities that you shouldn't pursue or that you're unlikely to win and, therefore, shouldn't waste your valuable time on.

These criteria you develop become your *qualification criteria.* You and your sales management colleagues need to agree on some of these criteria because they are such a vital part of the winning new business process. This chapter describes the importance of qualification, discusses different types of qualification criteria, and explains the value of tracking qualification information over time.

Qualifying: The Most Important Part of Winning New Business

Qualifying every new business opportunity is such an important part of your role in winning new business that it may be the most important part of your job.

REMEMBER

What do I mean by qualifying? With each new business opportunity, you need to think about three key things:

>> Can you measure the criterion?

>> Can you track the progress toward your goal?

>> Does the criterion help you decide what action you need to take?

If you answered yes to these questions, there's a good chance that the element you're considering should be part of your qualification process. If you can't answer yes to all three of these questions, there's a good chance that the element you're considering shouldn't be part of your core qualification process.

For example, you may decide that a prospect having a financial year-end within three months is an important criterion. You can easily measure this by either asking or checking fiscal records that are freely available. If you find that the year-end falls outside of this three-month window, then you can adjust your approach by delaying action until the timescale is within range, saving yourself the time and effort of starting a sales cycle before you know the prospect will be ready.

REMEMBER

In reality, you can use almost anything as qualifying criteria, and the key then becomes determining how important each qualifier is to your business and to your overall objectives. When I'm helping a client determine whether a project is worth pursuing, my rules are simple and include asking the following questions:

>> Do you know who the decision maker is or the key makeup of the decision-making unit?

>> Do you know the budget, and does it fit with your requirements?

>> Have you identified a real project?

If you don't know the answer to these basic questions or if the answers don't meet your new business objectives, then you don't have a qualified opportunity. If you continue to pursue it, you'll likely be wasting your time. In the rest of this chapter, I come back to these three key points, which I consider to be the absolute core qualification issues.

REMEMBER

Each business has additional qualification factors to add to these three fundamental ones, and all the qualification factors need to be met to consider a sales lead qualified.

If you don't use qualifying as a key in winning new business, what approach do you take? Chase everything and end up winning some wrong type of business while missing out on the key opportunities? Not such a great career move. Hope for the best that your prospects will work out for themselves that your solution is the best fit for them and buy it from you? An interesting approach and one that I've seen deployed too many times over the years but one that I'm delighted to see a competitor employ, because the competitor spends countless hours chasing shadows rather than going after new business on the basis of solid qualification.

Recently I was in a meeting with a client's management team, and we were discussing what approach they should take to win new business. The CEO was concerned with targeting and winning the right type and right mix of new business or, in his words, "If we get too much low revenue work, we will be swamped with work but not making any money." I advised them to qualify the type of business that they wanted in terms of the fit for their skill set but that also matched their growth and revenue plans.

WARNING

Winning any type of new business just for the sake of getting more work in through the door is rarely the right way to move ahead successfully.

Beginning with Basic Qualification Criteria

To qualify a potential new business opportunity, you need to first determine what tests, or criteria, you're going to apply to it. In the preceding section, I talk about the three core elements of knowing the decision maker, having a budget fit, and identifying a project. In this section, I go into more detail about these elements, and I show you why they're so important in winning new business.

The decision-making unit

Sometimes you'll sell to an individual who has both the need and the budget, but often, and especially in bigger sales situations, you'll deal with a group of people who, in turn, have a say in the outcome of the sale. When there's more than one decision maker, this is commonly known as the decision-making unit, or DMU.

If you ask an experienced salesperson what his biggest problem area is, you'll often hear that it's "selling to a committee" or something similar. Making a sale to an individual is usually much easier, but with the right understanding and approach, selling to a decision-making unit isn't a huge problem. You'll also want to understand and be comfortable with the decision-making unit because you'll encounter it frequently.

In its simplest form, a decision-making unit may be a cohabiting couple if you're selling a domestic product. In a more complex business sale, it may comprise a technical person, a finance person, someone who represents the end users of the product, and so on. (You may also come across a purchasing department, but I cover that separately in Chapter 13.) A marketing textbook tells you about users, initiators, influencers, decision makers, gate keepers, and buyers, which can all sound a bit daunting. The key things to note are that people have different roles to play in making a decision about a purchase and that you need to understand their motivation and be able to address their specific concerns as part of your selling job.

As far as qualifying new business opportunities is concerned, you need to be able to identify who the key players are. As an absolute minimum, you need to understand who will make the final decision or how that decision will be made. Sometimes the easiest way to find something out is to ask a simple question. Ask your contact or the person who appears to be the most senior you're dealing with to explain his decision-making process. If he's reluctant to tell you, push back until you get an answer. Knowing the client's decision-making process is important to your sales process, and asking your client to explain this to you demonstrates that you're being professional in your approach.

In those very rare situations where someone won't tell you about the decision-making process, you need to consider what this says about the relationship you're going to have with that business and whether it's worth pursuing. Explain this to your contact if necessary. You need the information to do your job, but you also want to conduct yourself professionally. If he's not going to provide the information you need, then you have a mismatch in this business relationship that you may as well stop before it gets any further.

After identifying the key players and understanding the roles they play in the buying process, you'll see that they each have different viewpoints and needs that you need to meet. You can handle these differences in a variety of ways depending on the size and complexity of your sale.

If you're presenting to or always meeting the key players as a group, then be sure to acknowledge each of them and demonstrate that you understand they have differing objectives to cover. Offer to meet with them individually if that is appropriate, or offer to communicate via email to address any specific issues. When meeting as a group, you need to make sure that while your primary focus is on the most relevant person (generally the ultimate decision maker you've identified), you also take time to involve the others as the discussion covers their areas. Sometimes you'll need to deliberately take the conversation in a direction that addresses key individuals, for two reasons: First, to demonstrate that you understand the importance of their areas, and second, to actively involve them. Keep in mind that they'll have a say in the final decision and you want them on your side.

TIP

Often in a decision-making unit, some people will have no apparent role to play in the decision. These are usually decision influencers rather than decision makers and often play an important role without necessarily having a specific area of interest. You need to keep them engaged, too, and make sure that you pick up on anything that they introduce. Influencers are just that — people who can sway a decision by influence rather than authority — and you need to discuss with them what their interest in the solution is and to be able to demonstrate how your solution addresses those concerns.

The budget

Every purchase, domestic or business, has a budget, but it may not be expressed in absolute terms, such as $5,000. Instead, it may be addressed as "affordable," for example. One of your important qualifying tasks is to determine what the budget is and to make sure that it fits in line with your proposed solution. How do you find out a budget? Well, you can ask, but don't be too surprised if you're not given a simple straightforward answer because often buyers are suspicious of being asked how much they're prepared to spend.

TIP

Imagine the reaction if, when asked what the selling price was, you took a similar approach and wouldn't say. Point this out to your buyers if they won't tell you their budget, and also inform them that your role is to ensure a good fit between your product or service and their needs and that part of the process is to ensure both affordability and no mismatch between expectation and reality. (Refer to the power of silence concept that I cover in Chapter 2 if you still have a problem.)

If you can't get an absolute value on the budget, ask for a guideline and let it be known that the process can't go much further without that information. Stop the phone call or even the meeting if necessary because you really don't want to get into game playing. But remember: Be professional in everything that you do.

Be as direct as necessary here, and tell your prospect that you can't continue to recommend a solution without knowing the basic parameters. Turn the situation around and ask how he proceeds when he's in the same position with potential clients of his own. Don't accept being fobbed off here because this is a vital piece of information and without it, you can't continue a sale. Any genuine buyer understands this, and if you continue to meet resistance, then walk away from the sale because it isn't going to be qualified.

Here are some other ways to find out budget information if buyers are reluctant to tell you outright:

>> Ask how they currently meet their needs and how much that costs (or you may discover this based on the information you gather).

>> Ask about the level of investment they think is necessary to get the results they're looking for.

>> Talk about similar situations you've experienced, discuss the approximate cost of those, and gauge a reaction.

When you find the budget, you need to check for a good fit to your solution. If the figures are reasonably close, then you're generally okay to accept that the deal is qualified in terms of budget. If there's a significant mismatch in the budget and your solution cost, then it fails this qualification criterion and you need to reassess accordingly. Budgets aren't always cast in stone, so find out through carefully considered questions whether there's any flexibility in the budget and, if so, how flexible it is. If there's no flexibility, then you should walk away from the deal, because if it's not affordable, it's not going to happen anyway and you don't have time to waste.

In addition to finding out the project budget, you need to determine who has the budget sign-off. This member of the decision-making unit (see the preceding section) will be a vital person for you as the sale moves toward a yes. The budget sign-off holder has the ultimate buyer's responsibility, so you need to make sure that you've covered all of his objections and that he is completely happy with your proposed solution.

Don't wait until the last minute to cover this sign-off responsibility as that will inevitably lead to a delay.

The timescale

A key qualifying area is the project timescale. You need to make sure that the buyer's timescale is consistent with the amount of effort you're putting in at this stage. For example, if your prospect is just at the information gathering stage and isn't going to make a decision for six months, then your job is to make sure he has access to the information he needs but not to commit lots of your time to it. At this point, you may simply direct him to your website and any literature you have to make sure he gets the info he needs.

Within a sales cycle, you have a window of opportunity for action. It's difficult to define hard-and-fast rules here because of the differences in products and services. You'll know what the typical sales cycle is like for your solution, how long information gathering lasts, whether a long gestation period exists, and how much planning is needed before prospects are ready to make a buying decision.

REMEMBER

You need to determine where the key points in your sales cycle occur. At these points, you need to be available to your prospect to cover any points he may have and to assist in moving the process forward. Understand the following triggers and be prepared to act on them:

>> What are your prospect's timescale drivers?

>> Why is he going to make a decision at the time he said he will?

>> Do internal or external factors have a bearing on this decision?

>> Is there anything that you could or should do to influence these factors?

In a long sales cycle, you don't have to be in constant contact with your prospect, as long as he knows how to contact you with questions. As key points approach, and especially as you get close to the end of the sales cycle, you need to spend more time with your prospect, but depending on your product or service, this doesn't always have to be face-to-face time because telephone time is often sufficient. Whatever the case, you need to show that you're committing time and resources to your prospect and that you're available to him.

Need and pain points

A need is best defined by the question "Does your prospect's business have a problem that your solution can solve?" A pain point can be best described by the statement "there is a problem that needs to be addressed."

Does your prospect have a real need for your product or service? If you don't quickly discover this, you risk wasting lots of time only to find out that he isn't going to buy from you because he doesn't actually need what you're proposing.

Amazingly enough, prospects don't always tell the truth or don't always explain their motives in looking at a product or service for different reasons. You need to be aware of all of these possibilities:

>> Some prospects aren't real buyers but rather mystery shoppers or even competitors who are trying to get a better understanding of your product, service, and sales processes. This does happen but not all that often thankfully.

>> Some prospects make a habit of collecting information but have no intention of doing anything with it.

>> Some prospects think they know what they want, but either they haven't thought it out well enough or they change their minds during the sales cycle.

REMEMBER

Anyone looking to buy a product or service is doing so for a reason, and as a salesperson, one of your first jobs is to discover these motives and the impact your prospect hopes to make by fulfilling them. Your job then becomes one of guiding your prospect through the process and demonstrating how your solution will address his needs and provide positive benefits.

A prospect usually has a set of needs rather than just a specific requirement, and you need to identify all of them as well as gain an understanding of their relative importance. This knowledge will put you in a good position to empathize with him as you build a sales relationship.

It may be that your prospect has to work weekends in order to catch up on work because his current mode of operating isn't time efficient. By demonstrating how your solution meets his business need, you can also show him how his time will be freed up.

Understanding your prospect's needs and their relative importance also enables you to quickly identify any show stoppers — that is, any benefit that your prospect wants to achieve that your proposed solution won't deliver. If such a show stopper is a need with high relative importance to your prospect, then the chances of you getting to a yes are slim to none, so it's vital to identify the needs and their importance very early in the sales cycle.

One of the best salespeople I've come across when selling to me didn't get a sale. He spent some time on the phone with me getting an understanding of my need and how his solution would meet it. It became obvious to him fairly quickly, as a result of asking searching questions, that my absolute core requirement was something that his solution wasn't able to deliver. It would do 80 percent of what I was looking for, but he recognized, correctly, that I wouldn't buy something that didn't fulfill my essential need. Instead of trying to change my mind or forcing a solution that was never going to be satisfactory, he told me that he understood how important my requirement was and thanked me for my time but said that he wasn't able to meet my needs.

You may think that losing a sale like this is a bad thing, but that's far from the case. This salesman recognized that his solution wouldn't meet my qualification criteria and therefore he wouldn't make the sale, so he saved a lot of time and effort by walking away. He also gained, in me, someone who is happy to refer others to him as a person who understood his solution and was open and straightforward to deal with.

REMEMBER

Don't consider it a failure if you uncover needs that your solution can't deliver. Sometimes you may find an acceptable workaround solution, but this comes down to understanding the relative importance. Often, a workaround won't be viable or acceptable. In this case, the sale is over because it has failed to pass a key qualification test. But this isn't a failure; this just shows you why qualification is so important. Without it, you can spend a lot of time and effort going after new business opportunities that are just not appropriate and will therefore never result in a yes.

The attitude to risk

REMEMBER

Your prospect's attitude to risk is also a qualification criterion. If he's ultraconservative in nature, then any sale is likely to be hard work and you need to factor this into your timescale (which I discuss earlier in this chapter). If he has more of a laissez faire character, you may have other problems to face if he blows hot and cold about a solution.

Risk is also a cultural consideration. In seeking to understand your prospect's attitude to risk and to use it as a qualifying criterion, you need to find a way to determine how important risk is to him. Unfortunately, you can't really ask your prospect, "How do you feel about risk?" You need to look for a set of clues that emerge during discussions and within his environment. The biggest clues will come from past performance, so ask how other decisions were reached and how he felt about the processes.

The biggest risk about risk (excuse the pun) is that your prospect will decide that doing anything represents a risk that he's unwilling to take, and this is a surefire way to a no.

An attitude to risk in a sales situation has no rights or wrongs. It's something that you need to be aware of, although you'll have no influence on it. If your solution isn't an exact fit or if you're asking your prospect to be an early adopter of a solution, you may lose the sale. Risk's qualification weighting will, to a large extent, depend on the type of product or service that you're selling.

For more on risk and its role in a sales situation, check out Chapters 5 and 18.

Your competitive standing

Your competitive positioning as a qualification criterion may not be an obvious one, but nonetheless it's important. First, you need to understand whether your solution is a good fit for your prospect's needs. Does your solution lend itself to his needs out of the box? How does your solution measure against competitive offerings that your prospect may also be considering? Does your solution offer some clear benefits? If so, then how are you communicating this to your prospect?

In a "tick the box" exercise, how does your offering compare to those of your competitors in terms of matching your prospect's needs? You can be sure that your prospect will compare your solution to your competitors' at some point, so you need to be on the ball with your own comparisons. And you need to be ready to discuss them in a solution-oriented way, not attempting to put down any competitor's solution but rather demonstrating a clear understanding of your prospect's needs as met by your solution in a way that fits better than any competitors' can.

Ensure that your sales support material is presented in the best possible light in order for this "tick the box" exercise to show you in the best possible way. Don't make it difficult for your prospect to make a comparison of your solution to others that he may be considering.

If your solution is a less obvious fit but can still deliver real benefits, can you change the rules to play to your strengths? The short answer is yes. But this goes back to my point about understanding the real needs of your prospect and the relative importance of each of them (see the earlier section "Need and pain points" for more information). If you score poorly on some areas, you can play to your strengths on others, really pushing the benefits to your prospect while showing that you're a good fit in the more obvious areas. Although this perhaps isn't the best way to win the business, this shows your prospect that your solution scores highly in other areas that can provide a real advantage to him.

TIP

A useful approach in this situation is to borrow tactics from guerilla warfare, where you lose if you take on the competition head-to-head because it's a better, more obvious fit. If you can take the focus toward the less obvious benefits, sniping away at the side of an issue where you have a clear advantage, then you can begin to change the weightings in your favor by persuading your prospect that these are the areas where he'll gain most advantage over time. In other words, change the rules. Don't play to your competitor's strengths; understand its weaknesses in areas where you're strong and focus on those areas.

WARNING

Before taking this approach, you need be sure you understand your prospect's attitude to risk as I discuss in the preceding section. If your prospect is very conservative in his approach, then you're unlikely to win with guerilla tactics. And in terms of qualification criteria, you'll lose in this example. You need to understand where this leaves you in prospect qualification. Are you better off walking away from a potential sale and focusing your attention on better qualified opportunities? Note that you're not going to win every sale, and you need to use qualification as the real guide to where you have the best opportunities.

A level playing field

One of the most basic qualification criteria — so obvious that it's sometimes overlooked — is to make sure that you have a realistic chance of winning the business right from the beginning of the sales cycle.

As I explain earlier in this chapter, you need to ask these questions as the sales cycle gets started and before you spend too much time and effort on it, ensuring that the project is real:

>> Is this a real project? Is it going to happen? Is it budgeted? Is it core to the prospect's needs?

>> Does the prospect have the authority to make a buying decision?

>> Has your prospect already decided what he's going to buy and from whom before you even begin?

>> Are you being given an equal opportunity along with any competitors, or have you been invited to discuss your solution merely to make up the numbers? Are you being used as a stalking horse for your prospect to put pressure on an existing or preferred vendor?

TIP

I strongly suggest that if you're not being given a level playing field, then you're better off walking away from a potential deal that wastes your time and effort when the decision is essentially already made.

So how do you find out about the playing field? Ask your prospect about other solutions he's looking at. Ask about existing suppliers and how you'll be treated in relation to them. Generally, it's difficult for a prospect to hide the truth from you given a direct question, so don't beat about the bush if you perceive that you're not being treated equally.

In some industries, competitive tendering is the accepted norm. Two schools of thought on this kind of sales situation: Either you accept it and give it your best shot, or you decline to take part, preferring to focus your efforts on prospects who have a more selective buying process.

TIP

My rule of thumb is not to get involved in a sales process where more than two other vendors are involved. Why? For the following reasons, each of which is a red flag that suggests that your sales effort will be better utilized elsewhere:

>> Too many vendors risk an artificially prolonged sales cycle.

>> It suggests that your prospect is unclear on exactly what he's trying to achieve.

>> It suggests that your prospect doesn't value your time.

WARNING

Another issue to watch out for is when you're competing against an incumbent supplier. In this case, it's essential to understand the client-vendor relationship and why you're being asked to compete against an existing supplier. Is it a real opportunity, or is the prospect using you to put pressure on the supplier?

Adding Objective and Subjective Criteria

Ideally, you have a comprehensive set of qualification criteria — that is, comprehensive in that it covers the basics. Next, you need to consider the objective information you need to know about a sales situation to understand the likelihood of it closing in your favor. Then you need to balance this information against some subjective criteria, such as human dynamics and relationships, because you need to remember the adage that people buy people first.

Earlier in this chapter, I cover some of the basic qualification criteria. You also need to consider solution-specific criteria by asking the following questions:

>> Does your prospect have the necessary infrastructure to implement your solution?

>> Does your solution meet your prospect's technical requirements?

>> Do any licensing considerations need to be addressed?

Then you need to meet the following basic sets of demographic and activity criteria to give a more complete picture:

>> Company size

>> Industry sector

>> Geographic location

>> Sales volume potential over a defined period of time

>> Source of the lead

>> Credit worthiness of the prospect

Some criteria, which have straightforward yes or no answers, are objective. Other criteria, which are just as important, are more subjective and have to do with feelings and decision making.

In putting together your qualification criteria, the real question you need to ask yourself is, "What do we need to know to be able to get this deal to a yes?" Answering that question will guide you to selecting the correct criteria for your specific needs.

Objective criteria

Objective criteria are fairly straightforward — something either is or isn't met. For example, either you know that the budget is within your defined parameters or you know that it isn't within your parameters. This is black and white. There is scope for shades of gray, however, in that you may not yet know what the budget is. In these cases, if the budget is within your parameters, then this criterion is met. If the budget isn't within your parameters, then it's not met. If you don't yet know, then this criterion is pending. You pass the criteria only when you have a positive answer.

When I defined the objective criteria we use in my business for each contact stage in a sales cycle, I selected the following set of criteria, known as explicit ratings:

>> **Role:** Does your prospect have the authority to make a buying decision? Is he the key decision maker or a key member of the decision-making unit?

>> **Budget:** Do you understand the budget that has been allocated? Is it in line with expectations and reasonable for the scope of the project?

>> **Timescale:** Is the decision-making timescale in line with both the complexity of the solution and your sales budget time frame?

>> **Project:** Is the project real? Is it funded? Is in it line with the ability of your solution to address its needs?

>> **Demographics:** Is the size of the company suitable for your solution?

When qualifying these criteria, we assign each item a weighting between A and D. These weightings aren't equal; a weighting of A, for example, is more solid than one of D. For both our implicit and explicit ratings (find out about implicit ratings in the next section), our CRM system automatically calculates the weightings, which are based on the answers to the subjective and objective criteria. By having the weightings automatically calculated, we remove some of the "gut feel" qualification and finish up with a much more realistic set of data that we're able to rely on. (I go into more detail on measuring and tracking qualification criteria in Chapters 9 and 21, where I look at different aspects of using CRM systems.)

We also add some overriding objective criteria, which must be met before we'll even begin a sales conversation with a potential prospect:

>> **Business sector:** Is your prospect operating in a business sector that's a good fit for your solution?

>> **Geographical location:** Can you cover support in your prospect's area?

>> **Source of the lead:** How reliable is the pre-sales information that you have? How was the prospect identified?

>> **Company turnover:** Ensure that the prospect is neither too big nor too small to be able to operate with your solution. Is the company big enough to be able to offer you future scope for expansion?

>> **Number of employees:** Does your solution lend itself to that scale of business?

TECHNICAL STUFF

We add to this a couple of other criteria that are specific to our business and so not relevant for inclusion here to avoid confusion.

REMEMBER

If we ever run into a sales problem with a prospect that we didn't expect to occur, our first point of reference becomes the qualification data, and we ask: Have we correctly qualified the opportunity?

Subjective criteria

Subjective criteria are based on what you know about factors that are open to human interpretation, such as the level of interest your prospect expresses. Prospects can be very interested, a little interested, or not very interested, and both the level of interest and the way you choose to measure and report it are open to interpretation.

WARNING

Because subjective criteria are — just that — subjective, you need to take care in how you set these criteria and the reliance you place in the results. Subjective criteria should never be used in isolation to qualify the sales potential but can provide good guidance when used correctly and in conjunction with objective criteria (see the preceding section).

When I defined the subjective criteria that we use in my business, at each stage of tracking lead progress, I selected this set of criteria, which we call implicit ratings:

>> **No interest:** This is a dead-end lead. Maybe revisit it in the future when personnel have moved.

>> **More information required:** The prospect seems interested and has requested more details.

>> **Follow-up agreed:** A set of follow-up activities has been agreed on and will be carried out.

>> **Very interested:** This is the ideal situation; the prospect has a need and understands what you're offering.

We assign a weighting from 1 to 4 depending on which category the prospect falls into. These ratings are subjective because they're based on feelings, or perceptions, of how the prospect is disposed toward the proposed solution. Clearly, these criteria differ in importance to the qualification score, with very interested scoring a 4.

Tracking Qualification Over Time

Tracking qualification over the life of a sales cycle is closely linked to using qualification criteria. In a well-structured sales environment, the data you continually collect on your prospects is a vital tool in being able to accurately forecast the outcome of any specific sales opportunity. Qualification never stops, and a good new business salesperson continually qualifies all his opportunities, especially because situations change and the nature of a sales cycle is dynamic.

TIP

It's a good discipline to keep track of how your qualification changes as a sale progresses because you get an even better understanding of your prospect base and the overall opportunities that your business has.

The following sections explain how often to qualify prospects and how to manage and use the information you gather.

Knowing how often to qualify

REMEMBER

Don't fall into the trap of assuming that qualification of a prospect or a sales opportunity is a one-off action. Nothing could be further from the truth, and this assumption can come back and bite you if you're not careful. Just because you identified the key decision maker at the beginning of the sales cycle doesn't mean that he will remain the key decision maker. Businesses are organic, and change is a daily occurrence, so you need to keep on top of developments and be continually checking and requalifying as a sales cycle progresses.

I had firsthand experience of this recently when helping a client to open a new business relationship with a major technology company. We identified the key decision makers, and we qualified that there was indeed a real project and that both the budget and timescales were a good fit. Demographically, everything was ideal. The sales cycle was underway with some good initial discussion taking place. What could possibly go wrong? It started as something that was on our radar but gave us no immediate cause for concern — a new senior management appointment. This new manager didn't have an immediate bearing on our project because he wasn't involved, nor was his predecessor. What did change was that the new senior manager issued a company-wide dictate about new procedures to be followed when any project was outsourced, and this introduced a new key player into the decision-making unit as well as a new set of decision-making criteria. The balance of the decision-making unit subtlety changed, and had we not been alert to this, our client would have progressed its sale based on an out-of-date set of qualification criteria. Had it lost the sale, this would have been the pivotal moment. As it happens, our client went on to win the project, which in large part was due to being able to quickly identify and react to new qualification criteria.

REMEMBER

You'll often find that pivotal moments in the sales cycle occur when you least expect them. Sometimes it can be insight gained in a conversation of a new piece or research that you uncover. The key is to always remember to update your sales tracking system (I cover more on this in Chapters 4, 9, and 21) and the qualification data. When you review your prospect list and look at your forecasts in detail, they should reflect these newfound changes, and you should revisit any existing assumptions in that light.

In almost any sales situation, your qualification data provides the answers to these questions:

>> Will it close?

>> When will it close?

>> Why didn't it close?

>> Why didn't it close on time?

Learn to love the data. If used correctly, it can give you some superb insights to the real status of your new business initiatives.

Managing information about the qualification process

I talk a lot in this chapter about the need to qualify and manage the qualification process, but how do you manage to keep track of all this information and turn it into useful knowledge? In Chapter 4, I show you how technology can be one of your best friends in winning new business. You shouldn't hide behind technology, though, and you shouldn't use the lack of it as an excuse for inaction. Good old-fashioned pen and paper and a well-thought-out filing system can go a long way to helping you, too.

Selling and communication skills are paramount in uncovering the gems of qualification information. It's amazing what you'll learn and what people will tell you if you ask the right question at the right time. Ask questions and probe the answers. Keep your eyes and especially your ears open.

TIP

Develop your own qualification checklist; see Figure 19-1 for an example. Write down the key things you need to find out from a prospect and check them off as you discover the answers. Whenever you can, add this information into your company CRM or database system so it becomes shared knowledge and you can use it to track and measure the prospect qualification and pipeline.

REMEMBER

You need to take ownership of qualifying your prospects and not expect anyone else to do it for you. It's as important as managing your calendar, and you need to treat it with the same degree of importance. Ultimately, your skills in qualifying prospects will be the measure of your new business success.

Using qualification knowledge to make new business decisions

Very few new business salespeople have an abundance of time and are able to devote large chunks of such a valuable commodity where it won't reap significant returns, but how do you know where to invest your valuable time?

REMEMBER

Use the knowledge that you gain from qualifying opportunities and from tracking that qualification over time to give you the answer to the question, "What shall I do now?" In days gone by, salespeople largely relied on instinct or feelings when determining which prospects they need to invest time on. If you're truly tracking and constantly qualifying, then the data you collect will point you to which opportunities need your time. I'm not suggesting that you do away with some of the basic selling skills or that you ignore instinct, but used in conjunction with real insight from qualification and tracking data, you can really be on top of your game all the time.

You'll likely have times when you need additional resources to assist with a sale. When that happens, you'll often have to make a case internally for being allocated scarce resources. Correctly using and recording new business qualification will quickly provide you (and whoever you need to convince to give you the resources) the necessary information to make quick and informed decisions.

Example Qualification Checklist

Add your own criteria to make it relevant to your business.

Decision-Making Unit	
Who is the ultimate decision maker?	
Who are the key influencers?	
What are each of the DMU members looking for?	
Budgets	
What is the budget for the project?	
Is the budget approved?	
Timescale	
When is a decision due to be made?	
What risks are there to this timescale?	
Are there any third-party issues that could cause delay?	
Needs	
Do you know the key project drivers?	
How important are each of the drivers?	
Does your solution meet the key drivers?	
Risk	
Does the prospect have to find a solution?	
What alternatives does the prospect have?	
Competitive Standing	
Who are your competitors?	
How does your solution measure up against competitors' solutions?	
Is there an incumbent supplier, and if so, why are you involved?	
Demographics	
Is the prospect a good fit to your objectives?	

FIGURE 19-1:
A sample qualification checklist.

Consider this scenario: If you were a sales manager and had two salespeople asking for the same resource at the same time, and one request was backed up with a well-qualified case showing that the bases had all been covered and that this resource could drive the sale to an early yes, and the other request was based on a gut feeling because the salesperson "just knew" it would make a difference, where would you invest the resource?

In the earlier section "Adding Objective and Subjective Criteria," I talk about the implicit and explicit ratings that we use in my business. With these ratings, we're able to quickly identify opportunities where, for example, the prospect is interested but we don't know budget or timescales. This case would wave a big red flag to me, and I would want to know what exactly the prospect was interested in when clearly we know next to nothing about him.

Another example would be where our qualification criteria tells us that we have a first-rate prospect where we know the budget, timescale, and role of the decision maker, that the project is right for us, and that the demographics are spot on, but the prospect has no interest or maybe worse still the prospect is waiting for more information. Situations like these do occur in all sales environments, but having knowledge of them before it's too late to do something about it can make all the difference between winning new business and losing it.

REMEMBER

Qualification and tracking systems don't need to be overly sophisticated, and almost any new business team can easily replicate well-thought-out ones. Don't use fear of the unknown, fear of change, or fear of being "too complicated" as excuses to not be able to derive the same sort of benefits in new business. It can be done, and it can be done easily. I expand on this theme in Chapters 4, 9, and 21.

Experienced sales managers are able to identify these key pieces of information from sales reports and discussions with the salespeople involved, but their job can be made a lot easier and they can discover and act upon these issues much faster if the sales cycle information is treated as valuable knowledge. This qualification and information gathering can sometimes require salespeople to make a cultural change when they've traditionally guarded their information and been somewhat selective in the information they've shared with managers and colleagues. I have to put my hand up here and admit that I've been guilty of doing just this before I understood, accepted, and bought into the collaborative information-is-knowledge school of thought and long before I became a management consultant focused on helping companies to win new business.

I used to dread Monday morning sales meetings when the managing director would pore over spreadsheets and want to know all this "unnecessary" information and, even worse, when he put me on the spot with direct questions about "my" prospects. Who was he to want to know "my" information? How times have changed over the years as the poacher turns gamekeeper.

REMEMBER

An individual new business salesperson may genuinely think that the sales situation he's involved in is unique and that no one has ever encountered it previously, so he has to find his own way around the issues. He would, however, be wrong. Almost no sales situation is unique. Salespeople have a lot of clues readily available to them on how best to proceed in any given situation but only if they communicate the situation and seek help. Colleagues can share knowledge they've gained from wider-ranging research and intelligence, including how to save time and improve chances of success, for the overall success of the salesperson. However, if he still operates in a secretive "my sale, my data" environment, then knowledge is never going to find him on its own.

Gaining competitive advantage from qualification knowledge

Knowledge gained from qualifying your prospects should deliver you a real competitive advantage in the sales cycle. It's often said that knowledge equates to power, and in winning new business, that is certainly the case. Knowing your prospect and understanding his motivation, backed up with real solid data, puts you in such a commanding position in a sales situation that you should be beating any competition much more often than you lose. In those hopefully rare occasions when you don't win a sale, you'll find the reason why in your qualification criteria. You should make it mandatory to review any lost sales opportunity in light of your qualification to see what happened and whether you should have seen the problems and been able to take corrective action. Apply those lessons, and you will have at least gained something from a lost sale.

REMEMBER

Knowledge is a two-way street, and you'll get more and better insight if you take the time to log and share your data. This is especially true in a situation where multiple new business salespeople are working for the same business. The nature of a salesperson has tended to be self-focused and somewhat secretive about his data. This needs a culture change to really begin to have a positive impact, but you can begin to educate people to expect to gain much more than they feel they may lose by sharing data, which in turn becomes knowledge when combined and analyzed.

If you get into the habit of routinely updating sales information systems with everything you discover during the progress of a sales cycle, this information builds up over time and patterns emerge, which can assist both you and others involved in similar situations. Strive to be the best you can be at logging information that you discover during the sales process. What may seem insignificant at the time could very well prove to be the key to unlocking your sale later on, or it could prove to be a priceless nugget of information in another sale.

Just gathering reams of information is of little use, though. You see the benefit only when you collate, examine, process, share, and act upon that information. At that point, the information becomes knowledge and a valuable asset in helping you to achieve competitive advantage in sales because you have access to an information network.

IF IT'S NOT QUALIFIED, IT'S NOT GOING TO HAPPEN

Old-school salespeople will tell you that gut feel or instinct for a sale are their best friends. This idea is more than a little outdated. It may have been true 20-plus years ago, but as the profession of sales has developed over the years, it has also become much more sophisticated. Today, I feel safe to say that the most important aspect of a salesperson's job is to qualify potential new business, not just once but continually over the course of a sales cycle. Done correctly, this will guide you toward knowing where to invest your time and will provide you with the best possible sales closing ratio.

One client asked me to look at why it hadn't closed a piece of new business that it was expecting to win during the month. All the signs apparently told the client that the sale was "in the bag," and the only negative sign was the sales forecasting system my business had implemented.

Sales forecasting works on both subjective and objective ratings, and this sale was flagged as a C2, meaning it was progressing okay but not forecastable. The client decided to ignore this rating, and it included the sale in the formal forecasting system anyway because it "knew it was coming in this month." Strangely, the sale didn't close, and we were asked as consultants to have a look at what was wrong.

In this type of situation, you can almost always find the answer by looking at the qualification of the lead. Sure enough, the answer was staring anyone who looked for it right in the face. It was also the reason the sale forecasting system had it as a C2 and not an A1 or A2 as our client expected.

Why didn't the deal close? Simple. It wasn't properly qualified and was never going to close during that month for one glaringly obvious reason: The client wasn't dealing with the budget holder; its contact was somewhere down the food chain. When we looked at the CRM system notes, right there in the first note was a comment that the contact would "discuss with the budget holder." The client never revisited this and never even mentioned it again. The sales forecasting system flagged it as an issue, but the client assumed it to be "wrong" because it "knew it was going to happen."

Although this was a foolish error, it proved to be a very costly one for the client. The moral is, if in doubt, check the qualification because 99 percent of the time the answer will be there.

If a sale isn't qualified, then you should not be forecasting it; and if you're not forecasting it, then why are you wasting time on it? Trust your qualification data. It really is one of your most valuable assets in winning new business.

TIP

An information network is generally company confidential and stored and processed by a CRM system, which I discuss in Chapters 4 and 9, but you're also able to tap into informal information networks, such as chamber of commerce or other business networking events that I cover in Chapter 17.

REMEMBER

As a new business salesperson, one of your key attributes needs to be uncovering snippets of information and turning them into knowledge that will lead you to be in a stronger competitive position than any other salesperson you're competing with for a specific sale. Knowledge really becomes power when you apply it to a competitive sales situation.

IN THIS CHAPTER

» **Letting your qualification criteria guide you**

» **Tackling personality and group dynamics**

» **Getting your time back**

» **Handling indecisive prospects**

» **Leaving when a prospect lies**

Chapter **20**

Knowing When to Move On

A s a new business salesperson, you need to recognize that some deals are just not going to happen, regardless of what you do to try to bring those deals in. And there comes a point in some sales cycles where you just have to move on and accept defeat. Recognizing when you've reached that stage isn't always easy because you're too close to the action, so in this chapter, I highlight the warning signs to look out for.

Some warning signs may be that too much of your time and resources are being consumed without moving the sales cycle forward, or the relationship you're building with your prospect is just not hitting the right notes. Another clear warning sign is if you realize that your proposed solution isn't actually going to fit the requirements. In this case, the decision to move on is fairly black and white. However, knowing when to cease your sales activity with a prospect isn't always as clear as that.

REMEMBER

Moving on is different from being prepared to walk away as a negotiating tactic that I discuss elsewhere in this book (in particular, Chapter 10); moving on is the end of the road for that sales opportunity.

Taking Action When Qualification Criteria Aren't Met

It should be obvious that a prospect who fails to meet your qualification criteria (see Chapters 9 and 19) is one who's unlikely to result in a sale being made, but there's always the temptation to give it a bit longer to see what happens.

REMEMBER

It's important to revisit why you have qualification criteria in the first place. Qualification is the sales mechanism that ensures that you don't waste your time chasing dead-end leads that aren't right for your company or spend too long with prospects who aren't a good fit for your solution. Issues such as affordability come into play here; if your solution is clearly not affordable or not in the scope of a prospect's budget, for example, then that's a clear sign that all is not well and that the prospect likely won't pass your qualification criteria.

Are there circumstances when you should ignore the qualification criteria? The absolute answer is no; however, in some situations you may delay making a final decision pending more research and discovery because the need and solution may require some further investigation to determine the right fit. The following sections provide more guidance.

TIP

If your solution almost fits but not exactly, then you need to decide whether to continue with the sale, knowing that your prospect will likely uncover a perfect-fit solution elsewhere, which would essentially kill your sale anyway. Use due diligence to examine the facts that you uncover before you make any final decision about moving on and dropping the opportunity.

Trusting your qualification criteria

In new business sales, little is more important than your qualification criteria; it drives the sales process, is vital in forecasting (covered in Chapter 21), and is an invaluable tool in sales management. Trusting the results of your qualification is important because they provide an objective view of where the sales cycle is and where it's likely to go.

REMEMBER

Some of your qualification criteria may be softer than others, and you need room for interpretation and some leeway here. Your new business experience will guide you; however, the following four basic pillars of qualification are non-negotiable, and you really do need to trust what they tell you:

» **Decision maker:** Are you speaking to the real decision maker, or the pivotal member of the decision-making unit, not some more junior information gatherer who's just passing the information along? If you're not speaking to the decision maker, your prospect isn't qualified.

» **Real project:** Have you identified the real need that your prospect is trying to address? Is the requirement a real one that delivers business benefits or solves a pressing business need? Without this level of identification, your prospect isn't qualified. A real project is one that actually matters to the prospect and that is seen as being vital to the business, not a vanity project that is a "nice to have but not essential" type.

» **Funded:** How is the solution going to be funded? What budget is it coming from? Who signs off on it? Is the budget allocated to the need sufficient to meet the requirements of your project? Without positive answers to all these questions, your prospect isn't qualified.

» **Time frame:** When does your prospect intend the project to go live? Working back from that, when does a decision need to be made? Are these timescales compatible with each other? Do they fit with your sales time frame in such a way as to justify sales resources being committed now? Again, without positive answers to these questions, your prospect isn't qualified.

TIP

Another factor to consider is whether your prospect has any specific rules or requirements that you need to address. If so, are they compatible with your company's mission, objectives, and terms of business? If not, you have another problem that points to a failed qualification. An example of this may be that your prospect will deal only with a corporation and not with someone who has a sole trader business status.

Avoiding "instinct"

WARNING

All too often, sales time and resources are wasted because new business sales-people ignored or overrode qualification indicators because they "knew better." Don't fall into this trap. Instinct is a way of rationalizing almost anything you choose, and although it has a place in guiding you through a sales cycle, it isn't something you should rely on as any form of methodology-driven parameter. You rarely "know better" than the facts and conclusions in your CRM system (see Chapter 9 for an introduction), so trust the data and avoid hiding behind instinct when the data tells you things that you may not want to hear.

For example, your CRM may have records of several previous attempts at selling your solution to a prospect, and each time he pulled out of the deal at the last minute. This information should sound loud warning bells about history repeating itself, and unless the prospect can persuade you that he is genuine — maybe by paying a deposit — I would consider this to be a case where you shouldn't continue with the sales cycle and risk wasting time and resources again.

REMEMBER

When challenged on why you're pulling out of a sales cycle and moving on, you need to be able to defend your position. Be objective in this, and back up your position with evidence from the CRM system and your contact reports. (Flip to Chapter 3 for a primer on these reports.)

Dealing with Personality and Group Issues

As well as the qualification issues I address earlier in this chapter, you also need to consider some human and relationship elements that may inhibit a sale from going ahead. Valid reasons for moving on apart from failing with qualification include the following:

>> **Personality clash:** As a new business salesperson, you're used to dealing with lots of different personality types, but on some occasions, you just won't see eye to eye with a prospect. If you need to be involved in a long sales cycle or if you need to have a continued involvement beyond the initial sale, then this is going to be a problem. If the clash is both ways, then you can be reasonably sure that your prospect isn't going to buy from you in any case. Cut your losses, and move on to another prospect.

>> **Goes against your values:** Some prospects you meet won't have the same morals or value set that you do or your company does. For example, it may become obvious that a prospect has a total disregard for paying license fees for products, and your solution may involve such fees. These cases always end in failure of either the sale or the implementation. Moving on as soon as you discover a problem is far easier and quicker than trying to tiptoe around it.

>> **Not "your type" of people:** People buy people first, which I discuss in Chapter 14. Corporate culture breeds certain characteristics, and people of a certain character are drawn to each other. I completely support the "not our type of people" reason for moving on as you know that particular personality types won't fit with your company's style of operating and that a sale will unlikely result from them anyway. Many times I've returned to the office after a sales meeting and declared that it wasn't going to happen because they weren't "our type of people," and I've never yet been wrong.

One particular case comes to mind; I met with a company that was interested in outsourced new business services but wanted to pay for the services only under a limited set of circumstances, and it appeared to expect us to work for nothing in all other cases. It quickly became clear in discussions with the company that it failed to understand the nature of the service it was considering using — I say using rather than buying because the company didn't want to pay! Rather than trying to re-educate, it was quicker, easier, and ultimately less expensive to just walk away.

You should also be wary of decision by committee. I'm not talking about the decision-making unit here. I'm talking, literally, about a decision made by a committee. You'll most likely come across this when selling into partnerships as a business type, where each partner has a personal investment and stake in the decision. It's like they're spending their own money, and not the business's, which in effect is what they're doing.

WARNING

If no clear decision maker and no clear leadership are present, and the committee wants to act in agreement with one another, then run away — don't just walk. This is a nightmare scenario for new business salespeople, and it will drain you of valuable time and resources, frequently going nowhere. At best, these types of sales situations lead to delay after delay as the prospects can't agree on a decision to save their lives, and at worst they'll just never make a decision.

Walking away always needs to be done with a degree of sensitivity, regardless of how happy you are to do so. I always tell a prospect that regretfully we are unable to work with him due to a difference in culture, values, or valuation; there is no need to go into great detail. I always ensure that I follow up in writing and document the situation in the CRM for future reference.

Handling the Reality of Time Wasting

Time is precious and one of your main assets. You have to use your time wisely, and having a prospect waste your time is frustrating.

REMEMBER

If you think that your time is being wasted, try to uncover the reasons behind that action. If a prospect seems to be deliberately wasting your time, you should immediately move on. In that case, the prospect is unprofessional, and you won't want to deal with him anyway. There's likely a more logical explanation, though. To find what it may be, ask the following questions:

>> **Is there a fear of risk?** I cover this in Chapter 18, but try to understand whether the prospect has a fear of risk. If so, address it as a risk management objection and act accordingly.

>> **Does your prospect actually have authority?** Have you qualified that your prospect has authority to conduct the buying cycle? Is the perception of time wasting linked to his uncertainty as to how to proceed and whether he actually has the authority to proceed? You may need to revisit your qualification (see Chapters 9 and 19).

>> **Is there a real need?** You should have determined this right at the outset, but has something changed? Or did you not qualify need sufficiently? Have a look at Chapter 19 about qualifying potential business.

The following sections provide additional pointers on how to overcome a prospect who's wasting your time.

Taking back your time

If you perceive that a prospect is wasting your time, you're likely right. Time is your asset, and it's your call on how to invest it to maximum effect in winning new business. Don't be afraid to value your time, and let it be seen that you do. It's professional and clearly defendable as a sales tool.

Some time-wasting actions that may lead you to determine that it's time to move on are a series of cancellations or no-shows at meetings or planned touch points, or the denial of key pieces of information that you need to progress the sales cycle and get the solution right for your prospect. There can be little justification for a prospect taking these actions, and they're real indicators that it's time to move on.

Another time-wasting experience is circular discussions. You just don't make any progress. The prospect raises objections, and you address them and of course log them into your contact reports, only to find that you cover the same ground at the next touch point. Your prospect seems not to "get it," and the sales cycle is stagnating. This is another case where your time is better invested elsewhere.

TIP

A quick and effective test of how your prospect values your time in establishing a winning solution to his business need is to take it away and see what reaction you get. Simply tell him that as you feel your time is being wasted that you're going to invest it elsewhere and that the solution you were proposing is no longer available to him. This will lead to one of two things:

>> The end of the sales cycle with no sale, which was where it was heading anyway

>> A realization by your prospect that he's going to lose the solution unless he changes his ways, in which case you may overcome the perception of time wasting

If you use the "going to move on" test, then make sure that you really are prepared to give up on the sale because there is no way back for you if he tries to call your bluff.

If your prospect fails to see the value that you're adding in your quest to find a solid solution to his need, then in reality the relationship isn't very strong and the sale isn't going to be of massive importance to him, so you may as well invest your time and effort elsewhere.

Prospects can be challenging, entertaining, fun, and frustrating in equal measure, and these emotions will shift during the sales cycle. That's life. However, if your touch points with your prospect become draining or increasingly frustrating rather than positive and engaging, then you need a reality check on where your deal is heading.

Setting deadlines

To try to overcome the perception of time wasting, you can give your prospect a deadline for action. Tell him that you need to get certain issues resolved by a given date if the sale is going to progress. This may seem like you're taking the lead and forcing him into action, and in reality you're doing exactly that. If he doesn't like it, then that sends you a clear message of where the sale is going — nowhere.

If you set a deadline, then you need to stick to it and move on if it's not met. Failure to do this will result in you losing face and, more importantly, in your prospect never believing anything else you tell him.

I'm reminded of a case some years ago when I worked for a very large computer manufacturer with an international presence. I was based in the U.K. doing a U.K. marketing job and had been asked whether I'd consider relocating to France to do a pan-European role. This was a big move as it meant moving my young family, but it offered a significant opportunity that I was keen on progressing. Discussions followed, and I went to both Geneva, which was European headquarters, and Paris, where the role was to be based, for internal interviews and planning sessions. The role was to take effect from the beginning of the new fiscal year on July 1 and so had to be agreed on and in place before then.

By the end of May, everything should have been ready and was from my point of view, but the ultimate decision maker, whom I knew and had discussed the role with, couldn't or wouldn't sign off on it. I gave him an ultimatum: "Sign it off within another seven days, or I'm withdrawing from the transfer and staying in my existing U.K. role." Seven days passed, and nothing had happened, so I carried out my stated plan and withdrew from the new role. It caused some uproar, but I demonstrated that I wasn't going to be messed about, and I continued in the U.K. until leaving the company about a year later as my confidence in it had been undermined.

Facing an Indecisive Prospect

Sometimes as a new business salesperson, you wonder how certain prospects ever got into senior roles within their company, and when you have to deal with an indecisive prospect, that's a case in point.

Human nature dictates that some people are naturally cautious, and that's fine, but being cautious and being indecisive are different things. If you encounter a prospect like this, you need to have endless patience and a fair degree of time to invest, and depending on the significance of the sale, you have some early decisions to make about moving on or guiding him through the processes.

TIP

Don't beat about the bush and give your prospect an opportunity to constantly delay everything. Make your information gathering and qualification style more direct than you normally would, and ask simple direct questions, expecting straightforward answers. Tell your prospect that you're there to help him to decide on the best solution, but to help him, he needs to help you and be open with you. If he isn't, the sale isn't going anywhere and you have to move on.

If you encounter an indecisive prospect, then your qualification is going to be more important than ever in helping to determine whether you can reach a mutually beneficial deal. Dealing with an indecisive prospect takes time, and you need to consider whether the potential deal is worth you making that time investment.

REMEMBER

Revisit the essential qualification issues of whether the need is a real one or not. If the need is real, consider how it's going to be met. What will be the business impact to your prospect of not meeting the need? You have to lead him carefully through the process and guide him to consider the real answers. (Check out Chapters 9 and 19 for the full scoop on qualification.)

If your prospect isn't "getting it" or is simply out of his depth and not prepared to make any decisions, then you have two options to explore before deciding to move on:

>> **Engage with the rest of the decision-making unit.** The easier option is to engage with the rest of the decision-making unit, in the hope that you'll encounter someone a little more dynamic who will make a decision and become your alternative champion. Covering the same ground with different people takes time, but if this is the way around the immovable object, then you have little alternative.

>> **Go over his head.** You shouldn't consider this option lightly. In old-school sales, IBM salespeople did this as a matter of routine as soon as they felt they weren't getting their own way, and although it may have delivered short-term success, it was at the cost of wrecking the relationship with the key prospect.

TIP

A way you can do this a little more subtly, while keeping your prospect on board, is to copy his manager on your contact reports. Do this often enough and if the need is real and the immovable object is seen to be a stumbling block, then internal pressure will usually be brought to bear, clearing the path for your sale to progress.

Moving on due to an indecisive prospect can be a difficult decision as you're likely to have already invested an amount of time on the sale. If it proves necessary to move on in these circumstances, do so while leaving the door open should your prospect finally make a decision. Let it be known that while you can't invest any more time on him, should he decide that yours is the solution of choice, then you'll be happy to conclude an order but not to revisit the essentials.

Leaving When the Prospect Isn't Telling the Truth

Why prospects choose to lie is beyond me. It may be a little thing like keeping some competitive information from you, or it could be a much bigger thing like overstating the budget or their own level of responsibility.

WARNING

Accept that sometimes prospects do lie, and ultimately the reasons aren't important. Whether your prospect is simply being economical with the truth, telling you only part of the story on what he considers to be a need-to-know basis, or is straight out telling you lies, the behavior is unethical. And if you discover this to be the case, then it's difficult to imagine circumstances where you wouldn't move on and end the sales cycle immediately.

I haven't had to do this very often, but when I have had to, my approach has been to tell the prospect that we are unable to work with him due to a culture clash, and leave it at that.

A prospect being untruthful during the sales process doesn't lend itself to filling your company with confidence if you progress to the implementation phase. Can he be trusted to tell the truth then? Longer-term implications of being untruthful can have an impact on the success of a project, and you don't want to be associated with it.

REMEMBER

Relationships in sales, as in all walks of life, need to be built on solid foundations if they're going to last the course, and one of those is trust. Without trust, you can't have a solid business relationship, and without a solid business relationship, you won't have a deal that delivers any form of satisfactory outcome.

Chapter **21**

Being Realistic with Forecasts

You may have seen posters and T-shirts that proclaim "Managing Director: We do precision guesswork based on unreliable data provided by those of questionable knowledge." Although this statement is funny on its face, there's more than a grain of truth in it. Actually, it makes me cringe because I've been one of those new business salespeople who provided unreliable data!

This chapter is all about forecasting as it's used in winning new business and its role alongside budgets and targets. Here's a brief definition to these terms:

» Forecasting is the operational numbers. Simply stated, they are the numbers that count the most because they deal with reality on the streets and not a wish list in the boardroom. By operational numbers, I mean the revenue forecast that you see as being achieved in practice from each of your live deals, and not a plucked-out-of-the-air planning number based on a standard project. The operational numbers may be higher or lower than the expected norm, but the point is that they have to be forecast as being realistic and achievable. The numbers themselves include revenue and profitability as a minimum and, depending on your business, may also include things like number of licenses or other specific measurements that your company needs to know about.

>> Budgets are the figures that the company bases its financial projections and profit and loss (P&L) plans on, looking at the big picture typically for the next 12 months. New business salespeople have little or no involvement at this stage because it tends to be done at board level and handed down the management chain of command.

>> Targets are the new business salesperson's driving force, dictated by sales management and usually set in stone for the year. They do sometimes change as the year progresses, and that is usually only in an upward direction based on other pressures being brought to bear. Targets are what commission plans are based on and, for the new business salesperson, are very important and meaningful figures.

REMEMBER

Forecasting is a key part of the new business role, so take it seriously. Don't forecast in isolation, and do take responsibility for it. You'll always have an element of guesswork involved when forecasting, but the new business sales role involves helping to eliminate as much of the guesswork as possible. You have tools at your disposal to help achieve this, which I explore in this chapter.

Introducing the Basics of Forecasting

The budgets and targets are set, and the year is underway. You likely have to produce forecasts on a monthly basis showing the new business wins and revenue that you're projecting. If not, then you may wonder what your sales managers are actually doing — forecasting is that important to the role. The following sections describe the importance of taking responsibility for accurate forecasting numbers and the fundamentals of the forecasting process.

REMEMBER

You need to be aware of and avoid the mindset of "it's just a forecast; it doesn't matter." Your forecasts *do* matter; they matter a lot for reasons that I explore in this chapter. Sometimes they seem like a waste of valuable selling time, but you need to avoid this way of thinking. That's often easier to say than to achieve — believe me, I've been there!

Taking responsibility

You've most likely heard the apocryphal story of the Great War coded signal passed from the trenches back to Command HQ via a series of intermediaries, where the original message of "send reinforcements, we're going to advance" got altered along the way to "send three and fourpence, we're going to a dance." Needless to say, the requested reinforcements never arrived.

The point is that messages can subtly change as they pass from level to level, not always deliberately, but they end up with a slightly different spin on them so that by the time senior management gets them, they can portray a different message from the one originally intended. In the field of forecasting, this can cause all sorts of problems, and you need to take responsibility to ensure that your actual figures are the ones senior management uses to make decisions. When forecasts are proved to be incorrect, you can be sure that the finger of blame points firmly in the new business salesperson's direction unless you're proactive here.

WARNING

A forecast isn't a wish list, nor is it a best-case scenario. It's intended to be a true reflection of the sales and revenue that you believe will be delivered in the forecast period. You need to base your figures on reality. If a deal isn't going to close in this period, don't forecast it. Take responsibility and set expectations accordingly. Errors at the source, your figures, are magnified as the data moves through levels of management, so make sure that your submissions are true and accurate. (I discuss accurate forecasts in more detail later in this chapter.)

REMEMBER

Generally, everyone in the chain of command has a go at working with your figures and is likely to defend this task as adding value. You may see it more akin to interference. I've seen situations where the forecast finally submitted bears little resemblance to the figures the new business sales team provided. In this case, it's important to push back and to maintain a sense of realism. They are your figures, so be prepared to defend them. There's nothing wrong with people checking them, and you should expect that, but you shouldn't expect massive changes, especially if they have your name attached to them.

Understanding the forecasting process

The forecasting process differs between companies. In your role as forecaster, you should understand both what you're expected to provide and how it will be used. Make sure you know who will see your forecast and how it fits into management planning.

At its most basic, forecasting is taking the most likely outcome of each new business opportunity closing in the current period and, considering the most likely invoiceable value, adding value to this number based on your unique understanding of the dynamics of each sales cycle. It is really only new business salespeople who can provide these accurate forecasts because they are the ones who are driving the process and have the on-the-ground view.

REMEMBER

My rule of thumb for accurate forecasting is this: If it's not qualified, then it's not going to happen, so don't forecast it. Add to this the fact that the better your qualification, the more accurate your forecast is going to be. Keeping these rules in mind will help you deliver accurate, achievable forecasts. See Chapters 9 and 19 for more about qualification.

REMEMBER

How much time should forecasting take? By utilizing a good CRM system, as I discuss in the next section, the time shouldn't be an issue, but you need to be prospecting, selling, and following up for as much time as you can, and anything that gets in the way of those key tasks needs to be managed carefully.

I once had a new business role where the managing director insisted on spending a full day each month going over forecast numbers with a fine-tooth comb and having me with him while he did it. He then proceeded to hound me several other times during a month to spend time on his forecasting spreadsheet. In all seriousness, I used to spend 10 percent of my working month "doing the numbers" rather than "getting the business," and 10 percent of the month on forecasting is way over the top for a new business salesperson. It should take no more than a couple of hours to check and revise your forecasts when aided by effective use of a CRM system. Forecasting should not be a once-a-month exercise, but a living set of numbers updated continually to reflect the changing sales cycles.

Eliminating Errors with a Good CRM

In Chapter 9, I outline the use of good customer relationship management (CRM) systems as a tool in winning new business. CRM systems are software systems that act as a central repository for all the information about clients, suspects, and prospects, recording and tracking each change as it happens and using the accumulated intelligence to produce accurate reports and sales forecasts based on real, hard data. If you use your CRM correctly, and assuming it's fit for purpose, it will make your new business forecasting much easier, automating a good part of the process.

REMEMBER

Take away the guesswork by relying on the sales data that you collect every day as part of your job. Computers never lie; they just interpret the information you provide them with, and CRM systems are no different. "Garbage in, garbage out" was one of my early lessons when training as a programmer many years ago, and it's true. Feed the CRM with real, accurate sales data, and you'll get real and accurate forecasts. Use the CRM system correctly, and it will provide most of the forecasting information for your submissions at the click of a button. Your forecast should be a dynamic entity, so instead of having to revisit it frequently during the month, let the CRM do the number crunching based on the sales data you update it with. Remember to add weighting data to opportunities to arrive at the most accurate level of forecast.

Of course, you need human interaction to compile, review, and amend the reports, but learn to deal with facts and realities and to avoid gut instinct, because it's rarely right.

Understanding your prospect's buying cycle, which will differ from your sales cycle, is also key to ensuring that you correctly interpret messages that you receive and guards against making rash forecasting errors based on misunderstandings. Earlier in this chapter, I say that forecasting is a moving target, and it is. But that is no excuse for inconsistency. Constantly refine your forecast data, or rather let your CRM do the hard work, as you constantly refine your prospect qualification. Apply the same rules throughout your forecasting to provide consistency and to be able to track forecast movement over time. Tracking over time will provide sales management with the insight that they need.

WARNING

If your forecast is inconsistent with your qualification data, that's a big red flag that something isn't right.

Providing Accurate Forecasts

Accurate forecasts are essential. People use them to determine the need for resources and to allocate those resources for the next period of time, and any mismatch between forecast and actual data will have a domino effect on the provision of resources. Forecasts are also important for cash flow planning, which is an essential element in running a business, so you can see that a lot rides on the accuracy of your forecast data, and it's much more than a tool to beat you up with.

Resourcing decisions are based on forecast numbers, so you need to be prepared to defend your numbers to ensure that you have the necessary resources in place to implement the deals as they come in. Don't complain if you don't have the necessary resources to implement your deals if your forecast was wrong — because it's your fault it was wrong. That's the bottom line with forecasting new business.

As a new business salesperson, you need to lead from the front. If you forecast new business, make sure you deliver it. Your business is counting on you, and this is why new business salespeople are so well rewarded in today's corporate world. Justify your elevated position in the company, and justify your salary by being the rainmaker — the one who goes out and delivers new business deal after new business deal, all accurately forecasted and therefore correctly resourced to ensure successful implementation.

WARNING

Beware of the following:

>> Especially early in your new business sales career, you may be tempted to build up your numbers to impress your sales managers. You have come into a job and have been given a set of scary-looking sales numbers to achieve, so

why not add a bit of poetic license to the forecast to show what a great job you're doing? This will come back to bite you in a big way, so avoid doing it at all costs.

» Equally important is to report fully and not hold deals back to look good as you bring them in as unexpected extras. This runs a severe risk of your company not being correctly resourced to implement your unexpected deals and in turn risks the customers being disappointed as the implementation fails. Finding that a deal has been compromised by you playing forecasting games won't stand you in good stead. You'll be the villain and not the hero for bringing in "unexpected" deals that you deliberately misforecasted.

» Forecasts need to be backed by solid qualification data; nothing else is good enough. The days of seat-of-the-pants forecasting have gone forever. Understand the risk, mitigate against it, and be realistic. You can no longer get away with (nor should you be able to) a "judgment call" forecast because you "know" that something unqualified is going to convert. Regardless of whether it closes or not, you now lose both ways.

Management likely won't take your forecast numbers as is, and you're probably going to have to defend them. They'll compare your numbers to their numbers and draw their own conclusions — high among them is that your numbers are wrong. If your qualification matches your numbers, then push back and fight your corner, equally when your numbers are increased. Own your forecast numbers and be prepared to defend them under pressure from your sales managers. If you know your numbers and your deals, then push back when challenged.

I've been in the position a number of times where I've been given some forecast numbers to achieve that bear little resemblance to my forecast, and I've fought my corner every time and made sure that my misgivings have been documented when I've been overruled. This is not playing politics; it's protecting yourself and your belief in your qualification. I don't recall a "revised" forecast that has been handed down to ever have been accurate when not based on solid qualification, which it rarely is. It's strange that "revised" forecasts are always higher, too!

You'll find that managers use both top-down and bottom-up approaches to assess your numbers, and you'd be forgiven for thinking that if sales managers spent as much time focused on competitors as they do on checking up on their own staff, that the business would do a lot better. You could do worse than to remind sales managers of the difference between forecasts and budgets (as I explain at the start of this chapter) and to introduce some realism into the forecasting process. Maybe giving them this chapter to read will do the trick.

5

The Part of Tens

Chapter **22**

Ten Key Metrics to Watch

I n any new business sales role, you have a number of measurements, generally handed down by your sales line management. Paramount among these is your revenue target. You may also get targets such as number of new appointments in a week or number of prospecting calls made. These secondary targets are actually worthless in nearly all cases, and although they may satisfy a sales reporting structure, they won't do anything to assist you in reaching your overall revenue goal.

This chapter explores ten key metrics to help you achieve your revenue goal and shows you how to set, track, and measure them. To succeed in winning new business, you always need to know your numbers. When you understand the ten key metrics, you'll be in a good position to determine how many suspects and prospects you need to have at each stage of the pipeline to meet your new business revenue target.

Initial Decision Maker Contact (IDMC)

The initial decision maker contact (IDMC) is where a sales cycle really begins; it's the point where the prospecting of that client turns into real sales activity. Until the IDMC point, all activity on that company is classed as prospecting or research rather than new business sales activity. IDMCs are the lifeblood of new business sales and in turn lead to everything else, and you just can't skimp on this activity.

REMEMBER

Your sales methodology will tell you how many IDMCs you need to make in each sales period. To get your daily target, you simply divide that number by the number of days in the period. Splitting down the number into a daily target achieves three things:

>> **It gives you a manageable number to hit.** Having a big number of new IDMCs to hit can be — in fact, *is* — a daunting task. Breaking it down into a daily target to run alongside everything else you need to do makes it more manageable.

>> **It keeps your pipeline topped up.** You need to keep the initial stage of your pipeline full so that you always have plenty of potential opportunities to work on and qualify, never having the excuse of "no one to talk to." Breaking down your IDMC into daily numbers helps you focus on your pipeline by always having a number to achieve.

>> **It makes it a habit.** You need to be in the habit of making daily new contacts at IDMC level and not let this task be daunting or allow it to consume vast chunks of time. Setting aside a specific day each week to work on new IDMCs, for example, isn't nearly as effective as building it into your daily workflow, because then it becomes a habit.

So how many IDMCs do you need? The absolute answer is unique to your new business sales situation. In my case, I need to hit ten new IDMCs a week, and this is the metric that I watch closely. Ten a week is only two a day, but don't be fooled into thinking that equates to only two phone calls — it doesn't.

REMEMBER

IDMC is contact with the decision maker — not an answering service, not an assistant, not someone junior as part of door opening, but an actual conversation with the decision maker. You likely won't achieve this on the first call to a company unless you strike lucky, so this metric needs its own pipeline to hit the daily target of IDMCs. You can't afford to take your eye off this metric because you need to stack the early stages of the pipeline, and you can't have a prospect enter the pipeline until you've reached IDMC.

Another metric that's interesting to watch, but not necessarily key, is the ratio of calls made to IDMCs. This tells you how efficient your early prospecting really is. I discuss this metric later in this chapter.

Subsequent Decision Maker Contact (SDMC)

Subsequent decision maker contact (SDMC) is, as the name suggests, each occasion after the initial contact that you interact with the decision maker. This interaction can be from any type of touch point: telephone, face-to-face meeting, or an email from the prospect (note that email only *from*, and not *to*, the prospect counts here).

SDMC is a key pipeline management metric and should be one of the first things you look at when reviewing sales activity within a named account. You need to track how many SDMCs you make each week. You should also measure the number of SDMCs you make each week within each target account in your pipeline.

You'll know from your methodology how many SDMCs you need to hit each time period, and as with IDMCs (see the preceding section), it's easier to split these numbers into weekly and then daily targets, for the same reasons that I outline earlier.

SDMCs within a named prospect are a good indicator of how well, or otherwise, the relationship is building up. With zero or just a few SDMCs, it'll be very difficult to accurately forecast anything.

Just as with IDMCs, SDMC targets need to become habits and need application to meet them. If you don't hit your SMDC targets, you likely aren't building strong enough relationships with the prospects in your pipeline; without those relationships, you'll struggle with qualification and therefore revenue targets.

Keeping track of SDMCs gives you and sales line management a good feel, based on real data, of how successful you are in really penetrating and getting to know your prospects. A weak SDMC number is a sign of a floundering new business salesperson, or one who needs support.

Qualification Key Stage Three (a.k.a. MCPQ)

Qualification key stage three is also known as MCPQ within my methodology. The name doesn't matter all that much; what matters is that it's a key metric to watch because it shows how your pipeline qualification is going.

The original meaning of MCPQ was meeting, confirmation, proposal, and qualification, and it was a measurement of how and when each of these stages was reached within a sales cycle. Although the acronym has stuck, because "key stage three" sounds like something from high school, the meaning has become much more relevant as years have passed.

MCPQ measures whether a prospect has moved forward during this touch point, in terms of qualification, and documents in exactly what way the forward move happened.

REMEMBER

If a touch point doesn't result in MCPQ, it's largely a waste of time. The number of touch points and the number of MCPQs within a target prospect will likely be close; if a large discrepancy occurs between those numbers, then something isn't right in the sales cycle and should set alarm bells ringing. In other words, if you're not moving a prospect forward during a touch point, then what are you actually achieving?

As your qualification kicks in, some of your prospects will inevitably fail the qualification tests and drop out of the sales cycle. (Flip to Chapter 19 for details on qualification.) Figure 22-1 shows a pipeline with lots of activity at the top to pour in raw unqualified suspects and then a filtering through various stages of qualification with a lot of them dropping out along the way. What you're left with is highly qualified prospects, which you should be closing the majority of and is certainly where you should invest your time. The further down the pipeline a prospect gets, the higher the level of qualification will have taken place and the closer he'll be to becoming a new client, which is of course the desired result.

REMEMBER

Prospects dropping out of the sales funnel is always going to happen, and depending on the nature of your business and solution, it may well be that the majority drop out. This is natural and nothing to be concerned about. Your qualification criteria are designed to eliminate as many of the prospects that stand no, or very little, chance of becoming a client without you having to spend valuable time and resources on them.

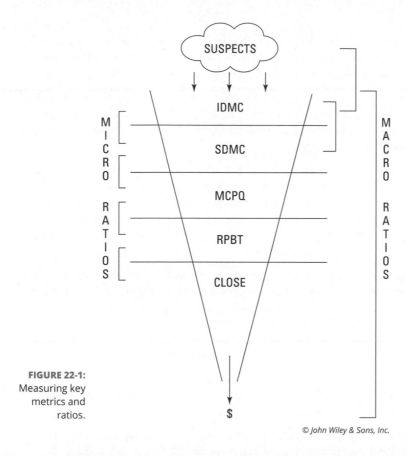

FIGURE 22-1:
Measuring key
metrics and
ratios.

Qualification Key Stage Four (a.k.a. RPBT)

Qualification key stage four is also known as RPBT within my methodology. RPBT originally stood for role, project, budget, and timescale. These remain the fundamental cornerstones upon which all other qualification criteria are built; without them in place, you simply don't have a qualified prospect. (See Chapter 19 for the full scoop on qualification.)

Note: The vast majority of companies will have industry- or solution-specific qualification criteria of their own to add, and they're included within the definition and scope of RPBT as far as metrics and tracking are concerned.

Here's an introduction to RPBT:

>> **Role:** This makes sure that the key person you're dealing with in your prospect's organization is in fact the key decision maker or a key member of

the decision-making unit. Unless he is, then the role element isn't qualified, and the sale isn't currently progressing. Dealing at the correct level of decision maker is vital because otherwise you're almost certainly wasting your time.

REMEMBER

It doesn't matter how much a subordinate within your prospect's organization likes you or your proposed solution. Unless you're communicating and selling at decision maker level, you're not dealing with a qualified prospect, and your sale isn't going to progress.

>> **Project:** This makes sure that you're dealing with a real need, something that your target prospect's company actually needs and is a real pain point for it. Is the company actually going to do something about it? Is it in the plan? This part of the qualification is absolutely vital because you need to make sure that you're dealing with a real, live project, and not somebody's wish list or a side project that hasn't been authorized.

WARNING

If you don't properly qualify this element very early in the sales cycle, you risk wasting your valuable time and resources, something you simply can't afford to allow to happen. Far too much sales time is wasted just because new business salespeople fail to qualify a real need. Obviously, in addition to qualifying that a real project exists, you need to ensure that it falls within the scope of your company's ability to deliver against those needs.

>> **Budget:** Another vital part of qualifying data is ensuring that the prospect has allocated a budget for the solution and that the scope of the budget falls within a level suitable for your likely solution.

REMEMBER

There's no point in progressing a sales cycle for a Rolls Royce standard of solution if your prospect sufficiently budgeted for only a Kia standard. A mismatch clearly exists here, and the quicker you find out, the better it will be. There's nothing wrong with a lower level of budget, unless you're selling a high-ticket item. This also works in reverse: If the project has a Rolls Royce standard of budget and you're selling a Kia standard of solution, then you also have a mismatch, and your prospect likely won't settle for a cheaper solution.

Here are some things to consider about budget. Does the budget contain any element of elasticity? Does it include ongoing support and maintenance costs, or is it a capital-only budget? Who has the ultimate sign-off? Is this person covered as part of the decision-making unit? Unless you know all these answers and the budget fits your level of solution, then your prospect hasn't passed the budget qualification.

>> **Timescale:** Understanding your prospect's idea of time frame is essential. If he's at the very early stages of his buying cycle and plans for it to take many months to complete, you need to factor this into any forecasting that you do on it, and you need to allocate your time and resources accordingly. Could you allocate some pre-sales support resources to provide your prospect with

REMEMBER

low-level information gathering if he's some distance away from getting seriously involved and where your time is required?

Don't get too excited and throw everything at a prospect who's months or more away from a decision point. You need to maintain your primary focus on short-term business wins while driving longer-term sales cycles.

Qualified Pipeline Value

The new business sales role is about securing sales revenue for your business, and you'll have a sales target to meet, generally agreed at the beginning of the financial year. The figure isn't always "agreed"; sometimes it's handed down from sales management as a "will do" figure that you have little or no control over.

Whatever your sales target is and however it's determined, your job is to at least achieve it and hopefully overachieve. To track progress against budget, you need to keep a close watch on the value of your qualified pipeline. You shouldn't count anything prior to a successful IDMC (which I discuss earlier in this chapter).

REMEMBER

Pipeline value and sales forecasting are different, although closely related in that one feeds into the other, largely based on level of qualification and weighting factors. Check out Chapter 21 for more about forecasting.

Weighting of pipeline value is done according to both explicit and implicit criteria by my methodology. Explicit criteria are

>> Role

>> Budget

>> Timescale

>> Project

>> Demographics

So they're the same as key stage four qualification (see the preceding section) with the addition of demographics. The more of these criteria that have been qualified, the higher the level of explicit qualification weighting is applied to the pipeline value.

Implicit criteria are

>> No interest

>> More info wanted

>> Follow-up agreed

>> Very interested

These are fairly self-explanatory criteria and are taken alongside the explicit criteria to form a weighting that you apply to the known project budget, giving a potential value to each entry in the pipeline. Clearly the weighting for no interest is much lower than for very interested; weighting increases as you go down this list. A word of warning here, though: Implicit criteria by their very nature are prone to rapid change, so make sure that you revisit them after each touch point.

REMEMBER

You need to keep a close watch in the weighted value of your pipeline to ensure that it's in line with your sales target. Any shortfall here is a clear sign that you need to do additional prospecting in order to fill up the early stages of your pipeline. Also keep in mind that you're not going to win everything in your pipeline, through natural wastage and competitive activity, so make sure that the value of your pipeline reflects this and is significantly higher than your sales target.

Conversion Ratio of Suspects to Qualified Prospects

The conversion ratio from suspects to qualified prospects — those who make it into the pipeline to begin with — tells you a lot about the success of your prospecting efforts and the quality of your raw data. Watch your conversion ratio carefully because it guides you in the right direction and is a key metric.

REMEMBER

Too low a ratio suggests that you're doing something wrong with your approach to prospecting or that your data sources aren't good enough. You need to address either of these cases because although prospecting is an extremely important activity, it needs to be time and resource effective and able to generate sufficient quantity and quality of leads that make it into your sales pipeline.

In Chapters 9 and 23, I discuss prospecting in detail. Take on board these thoughts; apply them to your prospecting efforts and try to be targeted in where you commit your time and resources.

Personally, I'm disappointed if any suspect I identify fails to make it into the pipeline as a qualified prospect, because I firmly believe in going for quality over quantity every time. Make this your goal, too. Spend less time on suspects by focusing on some key attributes that you identify, and prequalify out anyone who doesn't meet your criteria, leaving you free to invest your time on a higher level of suspect.

Touch Points

Touch points with your prospect are vital. These are your primary opportunities to both qualify your prospect and to build your relationship. As your sales cycle progresses, the number of touch points will increase. So if you discover a highly qualified prospect in the sales forecast with a low number of touch points, then I'd be suspicious of the accuracy of the qualification and forecast.

The volume of touch points should be an accurate indication of where you are in a sales cycle. This metric also shows you whether you're spending too much time on a prospect who isn't progressing through the sales cycle sufficiently.

Keep a close watch on your touch point numbers and make sure that you're using your time to maximum advantage.

New Prospect Identification

You need to keep your pipeline filled at the early stages because some of these new prospects will become your qualified prospects and new clients as time progresses. The last thing you want is to be floundering for prospects to sell to.

Having a regular flow of new prospects, emerging from your suspect pool (which also needs to be constantly topped up), is vital to your prospecting and sales efforts. See Chapters 9 and 23 for details on prospecting.

Have daily and weekly targets for the number of new prospects that you feed into your sales cycle, and don't let this figure slip because it will have a negative impact further down the line. The absolute numbers that you need vary depending on your sector and solution and the length of your typical sales cycle, but work out the figures that you need to achieve, and then don't let anything get in the way of achieving them.

Ratio of IDMC to SDMC

If you're achieving a reasonable number of IDMCs but not securing many SMDCs (both of which I cover earlier in this chapter), then something is going seriously wrong, perhaps with the way you're positioning yourself or with your prospect targeting. The ratio of IDMC to SDMC is a key metric to track.

REMEMBER

You should always achieve a multiple of SDMCs for every IDMC. Within a target prospect, the ratio is a significant figure to watch and ensures that you're covering the basis of the decision-making unit. Too few SDMCs will make any sales forecast or qualification a bit suspect.

If your ratio of IDMC to SDMC is too low, say, less than 1:2, you need to spend some time considering what the problem is and how to address it as a matter of some urgency. This low ratio implies that you're not getting second touch point opportunities. A ratio of 1:3 in the early stages of a sales cycle is about average, and 1:4 is good to achieve. The relative importance of the ratio numbers is a moving target and shifts as the sales cycle progresses, but it's a metric that you need to watch.

Close Ratio

Clearly, the number of sales that you close is of vital importance. To become more efficient as a new business salesperson, you need to pay attention to the ratio of IDMCs to close. This metric shows how efficient your sales activity and sales processes are.

When you have a good grasp of this number, you can work backward and determine with a fair degree of certainty how many prospects you need to have at each stage of the pipeline to deliver your target revenue figure.

REMEMBER

Closing new business is the pinnacle of your new business salesperson's role, but as you see from the ten key metrics in this chapter, the role can be made easier with a more scientific approach than just chasing everything that moves. Take the time to understand these metrics and how knowing your numbers can help you deliver more predictable new business success.

Chapter **23**

Ten Prospecting Resources

A s a new business salesperson, one of the key challenges you face is finding consistent and reliable prospecting data. You can't just wait around for leads to drop into your lap; you have to proactively search for new potential opportunities.

On the other hand, you don't want to go rushing around like a headless chicken. You need a structured workflow, and you need to be able to keep the early stages of your pipeline filled up. In this chapter, I look at some of the best resources for discovering potential opportunities. Some of these are specific to the United Kingdom and so are useful to those selling into or working in the U.K., although most other countries have similar resources geared toward them. (*Note:* In putting together some of these resources, I left out the most obvious starting point of Google as I assume that everyone already knows about it and uses it extensively.)

For a full introduction to prospecting, see Chapter 9.

REMEMBER

Keep in mind that you won't be the only one looking for prospecting data. Assume that your competitors can also see information that's in the public domain, so try to look beyond the obvious sources and give yourself an advantage.

WARNING

External suppliers will no doubt offer you chances to get all sorts of prospect data as soon as they get hold of your details. I must get at least four or five emails every week with "offers I can't refuse" on data, and on occasions I've subscribed and bought lists only to find in the vast majority of cases that the data isn't especially complete, accurate, or useful to me. Before committing to buy new data, ask the supplier to send you a random sample and check out the accuracy for yourself. It's easy to do a few Google searches and website checks to verify the accuracy of the information. Generally, I find it much more valuable to stick to known and trusted data sources.

Insider Media

Insider Media (www.insidermedia.com) is a U.K.-based business-to-business media company that specializes in providing daily news digests as well as selling lists of data. This daily news digest is an invaluable prospecting resource because it provides timely data that has always proved accurate to me and saves countless hours of scanning dozens of publications myself.

Insider Media is one of the main sources of prospecting data that I personally rely on for solid U.K. business-to-business information. It forms a big part of my daily workflow and feeds a number of potential leads into my line of sight on a daily basis.

Individual stories may highlight new business opportunities by using a bit of lateral thinking; for example, a story may highlight a merger, a new product launch, or personnel changes, all of which are classic signs of a pending change that new business salespeople need to know about and take advantage of. Information can be summarized into your CRM for future use, or it may trigger immediate sales action, depending on the article.

Figure 23-1 shows some news stories from a selected region. The publication produces digests on different regions of the country, allowing you to be selective in your requirements. This figure highlights some potentially interesting news items, including one that shows that a company has secured some significant funding.

TIP

You can subscribe to daily digests on different geographical regions. The digests tend to arrive in my inbox by the time I reach my desk in the mornings.

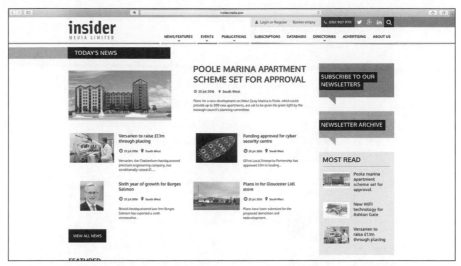

Source: Stewart Stuchbury

FIGURE 23-1:
Insider Media offers daily news digests.

Local Business Publications

Local business publications are available all over the world and provide some great prospecting resources. Figure 23-2 is a good example that highlights a number of opportunities that would be worth further investigation.

A Google search for "local business publications" is the ideal starting point, and you can then narrow your search to include more specific terms, such as the industry that you're researching. After you identify publications, you can then read both articles and advertisements to try to identify potential prospects to feed into the early stages of your sales funnel. I find that ads are a really good source of prospects, especially because a company that's advertising is actively engaged in doing something.

TIP

You may need to look at local business publications across a wide range of areas to cover your target geographic market, and not just the publications geographically close to you. Depending on the size of your target prospects, you may find that this is one of the best sources of data available to you because many organizations like to see themselves covered in the business press but are often considered to be too small or not noteworthy enough to warrant national coverage. For these businesses, local press is among its target audiences for press releases and stories, and if you're able to pick up on these they can offer some valuable information to you.

FIGURE 23-2:
Check local
business
publications for
leads.

Source: Stewart Stuchbury

Many local publications are available with online access, although the online versions don't always carry advertisements, which are another source of prospecting data.

TIP

Many publications will be happy to send copies directly to you if you're out of their distribution area, generally at no cost if you just ask them.

Lists from "The Sunday Times"

Although they are specific to the United Kingdom, *The Sunday Times* lists are amongst the first places I look when I want to target fast-growing companies or sector leaders. This publication produces many different types of lists at various stages of each year. Some examples include

>> Best 100 companies to work for

>> Best 25 big companies

>> Top companies by revenue

>> Fastest-growing companies

Although the data is U.K.-specific, these lists offer a great way for new business salespeople to target the U.K. market irrespective of where they're physically based. All the lists are available on the Internet and not just in the printed publication. (Head to www.thetimes.co.uk to get started.) Other countries have similar data available; just do a search for quality newspapers and you may be surprised at what you find. In the United States, try looking at Forbes (www.forbes.com) as a great starting point.

Figure 23-3 shows the typical type of information found by using this resource. As you see, this provides a useful summary of current activity as well as financial information.

FIGURE 23-3:
The Sunday Times offers lists that can help you prospect.

Source: Stewart Stuchbury

New Local Business Lists

Many media organizations publish data on new businesses setting up in or moving to their area, and these can offer a valuable data source as anything new can represent opportunity to a new business salesperson. A good way of locating this type of data is to source lists from your local telecommunication company on new business telephone lines being installed, or you can look at local business publications as companies on the move are super keen on attracting publicity. Dun and Bradstreet is a good source for this type of data, too; check out www.dnb.co.uk in the U.K. and www.dnb.com in North America.

You can subscribe to regular updates and set up alerts for anything that acts as a trigger for you. Be a little cautious here, however, because as I highlight at the start of this chapter, your competitors have access to the same data.

Figure 23-4 shows an example of this type of listing (from `www.brandnewbusinesses.com`), showing a record count and offering the chance to delve deeper into the data.

TIP

Often, local business lists like this provide an update option where you can choose to have copies of all new entries sent to you weekly or monthly on a subscription basis. If you can locate a good source and check the reliability of the data as I cover at the start of this chapter, then consider subscribing to one of these information sources.

FIGURE 23-4:
Organizations publish lists of new local businesses that you can prospect.

Source: Stewart Stuchbury

Industry Publications

Just about every industry that you can think of now has a myriad of journals and other publications focused on it, and these provide two different prospecting resource opportunities:

>> **Editorials and articles:** Editorials and articles give you insight as well as raw data and often contain names and job titles of key decision makers who can sometimes be difficult to get hold of.

>> **Advertisements:** Ads are obviously intended to attract inbound prospects for the advertiser, but they're also a good indicator of a company being active, potentially growing and potentially having needs that you have a solution for. They're a valuable source of prospecting data.

Check to see whether your business has back copies of industry publications so you can see the titles available and arrange to subscribe to the most relevant ones.

TIP

Subscriptions can be expensive, so you make sure you'll get the right type of information before you make a subscription commitment. A good way to do this is to phone the publication and say that you work in that industry and are considering a subscription, and then ask for a back issue so that you can understand the type of content and make a decision on the benefits of subscribing. I've done that myself many times and have never had that type of request turned down. Remember, you're a prospect to the publication!

Chambers of Commerce

Your local chamber of commerce can be a great source of prospecting data if you're looking for local contacts, and don't be afraid to contact a chamber from much further away as part of its remit is to help people like you. (Just perform an online search with the name of a town or city plus "chamber of commerce" to find the group you need.)

Membership lists, journals, lists of exhibitors, and visitors to events are among the types of information you can expect to find from a chamber of commerce. If you dig a little deeper, you'll often find offers of help in locating the type of information that you're looking for. In Chapter 17, I cover networking as a prospecting tool, and events sponsored and hosted by a chamber of commerce are a good source of networking data, too.

TIP

Becoming known within your local chamber of commerce can also result in prospecting information being sent to you without prompting, so getting to know your local chamber is worth the time.

Highly Specialized Researchers

If your particular prospecting need is very specialized, then sometimes the best solution is to contract with a specialized researcher, brief him on your requirements, and then leave him to use professional prospecting and research tools to provide you with prospect lists. This tends to be a rather expensive option because outsourcing to specialists always is, but if time is paramount or if you just don't have the necessary skills available to you, then it may be an option worth exploring.

TIP

Any outsourcing supplier is likely to begin with exactly the same resources that you have, so consider telling him in your briefing that you want him to ignore the more obvious data sources and to concentrate on information that's more difficult to access to maximize your value for money.

A good starting point for finding specialized researchers is www.fiverr.com, but select with care and check references, and before you commit to anything on a large scale, do a smaller test batch first.

LinkedIn

LinkedIn (www.linkedin.com) has become the favorite business networking tool and for good reason, because literally millions of businesspeople have created LinkedIn profiles. I find that it's rather limiting as a stand-alone prospecting tool, but when you use it in combination with some of the other resources that I outline in this chapter, it delivers excellent results.

LinkedIn is especially useful in two situations:

>> When you know the company that you want to target but are looking for names and job titles

>> When you want to find people similar to a contact that you already have

LinkedIn often changes the ways that you can search for information, but the general search bar is a good starting point, with a search as simple as "vice president finance U.K." returning lots of hits for you to explore in detail.

Facebook

It seems like the entire world is on Facebook (www.facebook.com), but Facebook business pages can provide a new business salesperson with some very valuable data, including both company and people information.

Facebook now includes what it rather grandly refers to as graphical search. This isn't a search using graphics as might be suggested by the name but rather a very powerful natural language search capability that can help you locate really useful information. Figure 23-5 demonstrates the use of graphical search in finding information that can feed into your prospecting file. Try typing a natural language search command in the search bar and see what you get (for example, "VP sales in greater New York area").

FIGURE 23-5:
Facebook can help you get prospecting information for businesses.

Source: Stewart Stuchbury

An Existing Company Database

Perhaps the greatest of all the prospecting resources available to you, and one that is all too often overlooked, is your existing database or CRM system (which I introduce in Chapter 9). This really should be an absolute goldmine of prospecting data and detailed research information.

REMEMBER

Get to know how your system works and push it to its limits in terms of reporting options and selections to see what you can discover. I guarantee that you'll be pleasantly surprised by some of the findings and some of the prospecting information that has been hiding in plain sight.

Index

budgets
  agreeing on sales budgets, 18
  determining, 259–260
  in forecasting, 287
  moving on, 280
  objective qualification criteria, 267
  overview, 259–260
  RPBT metric, 211
  time windows and, 122
  tracking qualification over time, 272
business cards, 107, 112, 240
business newspapers, 125
business sectors
  first-level qualification, 128
  objective qualification criteria, 268
  prospecting, 119
buyer's remorse, 31, 222–223

C

call recording systems, 38
case studies
  feeding into marketing, 93
  feeding into procurement departments, 190
  mitigating perception of risk, 78
  overview, 23–25
  positive versus negative, 39
chambers of commerce
  meetings of, 233
  as prospecting resource, 311
close ratio, 304
commission plans, 17–18
commitment
  guarantees and, 171
  of resources, 186
  risk of lack of, 246–247
  stage payments, 152
committees, 281
company databases, 313
company size
  first-level qualification, 128
  objective qualification criteria, 268

  prospecting, 119
company turnover, 268
competitive tendering, 265
compliance regulations and risk, 250–251
conditional agree strategy, 30–31
confidentiality, 83
conflict, 31, 223
consultative selling approach
  asking for the order, 187–188
  building trust, 200
  mitigating perception of risk, 253
  presenting solutions
    overview, 73
    solution orientation, 73–76
    thinking in prospect's terms, 76–83
contact reports
  addressing risk, 252
  continuing to deliver during implementation
    phase, 168–169
  dealing with procurement departments, 191
  elevator pitching, 112
  establishing trust, 46–47
  follow-up process, 53–54
  handling objections already covered, 145, 150,
    159
contracts
  avoiding ambiguity, 172–173
  clear payment terms, 174
  mitigating perception of risk, 79–80
  processes for dealing with changes, 173–174
  written terms, 173
control
  ad-hoc demonstrations, 68
  asking for contact details, 112
  moving on
    avoiding instinct, 279–280
    defined, 277
    indecisive prospects, 284–285
    lying prospects, 285–286
    not wasting time, 281–284
    personality and group issues, 280–281
    trusting qualification criteria, 278–279

guarantees
  maximizing chances of success, 172
  mitigating perception of risk, 254
  one-sided risk, 250
  overview, 170
  role of, 172
  structuring, 170–171
"guerilla" tactics, 264

H

hard (pressure) selling, avoiding
  building reputation for buyers, 199
  building trust, 200–202
  creating pleasant buying experience, 197–198
  fostering long-term buying opportunities, 198–199
  knowledgeable buyers, 196
  not forcing solution, 202–203
  overview, 195–196
headless chicken syndrome, 216
Hill, Napoleon, 207
house account management, 18–19

I

IBM, 81, 148, 191, 285
IDMC (initial decision maker contact), 209–210, 296–297, 304
implementation phase. *See also* asking for the order
  advance payment, 174
  changes during, 173
  commitment and resources, 79–80
  general information, 13
  ongoing communication during, 168–169
  planning for, 186–187
  stepping back if successful implementation is in doubt, 155
implicit ratings, 268–269, 273, 301–302
incentive programs, 163–165
incumbent suppliers, 147, 265–266

indecisive prospects, 284–285. *See also* risk; time
industry-specific publications, 125, 310–311
inequity
  asking prospect for help, 148
  being prepared to walk away, 146–147
  ensuring level playing field, 147–148
  overview, 145–146
initial decision maker contact (IDMC), 209–210, 296–297, 304
Insider Media, 306–307
instinct
  avoiding, 279–280, 290
  qualification versus, 275
integrity, 31–32, 153, 180, 236
ISO (International Organization for Standardization), 244

J

Jobs, Steve, 23–24

L

language. *See also* cultural awareness
  body language
    active listening, 37
    elevator pitching, 110, 113
    enhancing credibility, 201
    making customer comfortable, 95
  getting prospect engaged in the solution, 186
  making words count, 107
  plain, 107, 113
  positivity in, 33
  saying no, 176–177
  structuring solution in prospect's terms, 79–80
  tone of voice
    developing own style, 34–35
    importance of words, 33–34
    overview, 31–32
    serving as company's mouthpiece, 32–33
  using prospect's terminology, 98

tracking qualification over time, 272
understanding prospect's view of, 77–78
ways of dealing with
accepting, 247
avoiding, 247
exploiting, 247
limiting, 247–248
mitigating, 248
transferring, 247
RPBT (role, project, budget, timescale), 209–211, 299–301

S

Sale of Goods Act, 170
sales forecasting
accuracy, 291–292
buying versus sales cycle, 291
CRM systems, 290–291
defined, 287
importance of, 288
qualification and, 275, 289, 292
taking responsibility for, 288–289
targets in, 288
understanding process of, 289–290
satisfied clients, 16
saying no
how, 177–178
negotiating positions established by, 179
opportunities afforded by, 178
overview, 175
permission to change rules afforded by, 179–180
to protect interests, 180–181
when, 176
why
clear reasons, 176–177
hazier reasons, 177
saying yes, motivating prospects toward
covering all issues, 98–101
creating straightforward propositions, 96–98
making customers comfortable, 95–96
taking away risk, 101–104

SDMC (subsequent decision maker contact), 209–210, 297, 304
setting goals
customizing goals, 209
filling pipeline, 208–209
headline goals, 208
importance of, 207–208
qualification metrics, 210–211
resistance to, 207
reviewing goals, 208, 211
writing down goals, 207
silence
allowing for response to pitches, 110
knowing when to stop talking, 38–39
listening
active, 37–38, 43–44, 46, 74, 200
creating pleasant buying experience, 197
elevator pitches as opportunity for, 114–115
enhancing credibility, 200
twice as much as speaking, 36–37
overview, 35–36
when prospect plays hard to get, 179
slang, 33
social media
building reputation for buyers, 199
first-level qualification, 129
following up on networking, 240
networking, 232, 238
prospecting, 312–313
Social Media Marketing For Dummies (Singh and Diamond), 199
soft close, 185
solution orientation
attitude, 73–74
critical thinking, 74–76
as part of replicable process, 217
team-based approach, 74
understanding prospect's problem, 74–75
speaking opportunities, 199
specialized researchers, 311–312
speed networking events, 237
stage payments, 152, 254